D1529065

THE INNER ELITE

THE INNER ELITE
DOSSIERS OF PAPAL CANDIDATES

By Gary MacEoin and the Committee
for the Responsible Election of the Pope

SHEED ANDREWS AND McMEEL, INC.
Subsidiary of Universal Press Syndicate
KANSAS CITY

Photos by Religious News Service

Library of Congress Cataloging in Publication Data
MacEoin, Gary, 1909-
　　Inner elite.

　1. Cardinals—Biography. 2. Popes—Election.
I. Committee for the Responsible Election of the Pope.
II. Title.
BX4664.2.M32　　　262'.135'0922 [B]　　　78-17845
ISBN 0-8362-3105-8

CONTENTS

FOREWORD

This book of dossiers of papabili is one significant element in an effort at world-wide consciousness-raising regarding the importance of the office of the papacy. One of the men whose biographies are sketched in these pages will be the next pope. If we start with the assumption—as we do—that the papacy represents a position of preeminent moral authority in our world, then it is baffling that an attempt like this has never been undertaken in the past and that so little is known even in corridors of power about the inner elite who will elect from among themselves the next pope.

Two years ago Universal Press Syndicate assigned journalists to interview key cardinals to obtain their views on Pope Paul VI's reign and to elicit opinions and facts about their peers in the College of Cardinals. The occasion for this journalistic project was the eightieth birthday of Pope Paul VI—an appropriate date for a retrospective, since eighty is the age Paul has legislated as the cutoff age for participation by cardinals in the next papal election and five years past the date when bishops and cardinals must submit their resignations from active duty to him.

Paralleling the interviews with the cardinals were interviews with lay authorities, theologians, politicians, editors, and other concerned persons throughout the world.

The results of the interviews were intriguing, to say the least. While the cardinals knew each other, the knowledge was social and superficial. Some couldn't even pronounce the names of their fellow cardinals. More alarming was the fact that a cardinal's perception of another cardinal seldom matched the views of the men and women who lived in the prelate's domain and had an opportunity to view the man closely over a period of years.

We were incredulous over the lack of basic information available to the world community about this inner elite.

As a result, several of us formed "The Committee for the Responsible Election of the Pope." The purpose of the committee is to gather information and to make it available not only to the cardinals themselves but to interested individuals throughout the world. It is not a lobby for a particular candidate, although several cardinals do emerge clearly in this work as serious candidates. Our purpose, however, is to fill the information gap. We are aware of the inspiration of the Spirit at conclaves but believe it is irresponsible of electors to use that fact as an excuse for not informing themselves about the men and the issues that will confront them in their momentous decision.

The Committee owes special thanks to the untiring professional commitment of author Gary MacEoin. Dr. MacEoin coordinated reports from over one hundred sources throughout the world. Only a man with MacEoin's international reputation, background of extensive travel and writing, and fluent control of several languages could have coordinated this project.

It is obvious that each member of the Committee cannot be expected to agree with every judgment in this book. Their commitment is to focusing attention on the office of the papacy, creating discussion about the qualifications necessary in the next pope, and serving as a clearing house for information about the candidates.

JAMES F. ANDREWS
Cochairman
The Committee for the Responsible Election of the Pope

New York City
May 22, 1978

ACKNOWLEDGMENTS

More than a hundred persons with outstanding knowledge of the activities and outlook of one or more of the cardinal electors have contributed from all over the globe information and evaluation that have enriched this book substantially. Many have valid reasons for preferring anonymity. In consequence, all must be content with these words of recognition and deep thanks.

The major published sources used by the authors are listed on pages 297–298.

INTRODUCTION

Viewed in sociological terms, Roman Catholicism has taken hard knocks in this century; and its significance as a power bloc will decline further as those countries of Asia and Africa, in which it constitutes a small and often foreign element, grow in political importance and relative number of inhabitants. Even within its own membership, the institution no longer commands the blind obedience that until recently gave outside observers the sense of dealing with a monolith.

Paradoxically, the moral potential of the Catholic church was never greater. Pope John and the Vatican Council built a capital of goodwill that has been kept intact by Pope Paul VI, or if dissipated in some respects, recouped in others. But we have to recognize, more than a decade after the end of Vatican II, that the gains achieved by the Council have not been consolidated, that on the contrary strong countermovements have developed. It is also clear that Paul's efforts to reform the Code of Canon Law, remake the church's central administration as a service to the entire community, and implement the principle of collegiality in the selection of future popes, have not succeeded. Unless his successor moves vigorously to this task, the outlook for the church is bleak. The epitaph of Vatican II will be that of the Council of Trent, namely, that what happened after the Council was very different from what the Council decided.

It consequently becomes of transcendental importance to take a close look at the people who must agree by an affirmative vote of two-thirds plus one on the man who will become the 260th successor (more or less) of Peter as bishop of Rome. That is the object of this book.

In an area in which there are few guidelines or precedents, it will attempt to describe objectively who they are, what is the level and nature of their education, what are their interests and ambitions, how fitted are they for the task assigned them, to what extent they represent and reflect the joys and hopes, the dreams and aspirations of the people of God for whom they will choose a leader.

Popes, with few exceptions, have since the earliest times been elected, today the sole survival in the West of what was in the early church the standard method of choosing leaders. Eastern patriarchs in union with Rome continue to be elected by their Synods and confirmed by the pope. For a thousand years up to the twelfth century, the clergy and people of Rome chose their bishop in the same way as most other bishops around the world were then chosen.

The system of election by the College of Cardinals is just over eight centuries old and has been modified thirty-two times. The cardinals originally were twenty-five priests in charge of Roman churches, thirteen (later nineteen) deacons from Rome and its vicinity, and seven bishops of dioceses close to the city. In the twelfth century some prelates from more distant dioceses were also named cardinals. But as all posts were not usually filled, the actual number of electors in the thirteenth and fourteenth centuries seldom exceeded thirty, until Pope Sixtus V raised the number to seventy in 1586, a maximum not exceeded up to the time of Pope John XXIII. All cardinals are members of one or more departments of the Curia, the Vatican civil service, and each department is headed by a cardinal resident in Rome.

Pope Paul in November 1970 decreed that a cardinal, on reaching the age of eighty, ceased to be a member of curial departments and lost the right to participate in the conclave in which a pope is elected. He also decreed that the number of cardinal electors should not exceed 120. Cardinals under eighty currently number 117.

Thirty-four of these 117 live in Rome, and 30 of them are involved in the daily activities of the Curia. The others travel frequently to Rome to take part in the deliberations of the department or departments to which each is assigned. In addition, with the modern facilities for travel and the existence of not only national but regional conferences of bishops, the cardinals around the world today know each other well and have frequent opportunity to share ideas and experiences. This is very different from the past, when many cardinals arriving in Rome for a conclave had to be introduced to fellow cardinals by the curialists and often had to depend on the curialists for information about candidates for or against whom they were being asked to vote.

Limitation of voting to cardinals and exclusion of outsiders from the building in which they deliberated did not come about because of abuses, though there had been abuses as under any democratic system. What happened was that an elite succeeded in isolating itself gradually from its popular base and concentrated power in its hands, as so often in history democracies have been converted by power-hungry rulers into oligarchies and dictatorships. The change was spread over centuries, the clergy having marginalized the people and acquired a preponderant voice much earlier. Then, under the pretext of ensuring freedom from pressures, the conclave was developed, the locked building in which the cardinals remained isolated while they made their choice. Here was total segregation from the people, yet in practice a system that did not exclude the machinations of princes and governments. By the late fifteenth century, the papacy was auctioned to the highest bidder, the gold of the Borgias achieving the election of Alexander VI. Down to the twentieth century almost every conclave was dominated by the concerns of Austria, France, and Spain, each seeking a pope who would favor their ambitions, each wielding a veto to exclude an enemy.

With the loss of the papal states, Pius IX's great fear was that Italy would dominate future conclaves. His legislation, strengthened by his successors, isolated the cardinals more than ever before, and in the process widened the gap between them and the people of God. Only with Pope John was the trend reversed. For him, the papal election should be an ecclesial act, not a political one, a point he made by directing that every cardinal henceforth must be a bishop. He also took major steps to dismantle the walls of secrecy. Even more important, he ruled that notes and records made by cardinals during the conclave should not be destroyed, as before, but collected in a secret archive for such uses as future popes might authorize. This made the conclave knowable, an historical event capable of assessment as such.

Paul VI seemed at first committed to John's objective of making the papal election an ecclesial act. In 1973, he announced that he was seriously considering proposals to include 15 representatives elected by the Synod of Bishops as papal electors. But he had second thoughts after Asian, African and Latin American members of the 1974 Synod of Bishops carried the day with their program to end Europe's domination and incarnate the church in their respective cultures, following this up with an election of most of those who had led the movement for change as their representatives. Paul's reform of the papal conclave, announced in November 1975, not only continued to limit voting to the College of Cardinals but reversed Pope John's openings. The next conclave will be the most secret and controlled of all time. The electors will not only be locked within physical walls but surrounded with electronic defenses. Internal police armed with electronic spy detectors will patrol constantly, making systematic searches for transistors, videotape and other recorders, radio transmitters and all other devices for receiving, recording or transmitting information. Telephone calls will be monitored and mail censored. Where John had authorized two aides for each cardinal, Paul bans any assistant except in case of grave illness certified by a commission of cardinals. And all notes made by the cardinals must be delivered to be burned at the end of the conclave. All that will survive is the official record of the results of each vote, as made by the Cardinal Chamberlain, and this will be consigned to the Vatican's most secret archives. When it is realized that 104 of the 117 electors are Paul's own creation, these regulations are a measure of the Pope's evaluation of the honesty and honor of the men he selected to choose his successor.

It is tempting to think in national terms in assessing the cardinals and the positions they are likely to adopt in a papal election. Up to a century ago, that made some sense. Various European monarchs not only had an effective veto to prevent election of a candidate they disfavored, but often a significant positive influence on the supposedly secret voting. Such is no longer the case. What is of primary importance is the mind-set and values system of those admitted to what is one of the world's most exclusive clubs. There is no longer an Italian numerical majority, as there had been for centuries. Instead, more than three of every four members are non-Italian. All long-lived powers throughout history depended on a controlled infusion of blood and brains to extend their control and maintain their dominance. The Romans, the Turks, and the British, at the height of empire, not only drew their élite military units but their most brilliant statesmen from the periphery. Having conditioned them and loaded them with honors, they could command total obedience. Far from being a maverick, a Henry

Kissinger is a typical product of an imperial system. So is it with the typical non-Italian member of the College of Cardinals.

A study of the processes that bring a man to the cardinalate shows the extent to which each has been given a certain mind-set and imbued with a given system of values. A key element is isolation from the normal influences of human experience at an early age and immersion in a homogenized ecclesiastical culture. The official biography of each cardinal published in the Vatican's *Osservatore Romano* when the pope gives him the red hat does not always include the age at which he began his training for the priesthood. But it usually notes that he entered the seminary at the age of ten, eleven or twelve years, or "at a very early age." Cardinal Paul Zoungrana of Upper Volta entered at eight, a practice common in Africa in the colonial period, when missionaries from Europe and the United States believed they had to detribalize candidates to make them into good priests. Not surprisingly, Zoungrana is one of the most traditionalist of Africa's twelve cardinals.

A not insignificant sociological fact about the current cardinal electors is that almost all of them come from modest family backgrounds. Where the biography indicates the activity in which the father engaged, he might be a tailor, a butcher, a policeman, a school teacher, a minor government official. The sociological significance of this fact is that a child from such a home environment, especially in countries with strong class distinctions, tends to accept and assimilate without question the views and values offered by the one in authority, in this case the seminary professors and spiritual directors. If the youth is bright and ambitious, he will not only play according to the rules but interiorize them so totally that he will instinctively insist on others following the same drill when it is his turn to teach or command. And as he moves upward, he is conscious of the distance he has traveled and will instinctively and gratefully give his allegiance to those who made his success possible. If he is personally insecure, and most people are to some extent, he may even positively reject his background and insist that his only personality and concern is the class into which he has been incorporated. And the class of the cardinal is an exclusive one, a prince of the church, often carrying the honors and benefits of a secular prince, too.

After the seminary isolation normal for all candidates to the Catholic priesthood, most of those who will end up as cardinals have a further process of indoctrination in a papal institute of higher learning in Rome. With the exception of the Biblical Institute, at which only four of the present cardinal electors studied, all have long followed a similar pattern of instruction. The textbooks are the product of conservative authors of the so-called Roman school, legalistic, casuistic, steeped in the Aristotelian and Scholastic concepts of unchangeable essences, objective truths, definitions frozen for all time. The successful student asks no questions, absorbs passively the wisdom handed down to him by his professor.

Carlos Falconi, a profound admirer of Pope John XXIII, long a member of the Curia and still retaining close personal friendships with many of his former colleagues there, has summed up in a few words the essence of the function of these Catholic universities and educational institutions of Rome: "If they are formative at all, they are formative only as regards the intellect, even then only in a distorting sort of way, because their raison d'être is not to promote free scientific research, as in a free university, but to submit the student to a definite ideology under the pretext or illusion that it is identical with the truth."

Seventy-five of the present cardinal electors collected a total of some 120 degrees in these Roman institutions. About four-fifths of the degrees were laureates, the others licentiates. The *Osservatore Romano* translates laureate as "doctorate," but it is closer to the level of a master's in a good United States or European university. The licentiate given by many European universities is equivalent to a master's in the United States, but the Roman licentiate— except at the Biblical Institute and one or two new specialized graduate schools—is significantly less than the Roman laureate.

The Roman studies of the future cardinals were concentrated in three areas: theology (46), philosophy (23), and canon law (33). Actually all three courses produced the same basic mind-set, philosophy being presented within a rigidly Scholastic framework that defined its function as laying the foundations for rational proof of the "truths" of theology; and theology in turn being guided in its concerns and thrust by the dictates of the Code of Canon Law. A legalistic, casuistic, hairsplitting mentality, remote from the flesh and blood of real life, is the normal consequence of such training.

Equally significant is the absence of any balancing exploration of the vast range of contemporary knowledge in art, literature and the life sciences. Five cardinal electors have a degree in literature, four in sociology or other social sciences, one in political science, one in economics, none in biology, physics, computerization, cybernetics, communications, population, ecology, future planning, or other sciences that dominate contemporary thinking and are needed to make informed judgments on such religion-related issues as contraception or abortion.

The impact of the Roman system of instruction does not stop at the boundaries of the Eternal City. This "ideological barracks," to quote Falconi again, produces the officer-cadres responsible for operating similar institutions in various parts of the world "according to the methods and programs dictated not by the universities themselves but by the Department of Culture, that is, the Sacred Congregation of Seminaries [now the Congregation for Catholic Education]. . . . The methods used are all tested, decanted, sterilized, and directed above all toward immunization from outside contacts."

The next step up the ladder toward the cardinalate—for those who do not immediately enter the Curia after a course in Vatican diplomacy—is normally a long period as a professor and administrator in a seminary or similar Catholic institution. Those cardinal electors who did not study in Rome collected in such institutes twenty-two laureates in theology, philosophy or canon law. The remaining cardinals, mostly chosen under political pressures to establish the dignity of the new countries of Africa, Asia and the South Pacific, or to place on equal footing hitherto ignored small countries of Latin America, generally lack advanced degrees.

Significant improvement has occurred in the content and form of education in some seminaries and Catholic universities in Western Europe, Canada, the United States, and elsewhere, since Vatican Council II. Even some of the Roman institutions have raised their standards and made concessions to contemporary scholarship. But none of this is pertinent to the present papal electors, 56 of whom are over seventy; 94 over sixty; 116 over fifty; and the youngest forty-nine. And surveys among students in Rome indicate that the students generally regard the changes made there as more cosmetic than substantive.

How does one become a cardinal? Normally, the honor is conferred as a result of success in one of two fields, or perhaps in both. One is a lifetime of service in the Curia, and within the Curia the most promising career is as a member of the Vatican's diplomatic service. Practically every successful nuncio is in due course recalled to Rome and rewarded with a red hat. The other is by becoming the bishop of a diocese that is identified by reason of size and importance as entitling its head to be named a cardinal. Typical in the United States would be New York, Boston, Philadelphia, Baltimore, Washington, and Los Angeles. The primatial see in any country with a substantial Catholic population is almost sure to carry the cardinalitial dignity: Westminster in England, Armagh in Ireland, Santiago in Chile. This is a matter not of canon law but of convention and political judgment. A bishop in charge of a diocese will not be made a cardinal if the government in power at the time disapproves, or at least he will not be publicly disclosed to have been made a cardinal. That was the experience of Archbishop František Tomášek of Prague. Named a cardinal *in petto* by Pope Paul in May 1976, his name was not disclosed until June 1977, when relations between the Vatican and the Czechoslovak government had improved to a point where the government welcomed the nomination.

There is an element of luck in the process, being in the right place, knowing the right people; or alternatively, committing a gaffe and losing an opportunity. An occasional cardinal may have made the grade by political acumen or the ability to pull strings. But by and large, it is clear that those who succeed are men of superior ability, hardworking, clear-thinking, good executives and politically sophisticated. And when you take a hundred or more men who possess these qualities, you are bound to find some of such independence of character and intellectual curiosity that they have been able to rise significantly above their conditioning, develop wide interests, and think for themselves. This is undoubtedly easier for those who have studied in universities outside Rome, for example, Cardinals Evaristo Arns of São Paulo, Brazil (Sorbonne), Giovanni Colombo of Milan and the Argentine Sergio Pignedoli now in the Curia (Sacred Heart University, Milan), George Flahiff of Winnipeg, Canada (University of Ontario; Strasbourg; Chartres School, Paris), Basil Hume (Oxford; Fribourg), Joseph Parecattil of Ernakulum, India (University of Madras), Joseph Ratzinger of Munich (University of Munich), Victor Razafimahatratra of Madagascar (Lumen Vitae, Brussels), Herman Volk of Mainz (Fribourg; Münster). But even the Roman conditioning, though sociologically stable, admits of exceptions. The College of Cardinals is not only an exclusive club but a storehouse of unusual and disparate talents.

Among the leaders who have risen above their conditioning must be numbered Cardinal Paul Emile Léger (retired Archbishop of Montreal) who has asserted that the morality taught in seminaries "is neither principally nor fully Christian." Another is Cardinal Michele Pellegrino, recently retired archbishop of Turin, who said in August 1977 that "the church must still discover and bring about the values affirmed by the Council and engage herself in the cultural and political sphere to bear witness to justice and brotherhood in the world."

Such complaints, when voiced by individuals highly placed in the church and especially when voiced by cardinals, strike a responsive chord in the hearts of many within the church. But the institution rejects them, treating criticisms of its defects as a challenge to its existence. Even Pope Paul has fallen prey to this misunderstanding. "The church is in trouble," he said recently to a group of pilgrims to Rome, his voice and manner matching his concern expressed by the words. This is a long cry from the upbeat tones and optimistic phrases of his coronation address in 1963, but it has become for the past several years the leitmotif of his exhortations as he senses his inability to control the speed and direction of the changes he had earlier believed to have been inspired by "the Spirit and by grace." The critics, he now complains, want the church as it has been traditionally constituted to fade away and be replaced by "an easier, more rational and more scientific concept of the world, without dogmas, without a hierarchy, placing no limitations on any kind of pleasure." And these critics are not the church's bogeymen of the last century, the nihilists, the freethinkers, the deists, the Freemasons, and all the other conspirators against religion who haunted the imagination of Gregory XVI and Pius IX. No, these are termites boring from within, "those faithful who do not fear to be unfaithful."

Paul's fears have grown enormously with the success of the direct attack on his policies by rebellious Archbishop Marcel Lefebvre, and his fears have been played upon by cardinals sympathetic to Lefebvre including Oddi, Palazzini, Höffner and some few Latin Americans, as well as by cardinals close to the reactionary Opus Dei. These include Antoniutti, who was the curial candidate in the 1963 conclave in which Paul was elected, as well as Palazzini and Wojtyla.

The foregoing review of the makeup and mentality of the College of Cardinals, which is not merely the self-perpetuating group that elects popes but is also the board of directors of the Roman Curia, would suggest that other causes may exist for the universally admitted trouble. A study of the record, concentrating on the period from Vatican Council II (1962–65) as seen in the perspective of previous centuries, forces one to ask if the real villain is not institutional sclerosis. It is a well-known phenomenon. William H. Whyte, Jr., in *The Organization Man*, a sociological and psychological analysis of the managerial class of modern corporations, has sketched its essential elements. With the full consent of those it devours, he says, the Organization offers security at the price of depersonalization, destruction of the imagination, and interiorization of conformity.

Power is the Organization's purpose, a temptation of church as well as of business authority. Indeed, American Catholic theologian John L. McKenzie argues that power is the besetting or specific temptation of church authority. "It is not abnormal or surprising that power should be the most seductive temptation for men who have renounced the prospect of wealth and the pleasure of love."

The cardinals may have renounced the prospect of wealth at some stage of their career, but the reality of wealth has visited most of them, and that at a time when many know only frivolous ways to use it. Cardinal Wright is a connoisseur of whiskey; Villot of Italian wines; Nasalli Rocca a collector of rings and pectoral crosses; Sensi of fast cars to take him to his magnificent villa at Sila; while Guerri devotes his time to looking after the ranches he owns in Latium. Felici has a passion for all kinds of photography and audiovisual gadgets, a telephoto lens to follow the pope's movements in his palace right across from Felici's, a videorecorder on which he reruns the televised ceremonies in which he accompanies the pope. Pignedoli is another camera bug, with a miniature theater to show his enormous collection of transparencies from all over the world. He also maintains a file of 10,000 acquaintances and spends much of his time corresponding with them.

The Curia has monopolized power in the Catholic church for centuries, a reality expressed in the cynical saying with which its members reassure themselves whenever a pope tries to assert his theoretical control, "Popes pass; the Curia remains." It originally consisted of the ministries needed by the pope as authoritarian head of the Papal States to conduct the affairs of his Kingdom, a task which incidentally it performed extremely badly. The progressive centralization of decision making after the Protestant Reformation involved these ministries deeply in church matters, the naming of bishops, condemnation of heresies, prohibition of books judged dangerous to the faith, resolution of marriage issues, and a host of dispensations from church regulations. The loss of the Papal States with the unification of Italy in the second half of the nineteenth century concentrated the Curia's work in this area. The 1918 Code of Canon Law solidified its control of church activities all around the world.

The abuses of the Curia have for a thousand years been a commonplace of church history. The twelfth-century reformer, Saint Bernard of Clairvaux, reserved for it what Pope Paul VI has described as "burning pages." Every Council of the church since Basle (1431) and Constance (1514) has tried unsuccessfully to reform it. Much of the stimulus for the Protestant Reformation came from northern Europe's resistance to its bureaucratic, centralizing, and money-collecting methods. The break by Luther and Calvin, far from producing a reevaluation, spurred it to tighten further its grip on what remained of the church.

The 600 prelates summoned to Vatican Council I by Pius IX in 1869 were prevented from acting on the list of curial abuses they had compiled, when Italian troops occupied Rome in 1870 and ended papal rule over the city. "I am too old," Pius IX said wearily to a cardinal who urged that he himself should undertake the job of curial reform.

Pius XII, three quarters of a century later, did not think himself too old. Audaciously but unrealistically, he reserved all decisions to himself, building a private secretariat to short-circuit curial offices. He reportedly planned a force of supercardinals to roam the world and see that bishops carried out his directives. He couldn't crack the Curia, however. It smothered him in details. Archbishop Thomas Roberts of Bombay once said that delays were such that it could take ten years to get a ruling on the validity of a marriage. "Who cares ten years later," he commented, "even if the decision is favorable?" A Caribbean archbishop wrote appeal after appeal for five years for guidance on a conflict with his government that required urgent action. He finally went to Rome to discover that all his letters had piled up in the "in" basket of the first minor official they had reached.

The widespread dissatisfaction of Catholics with the arbitrary and often humiliating decisions of the Curia had reached boiling point when Pope John summoned the Council. John was well aware of the extent to which his freedom of judgment and decision was limited by the all-embracing curial apparatus, on the one hand restricting information input, on the other able to block implementation of papal directives. "Sono nel sacco" (I'm trapped) was his down-to-earth formulation of the strangling effects of ecclesiastical red tape. He hoped the Council would help him.

In this he was not disappointed. To the horror of the cardinals who headed the curial office, Cardinal Joseph Frings of Germany brought the conflict into the open. "The Holy Office is a cause of scandal to the world," he said. "Its methods are out of harmony with modern times." The immediate applause from the assembled bishops was followed by a flood of confirmatory charges and complaints, and by demand for reform and for the rehabilitation of theologians wrongly silenced for teachings to which the Council was giving the stamp of its approval.

Pope Paul, who succeeded John in 1963, promised to comply. The Holy Office got a new name and adopted a lower profile. Bishops and national conferences of bishops were authorized to make many decisions previously reserved. But the spirit of the Curia was not touched. Once the Council ended, it set out to reassert its monopoly of power. Nuncios and apostolic delegates were instructed to resume their former methods of keeping bishops in line. The apostolic delegate in Washington, for example, told the bishops to silence vocal progressive lay leaders, and to remove or keep lay people out of top editorial posts on Catholic newspapers.

By 1969, Cardinal Leo Jozef Suenens of Belgium could stand it no longer. Through the prestigious French Catholic news-magazine, *Informations Catholiques Internationales*, he appealed to world opinion. The Curia must be put in its place, the bishops restored to their rightful position as partners of the pope in ruling the church. Selection of new popes should be moved from the self-perpetuating College of Cardinals to the bishops. In this he was merely restating a proposal put forward by Cardinal Michele Pellegrino of Turin in 1966, namely, that the College of Cardinals should consist exclusively of the presidents of conferences of bishops, the mandate of each ending when he completed his term as president. And to meet the reasonable demands of the contemporary Christian, Suenens added, the bishops in turn should be elected by the people, as in the early church, thus restoring credibility and authenticity to authority.

The Curia's disapproving response, though deafening, was not nearly as deafening as the worldwide response of approval. Agreeing that the principle of collegiality proclaimed by Vatican II has not been properly implemented, Cardinal Pellegrino praised Suenens for insisting, and added that "participation of the Christian community in the election of bishops should be in the very nature of things." The *Times* (London) said that the Suenens manifesto gave new hope to the many Catholics in favor of reform and renewal who had lost faith in the hierarchy. "Suenens is no extremist," said Bishop Basil Butler, auxiliary of Westminster. "He stands in the 'extreme center' openly and prudently." To which *Le Figaro's* theologian René Laurentin added: "This is the jet age, yet the church still slogs along on foot."

It is significant that the Suenens criticism came two years after Pope Paul had reorganized the Curia in what was represented at the time as being the "reform" demanded by the Council. All that had happened, however, was an internal adjustment of the lines of power. Whereas the Holy Office had previously been the most powerful of a group of ministries among which there was no juridic order of precedence, the Secretariat of State became a superministry to coordinate the work of all the others and be the channel through which they communicated with the pope. Cardinal Jean

Villot was brought from France to head the Secretariat of State, and Archbishop (now Cardinal) Giovanni Benelli was brought in as his *sostituto* or assistant. Villot was well qualified for his job, but he always felt himself an outsider in the Curia; and almost from the start it was the shrewd, hard-driving Benelli who made the decisions. He was able to do this because it is a well established curial convention that the person who has the pope's ear and confidence is the real boss, regardless of the formal ranking; and in this case, Benelli was Pope Paul's man, as he still is. At first Paul tried to keep himself informed through Benelli, but with advancing years and more severe attacks of the arthritis that has long plagued him, he has become more withdrawn. His decision in 1977 to send Benelli to Florence to make him a cardinal, interpreted as inspired by his desire to have Benelli a member of the group that will elect his successor, makes it likely that the control exercised by the Secretariat of State over the other curial departments will decline. But whether this happens or not, it is clear that the formal changes made by Pope Paul have produced no substantive change in the relations of the Curia either with the pope or with the bishops and the people of God. Activities behind the Velvet Curtain are still so secret that even the number of employees is uncertain. Alberto Cavallari, who in an unprecedented but carefully staged public relations gesture was taken behind the scenes in 1965, put the total at 500. Giancarlo Zizola, correspondent for the leading French Catholic publication, *Informations Catholiques Internationales*, and one of the most respected of Vatican watchers, says it has grown from 1,322 in 1961 to 3,147 in 1977.

A substantial measure of internationalization has failed to make any worthwhile impact. Twelve of the thirty curial cardinals are now non-Italians, and the heads of six of the ten major congregations (ministries) are non-Italian. Of these six, three were already curially-oriented yes men, happy to enjoy the power they had sought. Three did try to make substantive improvements, the two Frenchmen Jean Villot (Secretary of State) and Gabrielle-Marie Garonne (Education), and the Yugoslav Franjo Šeper (Doctrine of the Faith). Villot, as already noted, was outflanked almost from the start by his assistant, Giovanni Benelli. Garonne started off amazingly well, but now he is a tired old man (77), lets his subordinates make the decisions. Šeper also started well but was worn down in a few years by the phalanx of reactionaries around him and today is solidly conservative.

In synthesis, none of the three goals set by Vatican II for the Curia has been reached. Bureaucracy has grown instead of declining. Decentralization of decision making has advanced in some respects but has regressed in others thanks to the more refined controls made possible by the computer, the teletype and the other instruments of information gathering and communication. Finally, nothing has been done to dismantle the structures of power and present the church as a service to all, but especially to the poor. The erection of the Secretariat of State into a supercuria controlling all the other offices and departments created yet another layer of bureaucracy between the pope and the bishops of the world, allowed the introduction of non-Italians into the lower departments without diluting real control. The survival of the rule of persons was documented by none other than Benelli himself. Shortly after he went to Florence as archbishop in 1977, he told listeners to Radio Florence that while Villot as head of the Secretariat of State had "formal" relations with Pope Paul, he (Benelli) as No. 2 saw the pope daily, sometimes twice. Meanwhile, the areas of greatest growth have been communications, finances (centralized in the Secretariat of State), and diplomacy. Paul has returned to Pius XII's idea that diplomacy is the best instrument to regulate the church and society, while simultaneously strengthening his own personal power as a response to the greater potential power of the bishops in terms of Vatican II's stress on collegiality. One of Paul's acts undermining collegiality was his placing of the cardinals—not in their quality of bishops but in their quality of cardinals (servants of the pope)—between himself and the bishops.

One thing that seems clear from all of this is that the deep philosophical divide within the church, which was made evident by Vatican II and all the subsequent discussion, has not been bridged over. We are still not agreed on the meaning of the *aggiornamento*, the updating of the church, that was the goal of Pope John's efforts. For the Curia, as for the other traditionalists still living in the realm of fixed and immutable essences dear to medieval thinkers, the life of the church must remain intact on the plane of institutions and theology; only a modernization of "systems" is permissible. The progressives, the existentialists who insist that our purpose on earth is to continue the creation and perfect the human condition, want a radical reinterpretation of Christ's message in order to bring into existence a living fraternity. So we face the alternatives: restoration or invention; fear of change or readiness to risk; a finished theology or a daily evaluation of concrete meaningful signs of the times. Pope Paul, himself a typical product of the Curia, his total training and experience within the framework of the Roman ecclesiastical machine, understandably settled for a modernization of systems.

Will his successor continue in a similar line, or will he make the radical break which many see as essential if the church is to realize its full moral potential, adjust its structures and practices to the needs of the contemporary world, and be a light and inspiration to its members and to all mankind? The overview already given of the processes by which the cardinal electors were prepared for their tasks would suggest that the prospect of a major departure is slight. The answer, nevertheless, is not so simple. As happened to Pope John during the years before he sprang unexpectedly into the world spotlight, even if not to the same extent, many of the cardinals have been sensitized to the needs of the people they have served. Many have been taught by Vatican Council II and other influences to read the signs of the times. So it becomes necessary to look more closely at the 117 electors, and in some detail at the outstanding members of the group, those who for one reason or another possess the qualifications that make them potential candidates for the papacy, those who by their personal gifts or the key posts they occupy are likely to sway a significant number of votes, or at least to direct the attention of the required majority toward one individual or one line of thinking rather than another.

The already mentioned Giancarlo Zizola presented an oversimplified but suggestive analysis of the main trends within the electoral college in a recent issue of *Informations Catholiques Internationales*. He divided the cardinals into three categories: Radical Evangelical, Moderate Reformer, and Conservative. The radical evangelicals would regard Christianity as committed to expressing a definite bias in favor of the poor and powerless, and they see the prophetic denunciation of injustice as the most urgent task for the church today. Asia has the highest proportion in this category, five of its twelve cardinals, led by Seoul's Kim Sou Hwan, courageous opponent of the Park dictatorship, and by Joseph Cordeiro of Karachi, the one most committed to a church biased in favor of the poor. The moderate reformers would in general support the thrust of Vatican Council II, some of them perhaps interpreting it largely within a framework of preconciliar theology. The conservatives would want to return to the greatest possible extent to the theology and attitudes of preconciliar days, while recognizing the need to make political concessions on lesser issues.

Zizola would give Europe twelve radical evangelicals, seventeen moderates, and twenty-seven conservatives; Asia, five, eight, and three; South America, four, ten, and six; North America (United States and Canada), two, six, and five. This would total twenty-seven radical evangelicals, forty-five moderate reformers, and forty-five conservatives. It must be stressed that the divisions represent trends, not blocs, especially in regard to the two first groups. Perhaps the only fairly definite conclusion that can be drawn on the basis of this analysis is that, if a conclave were to be held now, there would not be one candidate likely to attract immediately the required majority. The conservatives have a veto power, but as the other two groups are ideologically closer to each other than either is to the conservatives, a conservative choice would seem to be excluded. At the same time, the conservative veto would rule out a radical evangelical, so the ultimate question is where on the fairly broad spectrum of the moderate reformers a winning candidacy can be built.

But before the cardinal electors can even begin to consider who should be pope, they will for the first time—at least for centuries—have to try to reach some kind of consensus on what is the function and purpose of the pope in the church and the world of today and tomorrow. It was only after Paul had been elected in 1963 that the Vatican Council formulated its views on the nature of the church, stressing collegiality as an integral part of the exercise of authority. The implementation of this principle by Paul in the Synod of Bishops and the other postconciliar changes has been ambiguous and ambivalent. But if the continuing structural crisis is to be resolved positively and constructively, the new pope will need to know what kind of pope he is expected to be in what kind of church and in what kind of world. Given the vastly different views of the cardinal electors, this may be a long discussion. It will, nevertheless, differ essentially from past conclaves that dragged on for months or even years, in that the issues will not be political or personal, but basically ecclesial. It will be a clash between different theological understandings of what the church is and what it should be about. Included in this work are the cardinals, as well as some archbishops who are not now, but may soon be, cardinals who would be involved. The detailed analysis that follows of the personalities who are likely to dominate that debate will provide a basis for judging where each will stand, while simultaneously bringing into clear focus the inadequacy of the present system of papal election and the burning need for its reform.

The Americas

United States Cardinals

Nowhere is human fallibility more evident than in predicting the outcome of a conclave called to elect a pope. Subject to that caveat, one can safely affirm that none of the ten United States cardinals will be the choice of the electors. One solid ground for this conclusion is that the United States hierarchy has consistently throughout its history identified the interests of the church with those of the American state, particularly in foreign policy. In a period in which the United States is universally regarded as leader of one of the world's two great power blocs, and is additionally accepted as the policy maker for the rich capitalist orbit, an American pope is unthinkable. Moreover, with the possible exception of Cardinal Dearden (and his poor health excludes him), not a single United States cardinal is significantly qualified for the post.

The United States has many talented churchmen. The Jesuits Gustave Weigel and John Courtney Murray, to mention two who have since died, were but the most distinguished of an excellent group of United States theologians, scripturists, sociologists, and experts in other church-related sciences, at Vatican Council II. But as in business and in academia in the United States, so in the church those who fight their way to the top are not usually the most brilliant or selfless, but rather the pragmatists, the administrators and the string-pulling politicians. When Pope John announced his intention to convoke a Council, the United States high church leaders were aghast. From their point of view, things were never so good. Catholic colleges, thanks in significant part to government money under the G.I. rights and research contracts, were expanding at an unprecedented rate. Church attendance was up, and money was pouring in for churches, grade and high schools and all the paraphernalia that distinguished the church in the United States. Missionary activity was booming, and Catholic Relief Services were making an incomparable contribution around the world as the agency distributing the bulk of the grains and powdered milk supplied by the United States government from its bulging storehouses of "surplus" food.

When they reached Rome for the Council, in consequence, the United States delegates were for the most part quite unprepared, and that applied in particular to their cardinals, the ones who intervened most frequently in the Council debates. It did not take the Roman wits long to circulate cruel jokes about United States cardinals who, not realizing the need for advice from their experts or depending on experts as out of touch as themselves with the realities of contemporary theological thinking, presented as serious arguments the make-believe theses they had learned by rote from their textbooks half a century earlier.

Some of the names have changed since the mid-1960s but the characteristics of United States church leadership remain. This does not mean that the United States cardinals will have no impact on the conclave. On the contrary, they can be extremely influential, particularly because of the symbiotic relationship that long exists between them and the Roman Curia.

Much has been written about this relationship, but perhaps the best brief analysis is to be found in an article entitled "How the United States Church Looks from Latin America," written by Father Jesús García, a onetime member of the Vatican's Justice and Peace Commission and now director of the Mexican Catholic Social Secretariat. The article had been requested by the preparatory committee for the United States Catholic Conference's Committee for Celebration of the Bicentennial, to be included in a guide designed for mass distribution and intended to involve all United States Catholics in "a creative work of Christian discernment and decision." The article was apparently judged by the Committee too strong meat for tender United States stomachs. An emasculated version, omitting entirely the analysis of the Vatican-United States church symbiosis, appeared in the guide. The full text in English translation can be found in another United States Catholic Conference publication (LADOC #56; March 1975). Its circulation averaged 1,276 copies in 1975, a select group of readers to whom it told little or nothing they did not know already.

García's evaluation can be summed up in a few extracts:

> Everyone is talking these days about the transnational organizations that control the destinies of mankind. But the Catholic church is very definitely one of the most powerful of these. Does it realize the tremendous international influence and presence it has, and its consequent ability to bring about a worldwide liberation?

Secular transnational corporations have certain traits in common: they are obsessed with profits and power, they standardize their administrative procedures and controls, and in general they are super-efficient. But they also have a bad record of manipulating and homogenizing ideologies and cultures—so as to produce a uniform and worldwide consumer society.

For many observers, the Catholic church displays these identical traits, and of latter years, by an interesting sort of division of labor, the church's Roman headquarters, reserving to itself—as always—the vigilance over unity of dogma (theology and doctrine) and conduct (norms, discipline, pastoral administration), seems to have taken the United States church's "model" of administrative and financial efficiency as the ideal for pastoral government.

But is that model compatible with the role of the church within and vis-à-vis the twentieth-century consumer society? Should administrative and financial efficiency be one of the visible marks of the church? Doesn't the church's essential mission of proclaiming the meaning of human existence in and through the risen Christ mean that it should question the established society, prophetically and critically?

Unfortunately, many observers would say that the chief characteristic of the United States church is its smooth efficiency, not its prophetic proclamations or its desacralization of false gods. . . .

People cannot help noticing the impressive number of United States cardinals. Since almost every one of them is much more known for administrative ability than for the prophetic, pastoral stance that Vatican II praised, doesn't the cardinal's hat seem to say that good administration is a virtue to be singled out and rewarded? It may be that the cardinal's hat is becoming something more honorific and decorative than in the past, but it still brings a senatorial appointment that is important. The United States, by having 11 [now 10] cardinals—it comes right after Italy—has a decisive weight in the councils of the worldwide church. The United States has been rewarded beyond any other country of our hemisphere: Brazil's 100 million Catholics have six cardinals; Mexico's 57 million, two.

We have already seen something of the inevitable influence of the United States church on the universal church—an influence that one might wish were as prophetic and renewing as it is diplomatic and conservative. No one can fail to see this influence. It appears, for example, in the considerable number of United States prelates holding down key spots at the Vatican particularly in the Secretariat of State and in financial offices. Does this not reinforce the image of a powerful church, one specialized in what should hardly be a glory for a church: diplomacy and politics?

All this does not mean that the ten Americans form a solid bloc. Dearden is certainly not going to be influenced by Carberry, Krol, Manning and Wright, entrenched reactionaries. But they all fit into a certain pattern, pragmatic, likely to be influenced greatly by the atmosphere within the conclave, which in turn will have been affected by the overall problems of the church and the world at the given moment. If there is a solid curial position—and even the Curia is no longer as monolithic as in days of yore—most of them will accept it. In addition, because of their financial and other ties and weapons, they can exert considerable pressure on many cardinals from poor countries who turn to the United States to keep afloat.

Because of these factors, it is appropriate to sketch briefly the background of each of the ten, indicating similarities and differences of outlook and pastoral practice.

Cardinal William Wakefield Baum

A newcomer among United States cardinals who has kept an extremely low profile, Baum was born in Dallas, Texas, 21 November 1926. As a child he moved to Kansas City, Missouri, and attended Saint Peter's parochial school. At 13, he entered the minor seminary, moved up in due course to Kenrick Seminary, Saint Louis, and was ordained a priest in 1951 by Archbishop Edwin O'Hara, a pioneer of the Confraternity of Christian Doctrine.

After he had spent five years as assistant pastor of Saint Aloysius, Kansas City, and professor of theology and church history at the College of Saint Theresa, Bishop (later Cardinal) John Cody of Kansas City-Saint Joseph sent him to Rome for a laureate in theology at the Angelicum (1956–58), and on his return he performed a variety of pastoral and chancery activities. His ecumenical interests brought him to Rome in 1962 as an expert (peritus) at Vatican Council II. He was on several occasions a member of the mixed commission at meetings of the World Council of Churches, and from 1964 to 1967 he was executive secretary of the United States bishops' committee for ecumenical affairs. Three years followed as chancellor of the Kansas City-Saint Joseph diocese, and a further three years as bishop of Springfield-Cape Girardeau. Promoted to Washington as archbishop in 1973, he was made a cardinal in 1976. He is a member of the curial Congregation for Catholic Education.

He was chosen to head the Washington archdiocese, it is widely believed, precisely because of his low profile and his temperamental avoidance of conflict. His predecessor, Cardinal Patrick O'Boyle, had deeply offended many people in Washington and elsewhere by his harsh punishment of priests who disagreed with him. This conflict came to a head with the international publicity given to the theologians of the Catholic University who expressed publicly their reservations regarding *Humanae Vitae*. O'Boyle's rigidity was contrasted unfavorably with the flexibility with which his colleague next door in Baltimore, Cardinal Lawrence Shehan, had handled the same problem.

Baum has indeed succeeded in quieting the uproar. His negativeness is, nevertheless, already being resented by many of his priests. Even if they disliked O'Boyle's ruthlessness, they want leadership. They also object to the fact that he relies exclusively on a small coterie of priests, at least some of them lacking anything like his own culture and sensitivity. In the words of a professor at Catholic University, he is "a company man with eyes and ears only for the top; his lifestyle is princely; he is non-committal, aloof, shy and retiring; although personally compassionate in feeling, he cannot easily extend himself to assist in solutions." Another close to him would describe his lifestyle as upperclass rather than princely, says that he has an open personality and is receptive to reasoned argument. Nevertheless, his final conclusion is equally devastating: "A real disappointment. It's as though Jimmy Carter entered the White House and was never heard of again."

As cardinals go, Baum is extremely well informed in theology, but traditionally Scholastic in his views. His cultural and literary interests are wide. As a young priest he frequently visited London and Paris and got to know many people outside the usual ecclesiastical circles. He can, for example, join meaningfully in a discussion of Petrarch without advance warning. He is impressive on a one-to-one basis, but in public he avoids commitment. Even though personally very concerned about human rights, he is in practice highly supportive of the status quo, does little to advocate a juster social order, and is only mildly against racism.

As a company man, he will always carry out the directives of the Roman Curia, but he will do so with more finesse than Cardinals Carberry and Manning. Similarly, in a papal conclave, he would seek compromise within his own theological framework, a moderate conservative rather than an out-and-out reactionary.

Cardinal John J. Carberry

"On matters political he stands somewhat to the right of Barry Goldwater; on matters ecclesial, to the right of Pius IX." The devastating summing-up of Cardinal Carberry was made recently by one who has followed his career closely. A further interesting element in his composition is the defensive apparatus he has developed to ensure that no doubt will ever creep in among the certainties with which he lives comfortably. He can preside at a conference, in which everything he holds as given is rejected, without hearing a single word the speaker utters.

Born in Brooklyn 31 July 1904, he did his high school studies at the diocesan preparatory seminary, then went to Rome to the North American College, where he was ordained priest in 1929. On his return to the United States, he studied canon law at the Catholic University of America, spent some years as assistant pastor in parishes in Brooklyn diocese, then was loaned for five years to Trenton where he was secretary to the bishop and assistant chancellor. Returning to Brooklyn in 1941, he taught in the seminary for four years and was then made *officialis* (marriage judge), a post he held from 1945 until he was named auxiliary bishop with right of succession to the bishop of Lafayette in 1956, succeeding to the see the next year on the death of the incumbent. The next upward step was to Columbus, Ohio, in 1965, and from there three years later to Saint Louis, an archdiocese normally headed by a cardinal. The red hat was conferred at the consistory held in April of the following year.

He made no observable impact on Vatican Council II, which he attended from 1962 to 1965, nor did it make any on him. His theology, such as it is, is rigidly Scholastic, without flexibility or interest in such novelties as Teilhard de Chardin or the Theology of Liberation, and with little or no interest in ongoing theological developments. If anything, he has withdrawn to more conservative stands since Vatican II, implemented its decisions as little as possible, and gives tepid lip service to the ecumenical movement. His life-style is upper-class; his personality, aloof and authoritarian. He is little influenced by the views of his fellow bishops or his priests, and even less by those of the laity. He is highly sensitive to the vested interests whose support is helpful for the financial well-being of the diocese or whose goodwill would advance the diocesan institutions.

How little he is in touch with the reality of his situation is illustrated by his reaction to the news he had been made a cardinal. "This is a great day for the Irish," he proclaimed, in a city whose Catholic population is heavily of German background, or as they would say, in the heart of the *Gebiet*. Then he played his harmonica all the way to Rome. To be fair to him, he plays it rather well.

Carberry is a member of the curial Congregation for the Evangelization of Peoples (Propaganda Fide).

Where he is highly sensitive is when dealing with the vested interests whose support is helpful, while silent on the needs for a juster social order and for human rights. Similarly he is negative on such issues as the status of women, ordination of women, and married priests. In a word, he is threatened by a world he does not understand, thinks the pace of change in the church is excessive, and welcomes the curial attempts to halt further implementation of Vatican II.

Cardinal John Patrick Cody

It takes more than common talent to be simultaneously the bête noire of the Chicago Association of Priests and of Andrew Greeley. Cardinal Cody has that talent. Theologically, he is a canonist steeped in the Roman tradition. In addition, he is personally insensitive. On his arrival in Chicago as archbishop, he quickly offended many of the priests on whom his predecessor, Cardinal Albert Meyer, had relied to run the diocese smoothly. He had already made the same mistake in New Orleans, yet learned nothing from the experience.

Born in Saint Louis, Missouri, 4 December 1907, Cody studied in the minor seminary in that city, moved to the North American College in Rome in 1927, and was ordained a priest in 1931, having obtained laureates in philosophy and theology at the Propaganda College. After a brief visit to the United States, he returned to Rome to become assistant to the rector of the North American College. Shortly afterward, he joined the staff of the Vatican Secretariat of State. Meanwhile, he pursued studies in canon law at the Apollinare, receiving the laureate in 1938. That same year, he returned to Saint Louis as secretary to Archbishop John Glennon, later became a member of the marriage tribunal and chancellor of the diocese. Having gone to Rome in 1946 with Glennon for the consistory in which Glennon was made a cardinal, he was with Glennon when he died in his native Ireland on the return journey, and he officiated at the requiem Mass in Dublin's procathedral.

Cody was named auxiliary bishop to Archbishop Joseph Ritter, Glennon's successor in Saint Louis, in 1947. Seven years later he moved as coadjutor with right of succession to Saint Joseph, Missouri, and he became ordinary of that diocese the next year on the resignation of Bishop Charles LeBlond. Almost immediately, Saint Joseph was joined with Kansas City, Missouri, in the new diocese of Kansas City-Saint Joseph, and Cody was named auxiliary with right of succession to Archbishop Edwin V. O'Hara, formerly bishop of Kansas City and now head of the combined dioceses. On O'Hara's death in 1956, Cody replaced him. In 1961 he was transferred as coadjutor with right of succession to New Orleans, became archbishop of New Orleans when Archbishop Joseph Rummel died in 1964. The ecclesiastical merry-go-round finally stopped at Chicago in 1965, and two years later the cardinal's hat followed.

Cody is a member of the curial Congregation for the Clergy and for the Evangelization of Peoples (Propaganda Fide), and also of the Prefecture for the Economic Affairs of the Holy See.

Cody did not distinguish himself during the debates of Vatican II. His most commented intervention was during the discussion of Catholic education, in which he revealed a pragmatic and traditionalist attitude to Catholic schools. He continues to get himself involved in Catholic school issues, particularly in asserting his right to make all decisions about them in his diocese without input from others. He caused a major uproar in 1976 when he announced he was closing four all-black schools in Chicago's inner city. The archdiocesan board of education pointed out that its constitution provided it should be consulted before he could make that decision. His answer was to revoke the board's constitution, and it still remains without any powers.

Attempts to unionize the teachers in Catholic schools in the archdiocese have been fought with similar ferocity. Cody is currently appealing court decisions giving the National Labor Relations Board authority in the dispute, claiming that the constitutional separation of church and state prevents governmental intervention in Catholic schools.

Although he assumed a leadership role in the struggle for racial equality in New Orleans, he was rebuked in 1977 by the National Association for the Advancement of Colored People, when he ignored its appeal to speak out against the racial violence that had erupted in the 80 percent Catholic Bogan area on Chicago's southwest side. Harold Perry, a black priest of the New Orleans diocese since 1944 and an auxiliary bishop there since 1966 has called Cody "the prototype of the unconscious racist."

An opinion survey conducted among Chicago's Catholics under the auspices of the *Chicago Tribune* in October 1977 revealed that 33 percent of Catholics disapprove of the way Cody is handling his job, 25 percent have no opinion, and 42 percent support him. This level of support, the *Tribune* commented is "lower than the average performance rating among Americans for any president in the last forty years." Disapproval of Cody was strongest among devout Catholics, with four of ten who attend Mass weekly criticizing his performance. By contrast, 80 percent considered their pastors' performances acceptable, while having reservation on various issues (such as quality of sermons, understanding of parishioners' problems, rapport with teenagers).

The same dissatisfaction was expressed in a "statement of concern" signed by some fifty lay and clerical Catholic leaders. Without mentioning Cody by name, they deplored the decline of the "compelling vision of lay Christians in society" that had characterized the church in Chicago for decades and had been officially sanctioned by Vatican II. "We wait impatiently for a new prophecy, a new word that can once again stir the laity to see the grandeur of the Christian vision for man in society and move priests to galvanize lay persons in their secular-religious role."

In these circumstances, it is hardly surprising that persistent rumors emanate from Chicago to the effect that Cardinal Baggio as head of the Congregation of Bishops has made more than one effort to persuade Cody to resign. But he holds on, and in a papal conclave he will undoubtedly line up with the most reactionary United States and Roman cardinals.

Cardinal Terence J. Cooke

For well over a century New York has been the prototype of United States cities operated by political machines so organized that the interlocking power groups provided enough largesse to keep their constituencies reasonably contented and gave appropriate awards to the behind-the-scenes operators who oiled the machinery and pushed the appropriate buttons at the indicated times. The Catholic church has been a major force in civil politics as one of these power groups. In addition, it has run its own internal affairs on similar lines and with comparable ruthlessness. Not for nothing is the New York Chancery referred to by friends and enemies alike as the Power House.

Cardinal Cooke fits the tradition. Not long after Paul VI ascended the papal throne, an archbishop commented that if John XXIII had not intervened between him and Pius XII, nobody would have realized that one pope had died and another been chosen. That is how cardinals succeed each other in New York as archbishops of a 4,700 square mile area with a population of five million, nearly 40 percent Catholic, one of the wealthiest dioceses—if not the wealthiest—in the entire world.

Born in New York 1 March 1921, he is New York's first archbishop to have completed all his studies for the priesthood in the local seminary. Ordained in 1945, he spent two years in pastoral work in the diocese, then studied social work for two years at Catholic University in Washington. From 1949 to 1954 he worked with Catholic youth and was assistant in a city parish in New York, and from 1949 to 1956 he also taught in the School of Social Service of Fordham University. In 1954 he became procurator of Saint Joseph's, the diocesan major seminary in Yonkers, and two years later, Cardinal Francis Spellman called him to the chancery as his secretary.

He was the ideal man for Spellman's needs, gentle, self-effacing, low profile, always on top of his work, able to keep tabs on every person and activity that interested Spellman, and to carry out without hesitation whatever tasks Spellman assigned him. Here indeed was the epitome of what Father Jesús García, head of the Mexican Bishops' Social Secretariat, has identified as the outstanding quality of the church in the United States: smooth ad-

14

ministrative and financial efficiency.

Spellman rewarded generously those who did his will. Cooke was named vice-chancellor of the diocese in 1958, chancellor in 1961, and vicar general in 1965. He was also ordained an auxiliary bishop in 1965, and four months after Spellman died in December 1967 was named to succeed him. The cardinal's hat was conferred at a consistory a year later. As archbishop of New York, he is also head of the Catholic chaplains in the armed forces of the United States.

Cooke is a member of the curial Congregations for Bishops, for the Oriental Churches, and for the Evangelization of Peoples (Propaganda Fide), also a member of the Papal Commission for the Pastoral Concerns of Migrants and Tourists.

Spellman had run the diocese as a general runs an army in wartime, demanding absolute obedience, immediate compliance with orders and no complaints. Failure brought swift punishment. Although Cooke is smart, he is not very bright, and he tried to continue the same techniques of government in the late 1960s, as though Vatican Council II had never happened. It was the time a lot of priests were leaving the structures, and many of them would want to explain their reasons to Cooke. He was not interested. Gently but firmly, he would push them out the door, not even make any effort to expedite the papers from Rome that would release them from their canonical obligations. Slowly, nevertheless, he has learned that things had changed. Now he is much more considerate and helpful in such situations. This is, in fact, more in keeping with his personal character. He is a compassionate man, holds no grudges against people who have differed with him. But his conditioning was such that he felt compelled for the sake of the institution to act against his own instincts. In this he is a true organization man, pragmatic, untouched by theology or other theoretical influences.

Another example of the new flexible approach occurred a few years ago at an ordination ceremony in Saint Patrick's, when four Jesuits he had just ordained to the priesthood refused to give him the kiss of peace as a protest against his support of United States policy in Indochina and his identification of the church with the powerful in their oppression of the powerless. Without becoming in the slightest ruffled, he went to the microphone and explained that the kiss of peace was really a duplication of the ceremony just completed. They had all celebrated the Eucharist together, and that meant that they had already shared the peace of Christ.

In one area, nevertheless, whether because of the cardinal's own prejudices or the power of the organization within which he operates, urgently demanded change has failed to occur. More than half of the Catholics of the archdiocese are estimated to be Spanish-speaking, the majority from Puerto Rico, most of the others from the Dominican Republic, Cuba and Colombia. The fact was publicly recognized in 1977 when three Spanish-speaking priests of the diocese were made auxiliary bishops. But not even one of the three was of Puerto Rican or other Latin American background, two being of Irish ancestry, the third a Basque born and educated in Europe. The protests of the Puerto Ricans and other Latin Americans were so shrill when the appointments were announced that on the day of the episcopal ordination of the three in Saint Patrick's Cathedral, a contingent of New York's finest was moved in to surround the cathedral with police barricades to prevent a demonstration.

The public issue on which Cooke has been most vocal is abortion. He led the fight against the bill in the New York legislature that gave that state in 1971 the nation's most liberal abortion law. His slogan that "abortion is murder" backfired, polarizing the legislators and preventing compromises that might have limited the liberalization. But other social issues of a city scarred by burned-out buildings, rat-infested slums, and massive unemployment of youth and of minority groups receive low priority. Cooke is not interested in change. In a conclave, his vote would undoubtedly not go to an innovator.

Cardinal John Francis Dearden

The United States prelate most profoundly affected by the Second Vatican Council, the impact of which he continued to feel even after it ended, is undoubtedly Cardinal Dearden. As rector of the Cleveland seminary and then bishop of Pittsburgh before the Council, he was known as "Iron John." Such has been his odyssey that in recent years, the more conservative Catholics in his present see of Detroit refer to him as "the Red Cardinal."

Born at Valley Falls, diocese of Providence, Rhode Island, 15 October 1907, he was educated at the Cathedral Latin School and Saint Mary's Seminary in Cleveland, then studied for five years at the North American College in Rome from 1929 to 1934, being ordained priest in 1932 and ending up with a laureate in theology. After three years as an assistant pastor in Painesville, Ohio, he went to Saint Mary's seminary in Cleveland, first as professor of philosophy and later as rector. In 1948, he was named coadjutor bishop with right of succession of the diocese of Cleveland and succeeded as bishop in 1950 on the death of Bishop Hugh Boyle.

His gradual theological awakening became clear during the third session of the Council in 1964, when he opened the discussion on marriage with a report that spoke of the "principle of conscious and generous procreation," a significant modification of the bald statement in the Code of Canon Law that procreation is the primary purpose of marriage. Marriage, he continued, is an institution oriented to God, the specific love of the married, and the procreation of children, indicating a new order of priorities. He was even more outspoken a year later when a last-moment effort was made by Cardinal Ottaviani, head of the Holy Office and spokesman for the intransigents, to change the wording approved by the Council on the same issue. Ottaviani claimed that he was acting on the pope's instructions and Dearden openly questioned the truth of that claim, demanding the pope's signature as proof. After one of the Council's most bitter debates, Dearden won his point and the attempt to change the basic meaning of the Council document failed.

Renewal did not come to Dearden all at once. Two years later at the first Synod of Bishops, he lined himself up with very conventional positions. He deplored the many abuses that had resulted

from unauthorized liturgical experiments conducted under the
pretext of acting in the "spirit" of the Council. He asked for a
detailed declaration to clarify the real meaning of the word *experiment* and its relationship to ecclesiastical authority. And, he insisted, the processes should be conducted within the framework of
traditional ecclesiastical secrecy; things under study should not be
made known to the public. On the issue of marriage of a Catholic to
a Protestant, he favored the retention of the legislation which
obligated the Protestant—among other things—to make a written
commitment to have all children of the marriage raised as
Catholics. He also said that the United States bishops wanted the
matrimonial impediments to be retained in their existing form,
including the obligation to be married according to the canonical
prescriptions in order to have the marriage accepted as valid by the
church. The only change they sought, he said, was that the bishops
should be authorized to dispense from the canonical form in
specific cases instead of having to wait for an approval from Rome
every time.

By 1969 he had come a good deal farther. Perhaps also, having
just received the cardinal's hat that had been denied him at the
1967 consistory because of the maneuvers of Cardinal Ottaviani
and his associates, he felt he was speaking from a position of
greater strength. He was now also head of the United States
Conference of Bishops. In an indirect but clear rebuke to such
heavy-handed fellow cardinals as McIntyre, Krol, and O'Boyle, he
told a press conference: "It is not authority that is being questioned, but the way in which that authority is being exercised. And
one of the fundamental realities of our time is that in the church as
in other institutions authority must function in a way that differs
from the past if it wants to remain credible." That same year,
the authoritative Paris Catholic publication, *Informations
Catholiques Internationales*, rated Dearden as "one of the most
open of the United States bishops."

Dearden is a member of the curial Congregation for the Sacraments and Divine Worship.

Not everything was peace and light for Dearden as archbishop of
Detroit, where he has had some tough moments with rebellious
priests and laypeople who felt he should be pushing harder and
moving faster. But as head of the United States Bishops' Confer-

ence, he knew it would be suicidal to go faster than the pace at which he could move the majority of his fellow bishops. It was in that context that he became the inspirer and main implementer of one of the most innovative experiments ever tried in the Catholic church in America, the Call to Action. This was a 2-year consultation organized by the Bishops' Bicentennial Committee of which he was chairman, to "determine the mind of the church" and help develop a 5-year plan for church social action.

Parish discussions held round the country produced 800,000 responses for computer processing. Six regional 2-day hearings on domestic church issues were followed by a seventh on international concerns. They generated thousands of pages of testimony. The process built to a climax at Detroit in October 1976, when 1,300 delegates from ninety-two national organizations assembled with 110 bishops for three days of discussion, resolution drafting and voting.

It was the first time that unofficial groups representing every position within the church came together in the United States to talk with scholars, bishops and theologians about the church's problems and needs. The resolutions they voted—ordination of women, public accounting of all church wealth and spending, local participation in choosing bishops, etc.—so shocked the body of bishops that they avoided substantive decisions at their following meeting. But Dearden had achieved his purpose. He had the voice of the people on the record in a way that it never had been before. When Archbishop Joseph Bernardin, president of the National Council of Bishops, complained that special interest groups had too much weight, and Cardinal John Krol added that "rebels" had taken over and "manipulated a naive group of little ladies," Dearden hit back. He sent a letter to several bishops highly critical of the task force chosen by the bishops to prepare a response to the Conference resolutions. Significantly, Dearden had been excluded from that task force, as had Archbishop Peter Gerety of Newark who had chaired the hearings, but it included reactionary Cardinals Carberry and Krol.

To summarize his personal stands, he holds no brief for the status quo, but on the contrary vehemently advocates a juster social order. He is extremely active against racism and anti-Semitism, and is equally concerned about human rights and the status of women. He strongly favors both a married clergy and women's ordination. Although traditionally Scholastic in his theology, he maintains a very active interest in theological developments, being sympathetic to the theology of liberation and at least tolerant of Teilhardian theology. He has given full support to Vatican II changes, has not only not pulled back to a more conservative position since the Council but on the contrary has felt progressively more comfortable with the Council spirit. He is sensitive to the views of his fellow bishops and his priests, and even more to those of the people. He strongly resents the control exercised by the Roman Curia and equally strongly feels a need for substantial change in the way the church is governed, with far more independence for national hierarchies. He thinks the conservative reaction that has followed the Council has harmed the church, while he is strongly confident in the face of the contemporary world. Open and receptive to argument, he is all in all a very reasonable and balanced man.

His personal struggle to find himself and to share his new understanding of the function of the church and the place of bishops within it has taken its toll. A serious heart attack in April 1977 hospitalized him for two months and imposed a long period of convalescence and reduced activity. But a robust constitution combined with a self-control that enables him to keep to a regime gives promise of further years of positive contribution. In a papal conclave, he can be expected to exercise a good influence on at least some of his American fellow cardinals and to play a role with many others in promoting the kind of man who showed promise of pursuing his own vision of the church.

Cardinal John Joseph Krol

Keen intelligence and political acumen were outstanding factors in Cardinal Krol's rise to his present eminence. The fourth of eight children of a Cleveland (Ohio) butcher, he was born 26 October 1910, studied at Saint Mary's College, Orchard Lake (Michigan), and Saint Mary's Seminary, Cleveland, and was ordained in 1937. A year later, he went to Rome to study canon law at the Gregorian, then did graduate work in the same subject at the Catholic University of America, Washington, emerging with a doctorate in 1942.

Having taught canon law at Saint Mary's Seminary, Cleveland, for a year, he joined the chancery marriage tribunal as Defender of the Bond. Next he was named vice-chancellor and later chancellor of the diocese. In 1948–49 he was president of the Canon Law Society of the United States, then a bastion of legalism but since the Vatican Council one of the most thoroughly reformed of United States church institutions.

While in Washington studying for his doctorate in canon law, he had the good sense and initiative to go to the apostolic delegate, then Archbishop (later Cardinal) Amleto Cicognani, explain he had already stadied in Rome and knew his way around so that he was available to help at any time. One of the chores Cicognani assigned him was to drive when he went on vacation. One day, Cicognani was discussing a complicated canon law problem with a clerical friend in the back of the car. When they reached their destination, Krol said he thought he knew the solution. At Cicognani's request, he wrote it up, and the answer he offered pleased Cicognani. The apostolic delegate's esteem was quickly reflected in a series of papal honors: Secret Chamberlain to Pope Pius XII, Domestic Prelate, and finally ordination by Cicognani as auxiliary bishop of Cleveland in 1953.

Back in Rome as Secretary of State, Cicognani continued his interest in Krol, and when the archdiocese of Philadelphia fell vacant, Krol made the major jump in 1961 from auxiliary in Cleveland to head of one of the United States sees that ensures its bishop the cardinal's hat. Cardinal Francis Spellman of New York, long the unchallenged "kingmaker" of the United States hierarchy, had not been informed. The news reached him via the *New York Times* at breakfast one morning. "You'd think they'd let a fellow know before they do this kind of thing," he commented drily to the others at table with him. But he was not upset. He knew Krol well enough to recognize that they were in the same groove.

At Vatican Council II, he carried considerable weight as one of the six undersecretaries of the Council, a body very much under the influence of the dominating personality of the secretary general, Archbishop (now Cardinal) Pericle Felici. Krol had no difficulty in going along with the conservative Felici, with the possible exception of the maneuvering to eliminate or at least water down the statement on the Jews, a matter of concern to the United States hierarchy because of the major Jewish population and influence in their country.

Krol was particularly intransigent on the marriage laws. In 1964, a proposal was submitted to the Council to approve major changes for insertion in the ongoing revision of canon law. They included the suppression of "minor impediments" (such as consanguinity), procedures more in keeping with the Council decree on ecumenism (allowing nuptial Mass, recognizing validity of marriage of a Catholic and a Protestant before a non-Catholic minister, eliminating the promises by the non-Catholic spouse to bring up all the children as Catholics), and finally a revision of the canonical form for marriage, which normally required the marriage to be celebrated in the presence of a Catholic priest.

True to his legal training and his work as Defender of the Bond, Krol argued strongly that the prenuptial written promises be preserved, only allowing that a bishop might dispense for a non-Catholic "of deep religious convictions and strong church affiliations." He also opposed dispensations from the canonical form, because "experience teaches that when the availability of a dispensation becomes known, the requests for such invitations increase," and "the whims of the partners" would escalate into "grave reasons," to the scandal of the faithful.

When the same issue arose at the 1967 Synod of Bishops, Krol took an even more reactionary position. Hewing to the curial line, he asserted that—while the provisions of canon law in general are for the welfare of individuals—those regulating marriage of a Catholic and a non-Catholic are "for the supreme welfare of the faith." Non-Catholics must be told with charity but in all truth, that the church cannot yield on principles dealing with "the divine rights of the faith." To suppress the canonical form would not resolve any problem but would create additional problems. Here we have the quintessence of legalism offering us theoretical principles as prior to and independent of human beings and their rights.

His intransigence was again revealed by his reaction to the "Call to Action" congress at Detroit in October 1976. (See profile of Cardinal Dearden for background to this meeting.) When the 1,300 delegates—many of them handpicked by bishops—and 110 bishops assembled to recommend changes in church procedures and priorities and came up with demands for such things as public accounting of all church wealth and spending, local participation in choosing bishops, and ordination of women, he publicly denounced the "rebels" who had taken charge and "manipulated a naive group of little old ladies." He then had himself named to the task force to prepare a response, the result being that the next bishops' meeting avoided taking a stand on any of the major issues.

Traditionally Scholastic in his theological training, he takes little or no active interest in theological developments. Ecumenical at the social level in the tradition of the United States church, he is a hard-nosed opponent of ecumenism as understood by Vatican II and subsequent ecumenists. His support of the Vatican Council has been lukewarm, so that he interprets its decrees with a preconciliar mentality. He is only moderately sensitive to the views of fellow bishops, and even less to those of his priests and the people. A loyal servant of the Holy See, he is happy with the tone and style of Pope Paul's papacy, approves of the Curia's power and methods, and of the corresponding weakness and lack of power to decide of the Synod of Bishops. He strongly supported *Humanae Vitae*, thinks that change in the church has been much too fast, and is threatened by the dynamic movement of the contemporary church and world. His life-style is princely; his personality, aloof, domineering, authoritarian, and narrow-minded. In a papal conclave, he would be a leader of the reactionaries.

Cardinal Timothy Manning

Born at Ballingeary, Cork, Ireland, 15 November 1909, Cardinal Manning did his secondary studies at the Jesuit boarding school at Mungret, Limerick, then crossed the Atlantic to Saint Patrick's Seminary, Menlo Park, California, and was ordained in 1934. The next four years, spent in Rome, brought him a laureate in canon law from the Gregorian. He was secretary to Archbishop John Cantwell of Los Angeles from 1938 to 1946, in which year he was made an auxiliary bishop for the same diocese. In 1947 he was assigned to Fresno, California, as its first bishop, returned to Los Angeles as coadjutor in 1969, and became archbishop the following year on the death of Cardinal Francis McIntyre. He was made cardinal in 1973.

Manning is a member of the curial Congregation for Religious and Secular Institutes.

It is the consensus in Los Angeles that Manning is no leader, and some say that's a welcome improvement over his predecessor. But Los Angeles is a world in ferment, the wealth held by right-wing extremists and faddists, the future of the church with the Mexican-Americans who constitute a substantial majority of the Catholic population and whose numbers are growing astronomically both by their high birth rates and the movement north from Mexico. How little Manning is capable of being their leader is indicated by his insistence the first time he met the *Padres* (Spanish-speaking priests) that they remove their Mexican poncho-style vestments before he would concelebrate Mass with them.

They say he is learning, but in a papal consistory it would be a safe bet to find him in the same corner with Cardinals Carberry and Krol.

Cardinal Humberto Medeiros

People instinctively say nice things about Cardinal Medeiros, but by the time they have reached the third or fourth adjective, they have run out of steam. He is personable, decent, wonderful to the elderly, but not too bright. He was technically the second bishop of Brownsville, Texas, but in reality the first, his predecessor having died in Europe on his way to take up his appointment. It was a mainly impoverished rural area, with nearly 170 parishes, only 50 of which had a resident pastor, a quarter of a million Catholics mostly Spanish-speaking. He traveled around all over the place, very popular, very social-minded in the best sense. The people loved him, did not expect much because they knew he didn't have the means to offer much.

After four years in Brownsville he was moved to Boston in 1970 to succeed Cardinal Richard Cushing and assume responsibility for nearly 2 million Catholics, more than 2,500 priests, a network of seminaries, colleges, schools, hospitals, orphanages and other institutions, plus a 25 million dollar debt. He soon was made to realize he was out of his depth, and since then has kept the lowest profile of any United States cardinal.

Born in Arrifes, São Miguel, Azores, 6 October 1915, Medeiros came to the United States with his family at the age of 15, studied philosophy and theology at the Theological College of Catholic University, Washington, D.C., receiving a doctorate in theology, and was ordained a priest for the diocese of Fall River, Massachusetts, in 1946. He continued his studies at the North American College in Rome and obtained a laureate in theology at the Gregorian.

Returning to Fall River, he worked as assistant in various English and Portuguese speaking parishes until 1952, when he was named Vicar for Religious and diocesan chancellor, posts he filled until sent to Brownsville as bishop in 1956. In Brownsville, he was particularly concerned about the spiritual and material needs of the many migrant farm workers, spoke strongly in favor of the right to unionize and secure collective contracts, and often traveled with the migrants in their annual northward movement through the Midwest in pursuit of harvesttime work.

The reason why an individual is named bishop remains a closely guarded secret. Undoubtedly the nuncio or apostolic delegate in a given country has normally a powerful voice, and usually other cardinals and leading archbishops in the country are also heard, but the final decision rests with the curial Congregation for the Bishops and the pope. The choice of Medeiros for Boston surprised many. It would seem that the decision makers judged the time had come to break the traditional control of this major diocese by the clergy of Irish background and traditions, especially as various other ethnic groups, blacks, Italians, Poles, Portuguese, and Spanish-speaking had grown steadily more important. His success with the ethnic minority in Brownsville and his graduate study in Rome made Medeiros look the kind of bishop who could balance the many elements.

Named a cardinal in 1973, Medeiros is a member of the curial Congregations for the Bishops and for Catholic Education.

At the beginning he showed promise of major change. For example, he moved ten or twelve pastors who had built up their personal fiefdoms. One of them, it is said, came to him and demanded indignantly: "How dare you transfer me? I founded that parish, and without me it will die." To which Medeiros answered meekly but looking the pastor straight in the eye, "Jesus Christ told me to transfer you." It was a great moment but Medeiros lacks the personality to follow through. The story does, however, confirm the evaluation of others close to him in Boston, namely, that he is "a very cool man who hides under an outer cover of piety," and "a very tough fellow to work with."

Unlike Cushing, who was always ready to pontificate on any subject, Medeiros has grown hopelessly cautious in his public statements. When asked to appear on television, he requires a list of the questions in advance. He avoids comment on the racism that has racked South Boston for several years.

Perhaps his basic problem is that, in spite of two degrees in theology, he has no real theology of his own, has made no attempt to maintain an active interest in theological developments, and does not know how to apply traditionally Scholastic knowledge to the pastoral needs of the postconciliar church. In addition, he has an intense admiration for Pope Paul, strongly supports his stand on birth control and other issues, and is threatened by the changes taking place in the church and in the world. While extremely opposed to racism and clear in his belief for a juster social order and observance of human rights, he is noncommittal about the status of women, is opposed equally to the ordination of women and to married priests. This inability to integrate his values into a coherent whole marks him as locked into the mind-set produced in the traditional seminary, ensures that at a papal conclave he can be counted one of the Curia's men.

Cardinal Lawrence Joseph Shehan

The son of an Irish immigrant tailor, Cardinal Shehan was born in Baltimore 18 December 1898, attended a parochial school, moved to minor seminary at thirteen, to major at nineteen, and to the North American College in Rome at twenty-two. He received a laureate in theology at the Urbanian University and was ordained at the age of twenty-four. His first pastoral assignment was to a church in Washington, at that time part of the archdiocese of Baltimore, and he continued in parish work until 1945 when he was made an auxiliary bishop to the archbishop of Baltimore. In 1953 he was named first bishop of Bridgeport, Connecticut. Eight years later he returned to Baltimore as coadjutor with right of succession and became archbishop within a few months when the incumbent died.

His stands have been mixed in his efforts to represent traditional Roman positions faithfully while open to the new theology and not himself a theologian in spite of his laureate in that science. He was a pioneer of the ecumenical movement, a vigorous supporter of the principles of civil rights, and a strong advocate of Catholic schools. In 1962, he became a member of the Commission for Christian Unity, and in 1964 president of the Commission for Ecumenical Affairs of the United States bishops. This Commission set up a permanent office in Washington to inform the hierarchy on the practical application of Vatican II's decree on ecumenism.

At the Vatican Council he spoke frankly on papal infallibility, presenting the teaching—or rather what he called its misinterpretation—as an obstacle to ecumenical dialogue. He urged a statement by the Council that a papal definition could never be understood as "against the consent of the church." Criticizing a draft statement on church-state relations which sought to present the issue as one merely affecting the laity, he said that on the contrary it was a matter for the church as a whole. On divine revelation, he called for a clearer description of the part played by the human mind in receiving, interpreting and transmitting divine revelation. Stressing the notion of development of doctrine, he cited Cardinal John Henry Newman's statement that "a power of development is proof of life." Against various reactionaries who argued that earlier papal teaching had forever foreclosed a change of position on church-state relations, he joined John Courtney Murray in insisting that it was absurd to appeal to some popes while ignoring others and that conciliar documents can be understood only when allowance is made for doctrinal development or progress. He was also one of the strongest critics at the Council of the "official" Catholic teaching (a teaching later reaffirmed by Pope Paul in *Humanae Vitae*) on contraception.

Yet when it came to the issue of war, he adopted the traditional stand of United States top churchmen in support of the policy of the United States government, joining with Cardinal Francis Spellman in leading the opposition to a declaration by the Council condemning war.

As head of his diocese, he showed great sensitivity in dealing with people. Just when Cardinal O'Boyle a few miles away in Washington was furiously denouncing and suspending priests who questioned *Humanae Vitae*, Shehan had to deal with some forty priests who had similarly publicly rejected the papal teaching. He sent for them one by one and asked each if they believed in the Trinity, accepted the pope as head of the church and heard confessions. On receiving an affirmative answer to all three questions, he said: "Well, go home and take care of your business, but please keep out of the public press for the next couple of weeks."

Retired as archbishop in 1974 at the age of seventy-six, he remains in Baltimore, engaged in parish work and doing a little writing, a man at peace with the world and himself. When he reaches eighty on December 18, 1978, he will cease to be a papal elector. In a conclave taking place before that date, he can be counted on to support an open, moderately progressive candidate.

Cardinal John Joseph Wright

As a young bishop, a dignity to which he had risen at the early age of thirty-eight, Cardinal Wright was looked to by progressive young Catholic clerics and lay people as the great hope for the unfreezing of the icebound church in the United States, a figure he sedulously cultivated. Anytime he took a conservative stand or made a conservative statement, something he avoided whenever he was not forced to choose, his admirers assured the doubters that he had to play the game until he had built a power base. In due course he built his power base and hoisted his flag. It was and has continued to be the flag of black reaction.

Born in Dorchester, Massachusetts, 18 July 1909, Wright attended the Boston Boys' Latin School and Saint John's Seminary, Brighton, then completed his seminary studies at the North American College in Rome and was ordained at the age of twenty-six. After three further years of graduate studies in Rome, he returned to Brighton to teach at Saint John's Seminary. Cardinal William O'Connell of Boston made Wright his secretary in 1943, a post in which he was continued by O'Connell's successor, Archbishop (later Cardinal) Cushing. In 1947, he was ordained as an auxiliary bishop to Cushing, and three years later was moved as bishop to Worcester, then to Pittsburgh in 1959. After ten years in Pittsburgh, Pope Paul made him a cardinal and brought him to Rome to head the Congregation for the Clergy.

During these years, he had acquired a reputation for learning and for wide knowledge of the social and political problems of the times. So successful had he been in presenting himself as a progressive that even the astute Xavier Rynne in his epoch-making volume on the first session of Vatican II linked him with Paul J. Hallinan as one likely to make a positive impact on the Council's work. But when the moment came early in the session, during a discussion of liturgical reform, for United States bishops to show whether or not they accepted the conservative leadership of Cardinals Francis Spellman and James McIntyre, it was Hallinan that went to the podium to make a declaration of independence, while Wright remained discreetly silent. Subsequent interventions during the Council were carefully balanced and presented in such generalities as to keep alive the idea of an intellectual who saw all sides of a question and favored opening doors rather than shutting them. Even two years after the close of the Council, he was described by seasoned Vatican journalists during the first Synod of Bishops as "a middle-of-the-roader, publicly committed to the ideas of Teilhard de Chardin."

In the following years, sensing Pope Paul's change of mood, he revealed more openly what is now clearly seen as his true personality. He was a strong supporter of *Humanae Vitae* and showed total lack of human comprehension of the priests who left the structures in those years and married, two stands that may well have influenced Paul's decision to put him in charge of the Congregation for the Clergy. In an interview with the *Boston Globe*, before leaving for Rome in 1969 to assume his new duties, he said of these priests, "In my opinion, what they need is to go to confession, and that right away. . . . They gave their word. They should keep it."

His attitudes as head of the Congregation have been similar to those expressed to the *Boston Globe*, a stickler for unquestioning obedience, quick to reprimand anyone who steps out of line. He is credited with having been the main instigator of the harsh reprimands given in 1976 to Bishop Carroll Dozier of Memphis (Tennessee) for the public service of reconciliation that had aroused tremendous enthusiasm in his diocese and attracted national attention. Even in the Curia, many dislike his authoritarian methods. Some time ago, the pope named an assistant to him without previously consulting him, an action that within the curial protocol is a vote of no confidence that calls for the department head to resign. Wright, however, did not resign, an action the protocol-conscious curialists do not forgive.

In addition to his primary job as Prefect of the Congregation for the Clergy, Wright is a member of the Council for the Public Affairs of the Church (dealings with secular governments), of the Congregations for the Doctrine of the Faith (ex-Holy Office), for the Bishops, for the Evangelization of Peoples (Propaganda Fide), and for Catholic Education; a member, too, of the Commissions for the Revision of Canon Law, for the Interpretation of the Decrees of Vatican II, for the Vatican City State, for Oversight of the Institute for Religious Works, and for the Sanctuaries of Pompeii and Loreto.

Throughout his life, Wright has maintained his commitment to traditional Scholastic theology but has always kept an active interest in theological developments. He supported the Vatican Council's changes without enthusiasm and since the Council has withdrawn to more conservative positions. He remains a middle-of-the-roader on ecumenism and is only moderately sensitive to the views of his fellow bishops, the clergy and the people. He is careful not to offend vested interests whose support is important for financial reasons or because they could affect the control of church institutions. He is generally satisfied with the church the way it is, and he is fully convinced that the pace of change has been excessive. He is threatened by the acceleration of change of the modern world.

While an active supporter of a more just social order, a strong opponent of racism and of anti-Semitism and highly concerned about human rights in general, he does not extend his concern to the discrimination against women in the church. In particular, he opposes ordination of women, just as he opposes the idea of married priests. His lifestyle is princely; his personality, decisive and authoritarian. He has made many enemies and no longer wields the power he once did with the United States cardinals. But he is still an important element among the conservatives, and his contacts with international rightwing financiers give him a leverage that would undoubtedly be used in support of a traditionalist candidate for the papacy.

Wright told the press in December 1977 that, because of ill health, he did not expect to remain long in his Vatican post, and may return to the United States. He has grown heavy in recent years, and he suffers from a health problem that causes his left foot to tremble uncontrollably.

Archbishop Joseph Bernardin

Born at Columbia, diocese of Charleston, 2 April 1928, Bernardin was ordained a priest in 1952, made a titular bishop in 1966 and archbishop of Cincinnati in 1972. Theologically uninvolved and following unhesitatingly whatever line is laid down by the pope, he is highly pastoral in his concerns and he has acquired a reputation as a safe and cautious leader in the United States hierarchy. At the 1974 Synod of Bishops he was the only candidate to be elected on the first ballot to the twelve vacancies on the Synod Council. The following month he was elected to a three-year term as president of the United States Catholic Conference. The outstanding event of his presidency was the series of public hearings to poll Catholic opinion for a five-year program of social action. At meetings of the bishops, he has been consistently supportive of Cardinal Dearden, the most open of the United States cardinals.

Archbishop John Quinn

Two events in 1977 brought Bishop John Quinn into national prominence, suggesting that he may soon be in line to be made a cardinal. In February, he was promoted from Oklahoma City to San Francisco, and in November he was elected president of the National Conference of Catholic Bishops (NCCB) for a 3-year term, thus becoming principal spokesman for the Catholic bishops of the United States.

Born at Riverside, diocese of San Diego, California, 8 March 1929, Quinn studied at Saint Francis minor seminary and Immaculate Heart major seminary, San Diego, then went to the North American College in Rome for further study at the Gregorian. Ordained a priest in 1953, he spent two years in parish work before becoming a professor in the seminary. In 1962 he was named president of Saint Francis seminary, and in 1964 rector of the School of Theology of the Immaculate Heart seminary. He was ordained a bishop in 1967 and assigned as auxiliary to the bishop of San Diego. In 1971, he moved as bishop to Oklahoma City and Tulsa, and when the diocese was divided the following year, he became the first archbishop of Oklahoma City.

Quinn has been chairman of the NCCB Liturgy Committee and of the bishops' committee studying family life. He has also been a member of the NCCB committees for Administration, Doctrine, Liaison with Priests, Religious and Laity, National Catholic Directory, Pastoral Research and Practices, and Priestly Formation. He has also served on the administrative board of the United States Catholic Conference, and as a consultant to the NCCB Catholic Charismatic Renewal committee.

Canada

Canada's bishops are very different from those of its nearest neighbor, the United States. Sociologically speaking, they are more open, more approachable, far more progressive. The explanation generally offered is that the new theology from France had already reached Quebec before Vatican II and spread gradually from the French-speaking to the English-speaking church leaders, the result being that the Canadians threw themselves enthusiastically into the Council and equally into its implementation, while the United States bishops watched from the sidelines and obeyed out of a sense of duty.

The same difference can be seen in the cardinals of the two countries. Although Canada has only three, all are men of great culture, and all made a major impact on Vatican II. All are definitely in the progressive camp, at least two of them in what might be called the postconciliar attitude, that is, recognizing that Vatican II was only part of a process that must be repeated by continuous updating as world conditions change and humankind moves forward.

In recent years, the Canadian bishops, with the cardinals among their leaders, have devoted a very large part of their effort to the promotion of social justice, both for the Indians and other indigenous peoples of northern Canada, and for the oppressed peoples of the Third World. This concern, unparalleled in any other rich capitalist country, is well known to the bishops and cardinals of Latin America, Africa and Asia. It will give the three Canadian cardinals, who can be counted on to work in unison, a voice far greater than their numbers in the selection of the next pope.

Cardinal George Bernard Flahiff

"Scholarly, gentle, open, critical in his perception of things but loving and gentle in his affirmation of his positions; inwardly independent thinker, outwardly permissive, encouraging new trends, but such a gentleman that confrontation and dissenting pressure do not fit into his Christian universe." Such is the summing-up by one who knows him well of Cardinal Flahiff, who was born at Paris, Ontario, diocese of Hamilton, Canada, 26 October 1905. After studying at the College of Saint Michael, University of Toronto, and at the Ontario College of Education, he joined the Basilian Fathers and was ordained a priest in 1930. He then went to Strasbourg for graduate work, followed by four years at the Chartres School, Paris, specializing in medieval studies. From 1935 to 1954 he taught history at the Pontifical Institute of Medieval Studies, Toronto, and at the University of Toronto.

He was elected superior general by the Basilian Fathers in 1954 and elected for a second term in 1960. From 1958 he was president of the national assembly of Major Superiors in Canada, until in 1961 he was named archbishop of Winnipeg. Two years later he was elected president of the Canadian bishops' conference.

Always maintaining an active interest in theological developments, he sided strongly with the progressives at Vatican II. On the debate on revelation, he showed his understanding of the insights achieved by recent biblical research, and he was one of those who broke away from Scholastic definitions when describing the tradition and magisterium of the church as built—in St. Paul's phrase—"on the foundation of the prophets and apostles." At the 1967 Synod of Bishops, he deplored the slow implementation of the liturgical reform ordered by the Council. "The application of the general principles guiding the liturgical updating is not sufficiently bold and courageous. One has rather the impression of a timid and inadequate compromise, never getting to the radical solutions needed by priests engaged in the ministry. We still have many traditional elements that today are meaningless."

Since the Council, he has continued in the same open position, highly ecumenical, sensitive to the views of his fellow bishops, his priests, and the people. He is totally committed to the building of a juster social order, and he is strongly concerned for human rights, and particularly for the rights of women in the church, an issue he has repeatedly brought to the attention of the bishops and of the Catholic people. Though careful not to commit himself publicly, some who know him well say he does not exclude the possibility of married priests and of women priests. An open personality receptive to reasoned argument, he fulfils the basic requirements for a candidate for the papacy, although at seventy-two he is somewhat on the old side. The fact that he is a Canadian would be an asset to the extent that Canada is regarded by the Third World as probably the most concerned of the rich capitalist nations about the growing gap between the rich and poor countries.

Cardinal Paul Emile Léger

A cardinal who resigned after seventeen years as archbishop of Montreal, Canada, to work for five years as a missionary in Africa, then returned to Montreal in 1974 to take charge of a parish, Léger was born at Valleyfield, province of Quebec, 26 April 1904. From the local minor seminary he passed to the higher seminary in Montreal, for philosophy and theology, was ordained a priest 25 May 1929. After a period at the Sulpician retreat house at Issy-les-Moulineaux, France, he obtained a licentiate in canon law at the Catholic Institute of Paris in 1930, and the following year he began to teach canon law at the Paris theological seminary. A member of a society of priests who live together without taking vows, known as the Sulpician Fathers, he was made assistant novice master of the Sulpicians while teaching in Paris. In 1933 he was assigned to Fukuoka, Japan, to establish a seminary, and he was its head until 1939 when he returned to Canada to teach social sciences at the Montreal major seminary. In 1940 he assumed the additional tasks of vicar-general of the diocese and pastor of the cathedral parish. He returned to Rome in 1947 as head of the Canadian College, and in 1950 was back in Montreal as archbishop. Made a cardinal three years later, he is a member of the curial Congregation for the Evangelization of Peoples (Propaganda Fide); and of the Commissions for the Reform of the Code of Canon Law, and of Pastoral Concern for Migrants and Tourists.

At Vatican II, Léger became widely known and respected for playing a significant part in forming the Council's spirit. He was harshly critical of the seminary education cast in the Roman mold which presented a certain monolithic type of Scholasticism as the only valid theology. There are several radically different Scholastic philosophies, he insisted. Besides, it is in the nature of philosophy to begin with an investigation into reality and not with authority. Lay experts should be brought into seminaries to compare secular and religious kinds of philosophy.

His criticism of the moral theology taught in the seminaries was equally incisive. Moral theology, he said, should be founded on Scripture and centered on the love that sums up Christ's teaching. The morality taught in the seminaries is too preoccupied with casuistry and legalism, so that "it seems to me to be neither principally nor fully Christian."

A strong supporter of collegiality, he also called for a changed self-image for the church. Not only should bishops cut down on their insignia, but "we must pursue the truth in humility as well as charity. . . . When we say that the Catholic church possesses all truth, we use a misleading formula and forget that the mystery of Christ transcends our ability to understand it fully. We never possess the whole truth."

Time and again at the Council, he denounced the antiquated mentality of the Roman Curia, and at the 1967 Synod of Bishops, he returned to the charge. In the planned reform of the Code of Canon Law, he said, the pastoral purpose of law should be made more evident, and "every trace of Roman law should be eradicated." Of the draft document prepared by the curialists on dangers to the faith, he commented, "Truth can never be imposed like a law. It is a mystery into which we must search. . . . The document confuses errors with inadequate formulation of the truth. . . . Only an exploration conducted by the church, with all its trends and at all its different levels, can resolve the crisis." And in a jab at curial secrecy, he told the press that the Synod should be open because "a badly informed conscience is a badly formed conscience."

His biggest bombshell at the Council was his insistence on a full discussion of birth control after Pope Paul asked the Council not to make a formal statement on the subject. "Human love is a true goal of marriage," he insisted. "Marriage is primarily a community of love."

In recent years he has maintained a low profile, but there is no indication that his basic views have changed. That would mean that he would favor a progressive and dynamic candidate in a papal conclave.

Cardinal Maurice Roy

A man of immense energy and equal political sense, able to handle simultaneously two major posts in Rome and the diocese of Quebec in a state of ferment, Cardinal Roy was born in Quebec 25 January 1905, studied at the major seminary there, and was ordained a priest at age twenty-two. He continued his studies at the Angelicum in Rome, winning laureates in philosophy and theology. Returning to Quebec in 1929, he taught at the major seminary until 1940, when he joined the chaplains' corps and served in the Canadian Army throughout World War II. By 1944 he had become the head of all Catholic chaplains in the Canadian armed forces. He participated in campaigns in North Africa, Sicily and Italy, then moved to England to join the invasion of Normandy.

In 1945 he returned to Quebec to become rector of the major seminary, and a year later he was named bishop of Trois-Rivières in the province of Quebec. In 1947 he was transferred as archbishop to Quebec. His many activities there included the development of a faculty of theology at the new campus of the University of Quebec, of which he was made Grand Chancellor. He also had a new major seminary built as part of the university campus. In addition, he opened a seminary for English-speaking seminarians both of the archdiocese and of the entire province of Quebec. In response to Pius XII's call for volunteers for Latin America, he established a Quebec mission in Paraguay.

At Vatican II, he took a consistently progressive line, urging in particular that the church identify with the people in its use of language and its life style. Such expressions as "sacrosanct synod," he said, put an end to dialogue. He played a decisive part at the Congress of the Lay Apostolate in Rome in 1967, blocking the maneuvers of the Curia to control the proceedings. At the opening of the Congress, he told the bishops who headed national delegations that the object of the meeting was "direct and concrete dialogue between lay people," and that the bishops should avoid "too frequent interventions" that might restrict freedom of expression. When during the Congress a strong plea was approved that the church should leave the choice of scientific and technical means for achieving responsible parenthood to parents acting in accordance with the Christian faith and on the basis of medical and scientific consultation, the *Osservatore Romano* protested that the Congress was invading territory reserved to the pope. By no means, Roy answered publicly; it is not an invasion of the field of theology to make one's views known to the pope.

In 1967, Roy was made a cardinal and named head of two new curial offices, the Council for the Laity, and the Justice and Peace Commission, while continuing as head of his diocese. He was able to organize these two bodies in independence of the other curial structures and give them a contemporary outlook and concern. He was responsible for developing the main lines of the letter addressed to him as head of Justice and Peace by Pope Paul on the eightieth anniversary of *Rerum Novarum*, a letter which moved papal social teaching a considerable distance forward in recognizing the Marxist methodology as of possible use for evaluating the economic order.

In a long statement on the tenth anniversary of Pope John's *Pacem in Terris*, he repudiated war as today "not only a crime but an absurdity, . . . disastrously irrational, a non-sense, a self-destroying final step." He denounced the arms race and the waste of money on armaments. "Both nuclear and conventional armaments have launched a self-sustaining process with its own dynamism, regardless of aggressive intentions, so that states have ceased to control it. It is a machine gone mad." He approved of the growth of conscientious objection to bearing arms, and also "a conscience of a civil kind" which is beginning to be recognized as justified by the right to liberty of opinion formulated in the UN's Universal Declaration of Human Rights.

With a change in the status of the Council for the Laity and the Justice and Peace Commission in 1976, Roy ended his term as their head. He remains a member of the Congregations for the Clergy and for Catholic Education; and of the Commission for the Revision of the Code of Canon Law.

An extremely loyal servant of the Holy See, Roy is reasonably satisfied with the Curia as it now functions. If elected pope, a possibility that cannot be entirely ruled out because he has always been able to reassure both progressives and conservatives, he would not be an innovator or charismatic leader. He is a man of moderation, of the middle way, the virtues which made it possible for him to survive both in the labyrinths of the Roman Curia and in the turmoil of Quebec in the 1960s and 1970s.

Latin America

Some 80 percent of Latin Americans are baptized Catholics and regard themselves as Catholics. With 350 million people and a population growth that will raise the number of inhabitants beyond 600 million by the year 2000, it is a region of critical importance for the future of the Catholic church. But it is only since World War II that Rome has taken the church in Latin America seriously, and it is still far from having a voice in proportion to its importance in the decision-making processes of the universal church. It has only sixteen resident cardinals who are papal electors, five in Brazil, two in Argentina, and one each in Chile, Colombia, Ecuador, Guatemala, Mexico, Peru, Puerto Rico, Santo Domingo, and Venezuela. Mexico has a second cardinal who is not a papal elector because he is aged over 80. Two Brazilians and two Argentines are employed full-time in the Curia.

There is no such thing as a Latin American bloc. When Vatican Council II opened in 1962, it was assumed that the 600 Latin American bishops would constitute a monolithic group of conservatives, but it turned out that the majority of them supported the most progressive elements in the Council. It has, however, to be remembered that the church in Latin America was originally established as a part of the Spanish (and Portuguese) state, the higher clergy named by the state and entrusted with the supervision of various areas of social life, particularly education and health. Though the forms have changed, the concept of the church as subordinate to the state has in large part survived. The years of the Council were also the years of the Alliance for Progress, when Latin American states were committed—at least officially—to programs of rapid and radical change of structures. Like the society, the church is underdeveloped. Most of the bishops have relatively little education, and they followed the lead of a small minority of committed progressives both at the Council and for some years after it closed, the highwater mark being reached in 1968 with the issuance by the Latin American bishops as a body of the Medellín Documents committing the church to a position of leadership in the renewal of the material and spiritual life of the hemisphere.

In the 1970s, on the contrary, with the collapse of the Alliance for Progress and other efforts of evolutionary development, most of the Latin American states came under reactionary military dictatorships. While some segments of the church have resisted this trend, more traditional and conservative elements have increased their visibility and power within the institution. It is impossible to project whether this change will continue. When repression reaches a level where only the church remains to speak for those who suffer, one can see several examples of its emancipation from its traditional submission to the government in power. Such is the situation in El Salvador, where the hierarchy and clergy are solidly united in opposition to the institutionalized violence of the state and of rightwing vigilantes. In Chile, the majority of the bishops support the cardinal in a policy of cautious protest. And in Brazil, after a period of relative silence and acquiescence, the church leaders have taken a strong position in favor of the powerless and voiceless masses.

The changing political and social situation could exert a significant influence on the votes of nearly half the nineteen Latin American cardinal electors. Three or four can be counted on to maintain a strong progressive stand in any circumstances, the most outstanding of these being the Brazilians Arns and Lorscheider. Several have always been and will always be obscurantist and reactionary, led by Muñoz Duque of Colombia and Casariego of Guatemala. Given the rapidly increasing population without any corresponding increase in the level of production of goods and services in most Latin American countries, it may well be that the progressives will be able to rally a considerable number of the undecided to a candidate who stresses church commitment to social justice. This concern will be shared by many of the cardinal electors from Africa and Asia, and it may well be a major factor in the selection of the next pope. Of course, social awareness frequently coexists with conservative theology, and that may well prove the winning combination.

José Comblin, one of the main drafters of the Medellín Documents, surveyed the current status of the church in Latin America in the Jesuit review *Mensaje* (Chile) in October 1976. Belgian-born Comblin is a top expert on church affairs in Latin America, especially in Brazil and Chile. He distinguishes "evangelical" bishops or "bishops of the poor," listing Gerardo Valencia Cano (Buenaventura, Colombia), Enrique Angelelli (La Rioja, Argentina), Adhemar Esquivel (auxiliary of La Paz, Bolivia), Leónidas Proaño (Riobamba, Ecuador), and the Brazilians Helder Camara, Antonio Fragoso, José Pires, Waldir Calheiros, Marcos Noronha, Pedro Casaldáliga, and Helio Campos. Valencia Cano and Angelelli have died since Comblin wrote his article, the latter in an automobile accident that had all the appearances of a planned execution.

Next to the "evangelicals" come the "Ambrosians," those bishops who—like Saint Ambrose in Milan in the third century—are intellectuals engaged in defending the faith against the power of the world by their eloquence and the intellectual direction they give the entire episcopate. Here Comblin lists Cardinal Arns of São Paulo, and Bishop Candido Padín (Bauru, Brazil), and one who has since died, Bishop Ramón Bogarín (Paraguay). In the same line, Comblin continues, are the cardinals who for the past ten years have been the "moderators" of the Latin American hierarchy, following the pioneer efforts of the late Bishop Manuel Larraín (Talca, Chile), also killed in an automobile accident. They are Cardinals Avelar Brandão Vilela and Aloisio Lorscheider of Brazil, Landázuri of Peru, and Silva of Chile.

Comblin's rapid survey properly stresses the importance of the Brazilians in the updating of the church in Latin America and in its emergence as the principal defender of human rights. In the early 1970s the bishops of the poorest areas of Brazil, the Northeast, the Center-West, and Amazonia, in separate but parallel collective pastoral letters called for a radical change of structures to end the exploitation of the poor by the local oligarchs and the multinational corporations. In April 1977, the National Conference of Brazilian Bishops raised the challenge to the national level with a collective statement on the Christian requirements of a political order, a document that challenged the main premises of the socioeconomic policies of the dictatorship. Archbishop Geraldo Siguad of Diamantina, a leader of reaction at Vatican Council II and a big cattle rancher in the State of Minas Gerais, tried to diffuse the impact of the statement by stating publicly that the hierarchy had been infiltrated by communists, naming specifically Bishop Pedro Casaldáliga and Bishop Tomás Balduino. Casaldáliga has been primarily active in defence of Indians and squatters threatened by the multinational corporations who are seizing control of the Amazon territories and exploiting them without regard either for the inhabitants or the ecological consequences. Balduino is president of the *Conselho Indigenista Missionário* ("Missionary Council for the Indigenous Peoples"), the body that alone today protects the Indians, now that the Government's Indian Institute has taken the side of the land-grabbers. Government leaders in both houses of Congress supported Sigaud's charges, but the body of bishops stood firm. Even the conservative Cardinal Alfredo Scherer came to the defense of Casaldáliga and Balduino.

Cardinal Eugenio Sales of Rio prefers to stand aloof, to be seen as reconciler, diplomat, sometimes seeking the limelight that is more appropriate to the president of the conference of bishops. Unlike Cardinal Arns, he does not hesitate to be seen in public ceremonies with generals or to preside at Masses ordered by government officials. In this he shares the views of Cardinal Agnelo Rossi, his predecessor in Rio who is now a curial cardinal in Rome. Before leaving Brazil in 1970, Rossi visited the then president, General Medici, and promised him that he would create in Rome a center for promoting the true image of Brazil. Under Medici, Brazil lived the worst nightmare of political repression, tortures and censorship of the news media of its entire history.

Even though there are significant differences in style and even in substance between the Brazilian cardinals, the dynamics of the situation they are living drives them more and more clearly toward a stand in favor of major change both in their own country and in its relations with the rich countries. Writing in the Vatican's *Osservatore Romano* in 1977, Cardinal Lorscheider said that "the pastoral thrust of the church in the world's present situation tends more toward the intense development of the social and political responsibility of Christians." And coming from a very different direction, Cardinal Scherer criticized the United States harshly in one of his weekly radio talks for trying to block the Brazil-German atomic treaty. "They know how to enrich themselves and become more powerful," he said, "by sacrificing their poor brothers and cousins. We are watching with frustration the efforts of North American diplomacy to stymie a treaty that will greatly favor

Brazil's progress." Regardless of one's opinion as to the correctness of his judgment, what emerges clearly is the existence of a definite sense of solidarity and of common goals among the members of the Brazilian cardinal electors. They should carry many waverers from other Latin American countries to the progressive side in a papal conclave.

Cardinal Luis Aponte Martínez

Born to poor parents in Lajas on the outskirts of the city of Ponce, Puerto Rico, 4 August 1922, Cardinal Aponte at an early age become the protegé of Bishop James McManus of Ponce, who recognized his talent and encouraged him to continue his studies. Following the regular course of studies in the Boston seminary, he received a B.A. degree and was ordained a priest in 1950. He worked closely with Bishop McManus for ten years, then was made his auxiliary bishop. This was the time when pressure was growing in Puerto Rico for the elimination of bishops from the United States in favor of native Puerto Ricans. Aponte strongly promoted this movement, and it worked to his benefit when Bishop McManus resigned in 1963 and returned to the United States, passing the bishopric of Ponce to his auxiliary. Just a year later, Aponte succeeded in being transferred to San Juan, the capital, and he shortly had the additional prize of the cardinalate, conferred in 1964. He was the first native of Puerto Rico ever to be made a cardinal, an acknowledgement by Rome of the desire of Puerto Ricans to be seen as a distinct culture and society.

The church in Puerto Rico has been torn not only by conflict over control from the United States, but also by internal differences between progressive and conservative Puerto Rican bishops and priests. The leader of the progressives and long a thorn in the side of his colleagues is Bishop Antulio Parrilla Bonilla, a Jesuit. Aponte joined with the rest of the hierarchy in sidelining Parrilla, who still lives in Puerto Rico and promotes complete elimination of United States influence and control from the island but who no longer hold any office in the church. Aponte is by no means the most reactionary of the bishops, but he goes along with the others in clamping down on progressive priests, lacking the self-confidence to set a course of his own. On one subject, he and his colleagues are agreed. Given the enormous problem of surplus population, they make no attempt any more to challenge the government policies favoring birth control. In a papal conclave, he would probably be greatly influenced by the general atmosphere, avoiding premature commitments until he was sure which way the ball was going to bounce.

Cardinal Juan Carlos Aramburu

Of the three cardinal electors born in Argentina, Cardinal Aramburu is the only one now living in that country. The others, Umberto Mozzoni and Eduardo Pironio, live in Rome and work in the Curia. Mozzoni is a Vatican career diplomat. Pironio was in charge of a diocese in Argentina until 1975, when the Vatican authorities, fearful for his life because of his opposition to the military dictatorship, called him to Rome. Aramburu has no similar problem. He has always been careful not to offend the regime in power.

Born in Reducción, diocese of Córdoba, 11 February 1912, Aramburu studied at the seminary in Córdoba, then went to Rome for a laureate in canon law and moral theology. Ordained to the priesthood in 1934, he taught both subjects at the Córdoba seminary, simultaneously holding the office of vice-rector. Next he moved to the National University of Córdoba as professor of religious studies and philosophy. In 1946 he was made auxiliary bishop of Tucumán, and succeeded as bishop in 1953. He was promoted to Buenos Aires in 1967 as coadjutor with right of succession, and became archbishop of Buenos Aires in 1975 on the death of Cardinal Caggiano. Named a cardinal in 1976, he is a member of the curial Congregation for the Eastern Churches.

In Buenos Aires he undertook a major revision of the diocesan structures, dividing the enormous diocese into four pastoral zones, reorganizing the chancery, and setting up pastoral, liturgical and doctrinal councils. Although he participated in the 1968 meeting of the Latin American bishops at Medellín, Colombia, the impact of its historic statements was slight as far as he was concerned. Some months later, at Christmas 1968, several Buenos Aires priests made a public appeal for justice for the slum dwellers, and some of them also publicly asked pardon for the sins of a social order accepted too complacently by the church. Aramburu reprimanded them and issued an order forbidding any priest to speak or act on issues concerning the social and economic order without previous hierarchical approval.

In 1969, Aramburu was asked to intervene on behalf of the workers in Tucumán, his former diocese. Tucumán, a sugarcane area in northern Argentina, is one of the country's most depressed sectors. There were disturbances in 1969 following the closing of a sugar factory, and a priest was arrested as one of the demonstrators. Thirteen other priests issued a protest against the economic injustices and asked Aramburu to help as the most influential churchman in the country. "We wish to inform you respectfully," they wrote him, "of the criticisms we hear all around regarding the attitude of our bishops, namely, that the Argentine church seems to have become the church of silence." Their bishop, Juan Carlos Ferro, agreed, saying the church could not remain silent in the face of the anguish of the workers. Aramburu, however, refused to intervene. In his opinion, such stands were no part of the church's business.

All this was a far cry from his statement of principle during the debate on freedom of religion at Vatican II in September 1965. There he insisted that the church should never let itself be silenced by the civil authorities. "Christians have always troubled the public peace. Christ himself was an agitator. We should specify that public peace is founded on the universal rights of man; otherwise, public powers will be able to judge what constitutes a breach of public peace as they please." Regrettably, he was not the only bishop who found it difficult later to live up to brave statements made during the Council.

Cardinal Paulo Evaristo Arns

A Franciscan who heads one of the world's biggest dioceses—
some six million inhabitants—Cardinal Arns started out very
cautiously when made archbishop of São Paulo in 1970, seeking to
placate the military dictatorship. Gradually, however, he was
radicalized by the excesses of the military and their connivance
with wealthy landowners in oppressing the peasants. Particularly
since he was made a cardinal in 1973, he has shown fearless
leadership in the battle long waged almost alone by Archbishop
Helder Camara of Recife on behalf of the poor.

Arns was born in Santa Catarina State in the south of Brazil, 14
September 1921, the fifth of 13 children of working-class parents.
He did his high school studies in Franciscan preparatory schools in
Brazil and joined the Order at an early age. He studied philosophy
and theology in Franciscan seminaries in Brazil, was ordained a
priest in 1945, then went to France to obtain a doctorate in classical languages at the Sorbonne. Returning to Brazil, he taught at
various Franciscan institutions and at the Catholic University in
Petropolis. Also in Petropolis he was editor of *Sponsa Christi*, a
monthly review for nuns, and head of *Vozes*, the most important
Catholic publishing house in Brazil.

In 1966 he was made auxiliary to the archbishop of São Paulo
and succeeded as archbishop in 1970. An analysis he has made of
the pastoral needs of the diocese points out that the city grows by
300,000 to 400,000 every year. While there is much industry, there
is also desperate proverty, as well as very unequal quality in the
schools. University and intellectual people, he said, are able to
accept Christ's message. The middle class constitutes the most
religious segment of the population and has been affected by Vatican II. But there are three million poor people from the hinterland
who have lost their roots, including their religious roots.

This group constitutes his greatest concern. He tries to establish
contact with them by his pastoral action for human rights and his
insistence that society has a duty to provide for those now left to
starve in the slums. He has developed three alternative ways of
training candidates for the priesthood. One is the conventional
seminary routine. The second is for young professionals who work
at their jobs during the day and study the ecclesiastical sciences in

night courses. Finally, there are integrated courses of philosophy and theology combined with active pastoral duties under the supervision of a community of priests. The major pastoral activity of the priests in the slums is the formation of lay leaders to serve as "animators" and set up "base communities," nuclei of informed and committed Christians who will radiate their faith to those they meet at work or socially.

The resistance of the wealthy classes and of the military to the work of the priests in the slums, regarded by them as helping the communists to stir up discontent, played a part in radicalizing Arns. He was also influenced by the persecution of a young Spanish bishop, Pedro Casaldáliga, who was trying to protect the Indians and squatters in his remote diocese of São Félix in the Amazon basin. Each year he expresses himself more strongly. In 1973, he said that what Brazil needs is a "Christian socialism," a system he described as based on truth, human solidarity, dynamic peace, and love. It is the duty of every Latin American bishop, he added, to perform two very important tasks: to defend the fundamental rights of the human person; and to be the inspirer, as well as the center, of the changes needed by contemporary society.

Early in 1977, he visited Paraguay to express his support of political prisoners held by that country's military dictator, and to encourage the work of the ecumenical Church Committee for Emergency Aid. At that time he said that the problems of the hemisphere are not created by the prisoners but by "the iniquitous distribution of wealth." A few months later, the São Paulo arch-diocesan Commission for Human Rights issued a statement of support for students who had joined workers in technically illegal protests calling for amnesty for political prisoners, free elections, and an end to political repression. This statement came a few days after 10,000 students had marched through central São Paulo to protest the arrest of four students and four workers. It was the first major political demonstration since 1968, the year in which the dictatorship had by decree (Institutional Act #5) ended all civil rights. The demonstrators received a ticker-tape welcome from office workers along their line of march.

Because of the expression of such views in the São Paulo diocesan weekly newspaper, it is one of the few newspapers in the country that has to submit all copy for advance censorship, and

much of its content is cut. One issue in 1977 inserted an advertise-
ment in the space normally allocated to editorial comment. The
banned editorial, according to *Jornal do Brasil*, included the assertion that "it is much worse than trying to cover the sun with a sieve
for a state to try to confront the enemy outside without representing the people's will internally."

Arns has joined the growing number of advanced Latin American thinkers who are critical of President Carter's human rights
policy. Their objection is not to what Carter says but what he
leaves unsaid, namely, that even more important than the right to
freedom of speech or freedom from arbitrary arrest is the right to a
social system that gives all citizens access to material and intellectual wellbeing, to food, clothing, shelter, health services and education. "The United States should revise entirely its concept of
human rights," Arns has said. "It must not concentrate exclusively
on the practice of torture. The predatory action of wealthy countries against those peoples who fight to eliminate poverty and its
consequences should become an essential part of this new United
States sensitivity. Maybe this will even lead them to respect the
price of our coffee, the principal product of the labors of our people."

Theological reflection and understanding underlie the social
stands of Arns. Starting from a traditional Scholastic training, he
maintains an active interest in theological developments, sympathetic to the theology of liberation and enthusiastic about
Teilhard de Chardin's worldview. He places top priority on the
need for a juster social order, including radical land reform, and he
is confident in the face of the contemporary world. He feels the need
for a new papal style, favors more independence for national
hierarchies, and resents the control of the Roman Curia. He is
sensitive to the views of his fellow bishops, of his clergy and of the
laity, and he is unconcerned about personal risks or threats of
economic or political retaliation. While he has publicly supported
Humanae Vitae, he has expressed guarded reservations in private.
A compassionate man, with a pastoral, outgoing heart, he is receptive to reasoned argument and when he acts, he acts decisively.
Unspoiled by power, he lives a modest, middle-class life-style.

His curial appointments as a cardinal are membership of the
Secretariat for Non-Believers and of the Congregation for the
Sacraments and Divine Worship.

Cardinal Octavio Antonio Beras Rojas

El Seybo, where Cardinal Beras was born 16 November 1906, is a small (20,000 inhabitants) but historic city in the eastern part of the Dominican Republic. From this area came the leaders of the revolt against Spain in the last century, and the threads of the old traditions of political involvement of the oligarchs of El Seybo can be traced down to the present time. Beras forms part of that culture: conservative, traditionalist, with a provincial simplicity, an enormous appreciation of the past and respect for custom. His father was an important politician, president at one time of the Chamber of Deputies of the Dominican Republic. Beras knows his people well and appreciates their ways, is quick to laugh and most amiable; and in consequence, a good mediator and an administrator who can find areas of agreement among differing points of view.

After early schooling in El Seybo, La Romana and Santo Domingo, Beras entered the seminary in Santo Domingo in 1923 and two years later went to Rome to continue his studies at the Latin American Pontifical College. Reasons of health forced him to return to the Dominican Republic and he completed his theology courses in the seminary there and was ordained a priest in 1933. He worked for a time in a hospice for old people and the College of the Sacred Heart in Santiago, then moved to Santo Domingo as secretary general of the archdiocese. He was simultaneously pastor at the cathedral, editor of the weekly *Catholic Truth*, and director of a radio station. In 1945, he was named coadjutor with right of succession to the archbishop, and succeeded on the death of the incumbent in 1961, becoming at the same time bishop for the Armed Forces of the Dominican Republic.

A strange period followed, on which Beras's official autobiography in the *Osservatore Romano* throws no light. Beras had risen through the ecclesiastical ranks during the Trujillo dictatorship, and nobody in church or state advanced except through Trujillo's good graces. Beras undoubtedly had gone along with Trujillo's villainies but had certainly not been implicated as positively as the archbishop whose coadjutor he was. In any case, the feeling developed that he was a political liability to the church under the new regime that followed Trujillo's assassination, and a compromise was developed in a way appropriate to the devious plottings of Dominican politicians and the velvet-gloved fist of the Curia represented by Archbishop Emanuale Clarizio, the nuncio. In 1966, Bishop Hugo Polanco Brito was brought from Higüey as apostolic administrator to run the archdiocese of Santo Domingo, and Beras was suspended from all his episcopal duties but allowed to remain in Santo Domingo.

This situation, which lasted until 1970, brought out the best qualities in Beras. He made no attempt to create problems for Polanco, on the contrary maintaining excellent personal relations with him, and he continued to engage in church activities on a hemispheric and international level. An intervention Beras made at the Synod of Bishops in Rome in 1969 is said to have so influenced Pope Paul that he decided to reinstate him. A new compromise was effected in 1970. Beras was restored to full authority, and Polanco stayed on as his assistant until 1975. Polanco then returned to Higüey, and the process of revindication was completed in 1976 when Beras was made a cardinal. Although Santo Domingo is the oldest diocese in the New World, Beras is its first cardinal. His curial office is membership of the Congregation for the Bishops.

Beras is a man of extremely traditional piety and theologically simplistic. At Vatican II in 1964, he took advantage of an opportunity to speak on the issue of revelation to advocate a return to old-fashioned notions of tradition, and to give a plug to the International Marian Congress he had planned for the following year in Santo Domingo. His justification for raising these issues, he said, was that the theme of the Congress would be "Mary in Sacred Scripture." According to an observer, most of the Council Fathers, including the moderators, smiled in benevolent toleration of the self-advertisement, even though it was widely known that the instigator of the move was the Franciscan Mariologist, Father C. Balic, the organizer of the Congress. Balic, a henchman of Cardinal Ottaviani, then head of the Holy Office, had spent the previous months in the United States collecting funds for the Marian Congress and voicing fierce opposition to the progressive theology that dominated the Vatican Council.

Beras is incapable of understanding the temperament or values of the contemporary world. For all his good personal qualities, he has no idea how to, or of the need to, lead the church into the twenty-first century. That such a man is one of the small group who behind closed doors will elect the supreme leader of the biggest and most tightly controlled religious body in the world is a measure of the need to reform the process of choosing popes.

Cardinal Avelar Brandão Vilela

People who know Cardinal Brandão Vilela well speak of his aloof personality, his princely life-style, his authoritarian manner, his pride and lust for power, his refusal to take a strong stand on theological or social issues. Yet this is the same man who as president of the Latin American Bishops' Council (CELAM) in 1968 played a positive and constructive part in the preparation for and success of the 1968 Medellín Conference. He was not responsible for drafting the Documents which made that meeting historic, but he did work to have them adopted by the participants without the watering down desired by a small but powerful minority. The explanation of the contradictory elements would seem to be that this is a man more at home in administration than in creative construction, one who will follow the majority when he sees it is to his advantage to do so.

Born in Viçosa in the State of Alagoas, on the Atlantic coast between Recife and Salvador in Brazil's hungry Northeast, 13 June 1912, he was—against the wishes of his father—taken to the junior seminary of Maceió at the age of thirteen by an uncle who was also his godfather. In due course he moved up to the major seminary and was ordained a priest in 1935. After eleven years in parish and chancery activities, he was made bishop of Petrolina in 1946, transferred to Teresina in 1955, and finally became the head of Brazil's primatial see, São Salvador da Bahia, in 1971. The cardinal's hat followed two years later, and with it membership in the curial Congregations for the Clergy, for the Causes of Saints, and for Catholic Education.

As already indicated, he avoids taking strong positions on the social issues that are most critical in Brazil, such as land reform and the need for radical change of the socioeconomic structures. His concern for human rights is slight, as is his concern for the status of women. He is opposed to a married clergy, and even more strongly to the ordination of women. In public he has strongly supported *Humanae Vitae*, while privately expressing guarded reservations. He is definitely a loyal servant of the Holy See, is satisfied with the way the church is governed, and with Pope Paul's style of leadership. He is also strongly committed to maintaining a unified policy among Brazil's bishops and would consequently in a papal conclave tend to reach agreement with his Brazilian colleagues on a candidate.

Cardinal Mario Casariego

The epitome of obscurantism, reaction, and insensitivity, Cardinal Casariego was born in Figueras de Castropol, Oviedo, Spain, 13 February 1909. Both parents died while he was young, and he emigrated to Central America, where the Somaschi Fathers accepted him as a postulant, sent him to Somaschi, Italy, for his novitiate and accepted his profession as a member of the Congregation in 1930. After philosophy studies in Italy, he returned to El Salvador for theology and ordination as a priest in 1936.

A consummate political sense enabled him to win the support of wealthy and powerful patrons, so that he moved up rapidly as head of an orphanage and as a superior in his Congregation. In 1958, he was made auxiliary to the archbishop of Guatemala, whom he succeeded as archbishop in 1964. The red hat followed in 1969, and with it a curial appointment as member of the Congregation for the Causes of the Saints.

In Guatemala, both before and since he became cardinal, he has worked strenuously to prevent priests and church members from supporting the poor people of the countryside and city slums in their struggle for land and for work; and, as the only Central American cardinal, he has used all his influence to establish similar policies in El Salvador and other neighboring countries. While his actions have greatly helped the oligarchies by causing confusion among Catholics, most of his fellow bishops and priests openly oppose him. Already in 1969, when he was named cardinal, 50 priests protested publicly. "We oppose the institution of cardinal as it presently functions, and specifically the choice of Casariego. We oppose the obvious desire to gain influence and to extend it to the neighboring ecclesiastical provinces of Central America by his voyages and 'blessings.' We reject the official trip of the First Lady of the Republic and her entourage to Rome [for his installation]. It represents an unreasonable commitment for our country and a waste of money in a country where 58 percent of people cannot read and budgets for health and housing are miserable." They also noted that he had been named without consultation with bishops, priests, or the laity.

Protests brought no change. He absented himself from Guatemala in July 1976 while the conference of bishops issued a message entitled "United in Hope," in which they denounced institutionalized violence in Guatemala and insisted it was not accidental but "the concrete result of the actions of people who called themselves Christians." On his return, he publicly declined to add his signature to those of the other Guatemalan bishops, although the message was a mere reaffirmation of the 1968 Medellín Statements of the Latin American bishops.

Shortly afterward, Casariego sent a confidential letter to his priests warning them to refrain from actions leading to "delicate, bitter and prejudicial situations," such as those produced in other countries. He referred specifically to El Salvador, where various priests had recently been tortured and expelled and some murdered. He said that the church and its ministers did not have the right "to question constituted authority, nor are they competent to judge if these authorities are legitimate or not." Our mission, he added, is "to save souls."

FARO, a rightwing vigilante organization in El Salvador, congratulated Casariego, claiming that he justified FARO's earlier denunciation of "entities in El Salvador organized by the Jesuits and allied with other communist organizations or organizations led by communists." The archbishop of El Salvador, on the contrary, followed up a strong call from the standing committee of the bishops' conference with a demand that the government "stop torturing and threatening priests."

Meanwhile in Guatemala, the Confederation of Religious answered Casariego: "Central America's only cardinal writes his priests exhorting them not to live out the testimony of Jesus; to accommodate themselves to a situation of injustice that cries out to heaven; and to keep silent. We have to say to him, we cannot! We cannot be silent. We cannot be indifferent to the pain of so many people."

Without mentioning him by name, and in slightly more diplomatic language, the bishops of Guatemala concurred. "The church has an obligation to proclaim justice in the social sphere," they proclaimed in a joint statement, "and the right to denounce injustice, which is the fruit of sin, according to Vatican II. . . . No one can deny that excessive inequalities exist among us." The church in Guatemala, they added, is carrying out its function of creating better conditions, within the limitations of its resources;

and "it is unfortunate that some see this activity as a vehicle of internal communism and a promoter of class warfare. Instead, it is the persistence of these abysmal inequalities and the absence of brave and urgent reforms to bring about a more human, fraternal and just community that contribute to communism."

Violence in Guatemala has caused more than 28,000 deaths since Casariego became archbishop. Not only has he never commented on this continuing hemorrhage, but he recently declared that the priests and nuns who denounce it are in rebellion against him. He identifies publicly with the oppressive regime, having a radio patrol and two armed motorcycle guards accompany him at all times in the expensive automobile with Plate #18, an automobile replaced by the latest model each year.

Cardinal Juan Landázuri Ricketts

At least since the time of Vatican II, Cardinal Landázuri has ranged himself with the more socially progressive elements of the church in Latin America and been a defender of the theology of liberation. All this, however, occurred in a Peru in which the government was promoting modernization and social change. With the gradual change of the regime's policies in 1976 and 1977 to socioeconomic policies more in line with the reactionary regimes in neighboring countries, it is not certain that Landázuri will not trim his sails to match. Those close to him describe him as an adept maneuverer, a politician more concerned with protecting the church as an institution than with adopting prophetic stands.

Born at Arequipa in the far south of Peru of a well-to-do family, 19 December 1913, he received the names of Edward William at baptism, taking the name John when he was professed as a Franciscan monk in 1933. Six years later, having completed the regular seminary courses, he was ordained a priest. From 1939 to 1943, he taught canon law, pastoral theology and liturgy in Franciscan colleges, then was named secretary of the General Delegation of the Order, an office set up because of difficulty of communication with the central authorities during World War II. Tasks assigned to him in the following years involved travel to the United States, Spain, Switzerland, Italy, France, Belgium, England, Holland and Germany. From 1946 to 1949 he studied at the Antonianum in Rome and emerged with a laureate in canon law.

On his return to Peru, he taught at the Franciscan theological seminary and shortly was named Provincial Minister. At the Franciscan General Chapter in Assisi, Italy, in 1951, he was chosen to be the General Definitor for Latin America, a post which required that he return to Rome to reside there. Just a year later, he was sent back to Lima as coadjutor to the archbishop, and in 1955 he succeeded as archbishop of Lima on the death of the incumbent. Made a cardinal in 1962, he is a member of the curial Congregations for Religious and Secular Institutes and for the Clergy, also a member of the Pontifical Commission for the Revision of the Code of Canon Law.

He was one of the three cardinals who created a problem for the Technical and Organizing Committee of Vatican II because of his height, the others being Gracias of India and Rugambwa of Tanzania. As he was over 6 feet tall, a special De Gaulle-size bed had to be ordered for him. At the Council, he identified with the progressives. Speaking on the draft statement on the Church in the Modern World, October 1964, he said, "We cannot remain silent on the flagrant injustice of the hunger that plagues one third of mankind while another third lives in abundance. No peace will be possible as long as one person is hungry." He repeated this message in a talk at Notre Dame University, Indiana, in 1966. The bishops of Latin America are committed to the entire body of Vatican II constitutions and decrees, he said. Social revolution in Latin America is inevitable. It corresponds to a reality, to a fact.

In April 1969, he replied publicly to the papal nuncio who had attacked several Peruvian priests by name as hypocrites, clowns and unfortunate priests who recrucify Christ. Among those attacked was Gustavo Gutiérrez, one of the leading theologians of liberation, who had been one of CELAM's three theologians and Landázuri's personal expert at Medellín the previous year. The occasion of the nuncio's attack was a letter they had issued expressing their reservations regarding *Humanae Vitae*. Landázuri said the nuncio, Romolo Carboni, had done a great disservice to the church by bringing the issue to the notice of third parties, especially the civil authorities, whom the nuncio had asked to intervene. Carboni was quickly transferred as nuncio to Italy, a post he still held in 1977.

Also in 1969, Landázuri was on the platform beside President Velasco, as he launched his land reform program. He had just issued a statement that the church applauded this reform as "an instrument of justice in a fundamental sector of the national life and work, one that would help to bring true national liberation."

In late 1972, he declared that the Peruvian church recommitted itself to the "revolutionary process" in the country, calling on all the country's clergy to participate as direct actors in the search for social and economic progress. The military junta that had seized power in 1968 was still then openly committed to programs of reform, including nationalization of big estates and foreign-owned business, and the cardinal's strong words have to be read within the traditional "legitimating" function performed by the church in Latin America. No similar protests have followed the switch of policies that by 1977 had effectively tied Peru to the neighboring right-wing dictatorships.

People close to Landázuri say his personal commitment to a juster social order and to human rights is mild, that his concern for the status of women is even less, and that he is against the ordination of women. He does maintain an active interest in theological developments, is more sympathetic to the theology of liberation than to traditional Scholasticism, is highly sensitive to the views of his fellow bishops and sensitive to a significant, if lesser degree, to those of priests and lay people. His life-style is middle-class, his personality open, if somewhat pompous. Though nervous about ONIS, the Peruvian movement of progressive priests, he tolerates it. He defends Gustavo Gutiérrez and other liberation theologians, and is supportive of the work of his auxiliary, Bishop Luis Bombarén in Lima's teeming slums. For all his caution, he would be a positive and progressive influence in a papal conclave.

Cardinal Aloisio Lorscheider

Like his colleague, Cardinal Evaristo Arns, Cardinal Lorscheider is a Franciscan who has shown himself to be one of the outstanding church leaders of our time, with a reputation that has spread far beyond his native Brazil.

Born at Linha Geraldo, archdiocese of Porto Alegre, in Brazil's southernmost state, Rio Grande do Sul, 8 October 1924, Lorscheider entered the Franciscan minor seminary at the age of nine. From there he went to Divinopolis in Minas Gerais State for philosophy and theology. At eighteen he took the Franciscan habit, and six years later was ordained a priest. For a time, he taught Latin, German and mathematics at the minor seminary in Taquari, then went to Rome to obtain a laureate in dogmatic theology at the Antonianum. On completing this program in 1952, he returned to teach dogmatic theology at the seminary in Divinopolis and to write a number of articles in theological reviews that so impressed his superiors that they brought him back to Rome to teach at the Antonianum.

In February 1962, Pope John named him bishop of Santo Angelo not far from his birthplace in Rio Grande do Sul. Here he quickly revealed the characteristics that have continued to dominate his career: life-style of evangelical poverty, a kind, human personality, receptive to reasoned argument, a spirit of love and commitment to service, a social awareness, commitment to collegiality and the ability to radiate his personal dedication to a life of prayerful spirituality.

During Vatican II from 1962 to 1965, the bishops of Brazil established much closer working relations among themselves, including a series of programs of coordination of their pastoral activities, than had previously been the case. In this work, the young Lorscheider attracted the attention of his fellow bishops, and he was given various offices in the National Conference of Bishops, leading up to that of secretary-general, and finally president. After the military takeover in 1964 and the start of the dictatorship that still holds power in Brazil, the hierarchy tried for a time to maintain a low profile in the hope of achieving a modus vivendi with the generals. They elected Cardinal Agnelo Rossi, who had just become Archbishop of São Paulo, Brazil's biggest city and the world's most populous diocese, as president of the Bishops' Conference, because he was known to have no particular orientation. To placate the generals, who were opposed to the socially progressive orientation of the Conference, Rossi effectively emasculated it, starving it of funds and putting an extremely conservative bishop in charge of day-to-day operations.

When Lorscheider became secretary-general, he remained for a time rather uncommitted to the Conference, but between 1968 and 1970 he decided to revive it as a dynamic institution with an important role to play. He incorporated into it the Plan for Joint Pastoral which had been developed by concerned bishops when Rossi had halted the Conference's social work. In 1968, Lorscheider took a clear stand against the regime after several priests had been tortured until they signed false confessions. As secretary-general of the Conference he issued an official defence of the social mission of the church, insisting that "the judgment concerning whether preaching is authentic or not is for the exclusive competence of the ecclesiastical authority." The regime replied with Institutional Act #5 which gave it unlimited powers of search, seizure, holding without habeas corpus, and censorship, and also in practice an unlimited use of torture on suspects.

From that time, Lorscheider never wavered. In May 1969, Antonio Pereira Neto, a chaplain to university students in Recife and faithful supporter of Dom Helder Camara, was brutally tortured and strangled with barbed wire. Dom Helder charged that rightwing groups allowed to function freely by the regime, the Death Squads and the Anti-Communist Commandos, were responsible. The regime clamped down on all publicity, even forbidding radio or newspapers to give the place and time of the funeral services. Lorscheider as general-secretary of the Bishops' Conference went to Recife to join with Dom Helder in a funeral cortege of 5,000 people harassed on their march to the cemetery by armed police and military.

The bishops were still undecided as to whether they should continue to challenge the regime, and the internal conflict came to the test in 1971 when they met to elect a successor to Rossi as president of the Bishops' Conference, and also a new secretary-general. The candidates for president were Cardinal Scherer and

Lorscheider. Scherer was known as authoritarian, conservative in political and social matters, a believer in church-state cooperation, and a friend of President Medici. Lorscheider had by this time reached a position of such open opposition to the regime that some months previously he had been held five hours for questioning by the military in Rio de Janeiro. The bishops opted for Lorscheider, then picked his cousin, Bishop Ivo Lorscheider, also a progressive, to succeed him as secretary-general.

Lorscheider deplores the spread throughout Latin America of so-called governments of national security based on the Brazilian model and seeking to subject the citizens to a fascist-type indoctrination and persuade them that they should eschew politics and leave the decisions to the armed forces. In a radio panel discussion in Bogotá, Colombia, in April 1977, he said the attempts being made by various Latin American governments to "depoliticize" the young people were a source of danger and preoccupation. "This kind of government activity constitutes a true and serious evil for the entire country, and the Catholic church is worried about it, because under the pretext of national security, the State presents itself as the sole form of human life. The State, however, should be not a threat but a guarantee of the liberty of the citizen."

Also in 1977, as president of the Bishops' Conference, he issued a strong criticism of the regime for its attempt to push divorce legislation through Congress with what he called "indecorous haste." Supporting an earlier statement by his cousin, the secretary-general of the Conference, that the regime's strategy was to create an embarrassing situation for the Opposition (whose strength has grown enormously in a few years), he said, "Divorce is distracting the attention of public opinion from a desirable confrontation between the present political situation and the text of the bishops' statement on 'The Christian Requirements of a Political Order.' Everything is now outside constitutional order. There are much more serious topics to be studied." The document to which Lorscheider referred is a recent collective statement of the bishops emphasizing concern for the public welfare, freedom and citizen participation, individual and national security, and the organic harmony of powers. Many of Brazil's bishops, perhaps a majority, would not oppose civil divorce; but they recognize it is strategic at the moment to stand united against it, both to avoid a rupture within the body of bishops, and not to create enemies at the Vatican when they need its total support in their stand against the regime. Actually, divorce legislation would make a difference for less than half the population, since some half of couples in Brazil live in common-law marriages.

Lorscheider is wholly committed to the ecumenical movement and he maintains an extremely active interest in theological developments. He is mildly supportive of the theology of liberation and of the worldview of Teilhard de Chardin. He remains highly sensitive to the views of his fellow bishops, his clergy and the laity, and continues to promote the implementation of the decisions and spirit of Vatican II. He is highly concerned with human rights, as is clear from his entire history, and he is also aware of the need to promote the rights of women. He has indicated some reservations in private about *Humanae Vitae*, and while he is not acutely concerned with the role the Curia plays in the church, he would strongly support more independence for national hierarchies and would like to see a papal style more in keeping with contemporary opinion. Unfortunately, the state of his health rules him out as a candidate for the papacy, but his voice will be one of the most impressive and convincing in the next papal conclave.

He is a member of the curial Congregation for Religious and Secular Institutes.

Cardinal José Clemente Maurer

A missionary from Europe who landed in Bolivia at age 26 and worked his way to the top by hard work, apostolic commitment and organizing ability, Cardinal Maurer was born at Püttlingen, Trier, Germany, 13 March 1900, did his early studies at a Redemptorist school in Fribourg, Switzerland, then went to the major seminary at Echternach, Luxembourg, for philosophy and theology. Ordained a priest at twenty-five, he began the next year to work in Bolivia among the Aymara and Quechua Indians of the high Andes, traveling by muleback and wrapped in a poncho against the cold. Several years later he was made superior of the Redemptorist house in La Paz, then in 1947 head of the Redemptorist vice-province. In 1950 he was named auxiliary to the archbishop of La Paz, and a year later he was back in the high Andes as archbishop of Sucre. He was made a cardinal in 1967.

While by no means a great theologian, he showed at the Vatican Council and the subsequent Synods of Bishops that he recognized the need for updating the church. He was one of the first to speak out, at the 1967 Synod of Bishops, on a subject that has since been deeply debated, the role of foreign missionaries. Formerly, the missionaries from Europe and North America arrived in Latin America with the idea that they could implant the techniques and life style of their churches of origin. Maurer's insistence in 1967 that instead they had to adapt themselves has since become the common view of missiologists.

Bolivia has for more than a generation been racked by deep divisions between rich and poor, Indians and non-Indians, labor and management. These issues are reflected in the church, and Maurer has shown considerable skill in maintaining an uneasy status quo. His experience would make him cautious toward change, but he would tend to lean toward a moderate progressive in a papal conclave. While generally satisfied with the way the church is run, he would welcome some downgrading of the Curia and has more than once complained in private about the power of nuncios.

Cardinal Umberto Mozzoni

The son of Italian immigrants to Argentina, Cardinal Mozzoni was born in Buenos Aires, 29 June 1904. After primary and secondary studies in Buenos Aires, he entered the seminary of Macerata in central Italy, the city from which his parents had emigrated, then went to Rome to obtain a laureate in civil law in one of the pontifical universities and a laureate in philosophy in the state university. Ordained to the priesthood at age twenty-three, he was engaged in parish work for a time in Macerata, simultaneously teaching in the seminary, then returned to Rome to join the papal diplomatic service. After service in papal delegations in Canada, England and Portugal, he was made an archbishop and sent as nuncio to Bolivia in 1954, then four years later to Argentina. His final post was Brazil, from where he was recalled to the Curia and made a cardinal in 1973. His substantive position, a sinecure, is president of the Commission of Cardinals for the Pontifical Sanctuaries of Pompeii and Loreto. He is also a member of the Congregations for Religious and Secular Institutes, for the Eastern Churches, for the Clergy, and for the Causes of Saints; a member of Segnatura Apostolica, the highest curial court; and a member of the Commission of Cardinal Inspectors of the Institute for the Works of Religion, one of the major financial institutions of the Holy See.

Mozzoni's claim to fame is that he is nowhere on record as having made a wave in his life. He can be assumed to form part of the conservative bloc that dominates—though it no longer monopolizes—the Curia.

Cardinal Aníbal Muñoz Duque

More sophisticated in his expression of his reactionary views than his colleague in Guatemala (Cardinal Mario Casariego), Cardinal Muñoz Duque of Bogotá runs a close second to him in support of the rich against the poor. He was born at Santa Rosa de Osos near Medellín in the Colombian Andes, 3 October 1908. After the customary studies in the local seminary, he was ordained a priest in 1933 and assigned to teaching and administration in the minor and major seminary until 1950, when he became assistant vicar-general of the diocese. A year later he was made bishop of Socorro y San Gil, moved to Bucaramanga in 1952, to Nueva Pamplona in 1959, to Bogotá as coadjutor with right of succession in 1968. He succeeded as archbishop of Bogotá in 1972 and was named cardinal the following year. His curial post is member of the Congregation for the Sacraments and Divine Worship. He is also chaplain general of the Armed Forces and, to the great scandal of many Colombians, in 1977 accepted nomination as an honorary 3-star general.

As early as 1969, when he was apostolic administrator of Bogotá, he and other Colombian bishops encouraged the secret police (DAS) to bring pressures to bear on the progressive priests who constituted the Golconda Movement under the leadership of Bishop Geraldo Valencia Cano of Buenaventura, and at their instigation DAS expelled many foreign priests who belonged to the movement from Colombia.

While in most of Latin America, important segments of the church are taking a strong stand on behalf of the poor, the hierarchy of Colombia under Muñoz Duque's leadership is solid in its support of the ruling groups who describe themselves as liberal and conservative but who are all equally intransigent in their resistance to needed social reform. Just before the national election of 1976, a joint pastoral letter of the bishops came out flatly in support of the candidates of these reactionary parties. Many priests and lay people protested, but to no avail. Shortly after, Muñoz Duque refused to intercede on behalf of striking bank workers, and when the strikers occupied various churches to dramatize their plight, he condemned them in quaintly archaic terms. A hundred priests who came to his palace to intercede found the door locked against them. Priests who concelebrated Mass in a city park at the request of the strikers were suspended.

In a similar vein in 1977, he handed over the priest Saturnino Sepúlveda to military penal justice to be tried for subversion, sedition, and rebellion. His diocesan chancery told the judge that Sepúlveda was a priest but had been suspended and might consequently be arrested, this in spite of the fact that lawyers for Sepúlveda argued that under the 1973 Concordat, only high court civilian judges could initiate legal action against a priest. The charges against Sepúlveda were that he had conducted subversive activities through the Colombian Institute of Social Studies (ICIS) which conducts and publishes studies on political, economic, and social issues.

Also in 1967, under Muñoz Duque's leadership, the conference of bishops issued a long document condemning outright all Christians who engage in challenge to the regime in power in Colombia. It charged that they were attempting a synthesis of Christianity and Marxism that would end up by substituting Marxism for the gospel. Such people by their actions place themselves "on the edge of ecclesial communion." This document follows literally the line long promoted by Belgian Jesuit Roger Vekemans, leading opponent of the theology of liberation. Vekemans, linked to many CIA-subsidized activities in Latin America, tried to transfer his center of operations from Chile to Venezuela when Allende came to power in Chile in 1970. The Venezuelans would not take him, so he set up in Bogotá's sympathetic climate, where he quickly built up an elaborate center for the diffusion of his views, an operation in which he had full support of Muñoz Duque.

Traditionally scholastic in theology, Muñoz Duque has since Vatican II withdrawn to more conservative stands. He is insensitive to the views of priests and people but highly influenced by government pressures and the threat of losing support of wealthy benefactors. His life-style is upper-class; his personality, power-wielding and domineering. He has little time for the ecumenical movement.

Cardinal Pablo Muñoz Vega

A man who took Vatican Council II seriously and has since continued in its spirit, Cardinal Muñoz Vega was born at Mira, diocese of Tulcán, close to the Colombian border in northern Ecuador, 23 May 1903. Having joined the Jesuits at the age of 15, he obtained a laureate in philosophy and a licentiate in theology at the Gregorian in Rome, and was ordained a priest in 1933. He taught at the Gregorian from 1937 to 1939, then returned to Ecuador as head of the Jesuit vice-province. Expansion of the vice-province during the six years he was in office caused it to be established as a separate province. Meanwhile, he also founded the Pontifical Catholic University of Ecuador at Quito.

His next assignment, from 1954 to 1957, was as head of the Latin American College in Rome, from where he returned to the Gregorian as *Rettore Magnifico* (president) for six years, simultaneously teaching the psychology of religion in the Faculty of Philosophy and Missiology of the university, and serving as a consultor on various curial bodies.

In 1964, Muñoz Vega returned to Ecuador as coadjutor to the archbishop of Quito, and succeeded as archbishop three years later. Named a cardinal in 1969, he is a member of the Congregation for Religious and Secular Institutes.

In Quito he inherited a highly integrated and reactionary diocesan chancery. He did not, however, become its prisoner. He named a new secretary with teaching and journalistic experience, and he rejected the recommendation of the chancery officials, in 1968, that he should take a hard line with more than fifty priests who had asked that they be consulted before bishops were named. Instead, he met their representatives and agreed that some of the issues they raised were reasonable. He followed this up with a very thoughtful pastoral letter in which he warned of the danger of "a psychological schism" because of the conflicting assumptions and hopes among different sectors of the clergy. To avert this, he called on them to search for unity through dialogue.

A little earlier, at the 1967 Synod of Bishops, he adopted the position that the church needed more theological study, with its corollary of more freedom for theologians in their investigations. Listeners were impressed by the evolution in his thinking. At

Vatican II, he had opposed the declaration on religious freedom as calculated to encourage the spread of Protestantism in Latin America. His subsequent career has shown a similar growth. In 1976, when the government of Ecuador arrested and held for twenty-four hours several bishops from the United States and various Latin American countries who were meeting with the bishop of Riobamba, Muñoz Vega expressed his outrage in very strong terms. In August 1977, commenting on a statement on social justice in Ecuador issued by the Conference of Catholic Bishops, he said that the spectacular new oil wealth had widened the gap between rich and poor, with "a worsening of conditions regarding social justice." One can expect to find him on the progressive side in a papal conclave.

Cardinal Eduardo Pironio

With the enormous increase in the number of cardinals around the world and the elimination from papal elections of cardinals aged over eighty, both changes introduced by Pope Paul VI, the proportion of Italians in the Sacred College is now slightly less than a quarter. The Italians, nevertheless, still constitute the biggest bloc and they have a long tradition of Italian popes in their favor. The general feeling of Vaticanologists is that the next pope will be an Italian, but the possibility of a non-Italian can no longer be excluded. And if the electors decide to explore that possibility, the obvious front-runner is Eduardo Pironio, an Argentine of Italian descent, a member of the Roman Curia since 1975, first as Pro-Prefect and now as Prefect of the Congregation for Religious and Secular Institutes.

One normally reaches the cardinalate by one of two routes: entry into the Roman Curia following attendance at Roman universities and at the Pontifical Academy for training in the curial methods and procedures; or becoming archbishop of a major archdiocese that by usage has acquired a claim to be headed by a cardinal. Pironio's career was slightly abnormal. The highest rank he reached in the Argentine church was that of bishop of the relatively unimportant diocese of Mar del Plata. What placed the spotlight on him was his outstanding performance in various offices of the Council of Latin American Bishops (CELAM), that and the accident of political changes in Argentina that caused the Vatican to fear for his personal safety and find an excuse to summon him to Rome.

He did have a further advantage in that he had studied for a time in Rome, completing at the Angelicum University the courses in philosophy and theology he had begun in an Argentine seminary. After ordination to the priesthood in 1943 at the age of twenty-three, he taught theology in a seminary in Argentina for sixteen years, then moved to Buenos Aires to head the metropolitan seminary in that capital and to become dean of the Faculty of Theology in the Catholic University of Argentina.

A personal turning point was his selection by the Argentine bishops to accompany them to Rome for Vatican Council II as theological adviser (*peritus*). His preparation for that catalytic event was not significantly different from that of the Argentine bishops or the other Latin American bishops who attended to the number of six hundred. During more than four centuries, Latin American Catholicism had made no original contribution to theology. The seminaries were content to repeat the curricula and study the textbooks offered by Rome. Rome, for its part, had steadily narrowed the areas of free discussion. From the nineteenth century, in particular, it had reacted violently against the burgeoning secular culture that has led to the great scientific advances of the twentieth century. Seminarians were presented with only one side of a question. Starting with an answer, they were taught to develop arguments to prove that this answer was the only correct one. They were taught, for example, that the only community in which the Holy Spirit works is that of the Roman Catholic Church; that infallibility, as defined by Vatican Council I, extended to every official teaching of the pope, including encyclicals addressed to all Catholics, and spilled over into the acts and decisions of the various bodies acting with the authority of the Holy See, that is to say, the curial offices.

For Pironio, as for Latin American bishops and theologians in general, the Council was an initiation into the new theology, especially the biblical movement and a changed understanding of the nature of the church. The new theology had come to fruition in France and Germany and the other countries of Europe north of the Alps, thanks in particular to the sufferings these countries shared during and after World War II, sufferings that led to a personal communion of Catholics with their Protestant fellow Christians and convinced them that the official Roman theology ran counter to the reality of their life experience.

The majority of the Latin Americans responded positively to the new European theology, as their votes at the Council demonstrated. It did not take them long, however, to realize that in Latin America it was not enough to substitute one European formula for another. It was necessary to rethink the principles in the light of the reality of Latin America's own religious and cultural history, the first step in the process that would soon acquire worldwide notice as the Theology of Liberation. How quickly Pironio, who had been made an auxiliary bishop in 1964 and secretary-general of CELAM in 1967, grasped this radical concept was shown by an intervention he made at the first Synod of Bishops in Rome in October 1967. The subject of discussion was a document on "Dangers to the Faith," prepared by the Congregation for the Faith (ex-Holy Office), which if approved would have provided the basis for a papal statement listing—in the tradition of Pius IX's Syllabus of Errors—a catalogue of contemporary beliefs and attitudes regarded by the Roman school of theology as calculated to deceive or pervert the unsophisticated believers.

Bishop Pironio, then aged forty-seven, took the floor to support the reaction expressed by Archbishop Marcos McGrath of Panama that the document was "quite incomprehensible to a Latin American mentality." The modern way of speaking, Pironio continued, is much more positive; and, in addition, the document does not apply to the contemporary situation. What the church should do in this age of secularization is "to preach the mystery of Christ, especially his humility and his poverty." A further indication of his theological updating is provided by the titles of some of the many books he has published: *The Church as People of God, The Church that is Being Born Among Us, The New Man in Latin America.*

As secretary-general of CELAM, Pironio maintained the spirit instilled by his two immediate predecessors, Bishop Manuel Larraín of Talca (Chile) and Bishop—now Cardinal—Avelar Brandão Vilela of Teresina and later of São Salvador de Bahia (Brazil). CELAM was something new among ecclesiastical structures when started in 1955, but its activity was confined to traditional models until Larraín—a man of extraordinary vision and commitment to social change killed in an automobile accident in 1966 as his ideas were starting to bear fruit—created various departments in which bishops and experts cooperated in pastoral initiatives. Dom Avelar Brandão Vilela, for his part, organized regional meetings, some of which produced challenging statements and started the dialectical process of reflection and commitment. They paved the way for the General Conference of Latin American Bishops in 1968, of which Pope Paul named Pironio secretary-general, a meeting that produced the historical Medellín Documents, the charter of church renewal in Latin America.

Pironio's political acumen and diplomatic skill were tested and confirmed at Medellín. A small but intransigent minority, headed by Archbishop Geraldo Siguad of Diamantina, a big cattle rancher in the Brazilian state of Minas Gerais and a leader of the traditionalists at Vatican II, used every wile and pulled every political string to prevent the church from changing what had long been its primary role in Latin America, legitimizer and supporter of the status quo. Pironio managed both to avert an open break and to end up with statements that substantially reflected the will of the vast majority.

Medellín was an interpretation of the signs of the times. The bishops described an oppressed continent, victim of both internal colonialism (the neocolonialism of the national oligarchies), and of the external colonialism of "the international monopolies and the international imperialism of money." They made an unambiguously clear choice for radical transformation, a commitment to the search for ways to liberate the poor, and an undertaking to change from their habitual way of thinking and living in order to respond appropriately and become an evangelical sign to the hemisphere. "It is the same God," they proclaimed, "who in the fulness of time sends his son in the flesh, so that he might come to liberate all men from slavery to which sin has subjected them: hunger, misery, oppression, and ignorance; in a word, the injustice and hatred that have their origin in human selfishness."

In the years that followed, CELAM under Pironio created institutions and developed trends calculated to give substance to the commitments made at Medellín. Thus, its pastoral institute, IPLA, was located at Quito, where it taught some 500 students in nine sessions lasting four months each. The institute for catechetics, ICLA, was similarly active. These and other institutes of CELAM started with certain common guidelines and attempted to apply them to the overall Latin American situation. This was the start of a general awareness that in theology, as elsewhere, Latin Americans had been the victims of cultural oppression. The groundwork was laid for the meteoric rise of the Theology of Liberation. While Pironio is not identified as himself a contributor to the development of the Theology of Liberation, he "always defended and participated in it," according to Father José Comblin in an article in *Mensaje* (Chile), October 1976. Comblin played a major part in drafting the Medellín Documents and is one of the most authoritative historians of the contemporary Latin American church.

Typical of Pironio's work at CELAM is a report he made in 1969 to the General Council of the Commission for Latin America, the Vatican counterpart of CELAM. It dealt with the subject of foreign priests in Latin America, and it was based on the replies to a questionnaire he had sent to all the presidents of Latin American national conferences of bishops, and also to seventy bishops he had selected because of their known interest in the subject.

The report sets out at length the positive and negative contributions of the many priests working in Latin America who come from different language and cultural backgrounds and with a variety of preconceptions and expectations. It then focuses on the ways to improve the situation. The first task is for Latin Americans themselves to increase vocations and thereby reduce the need for outsiders. The sending countries for their part should take more care in selecting only those with human and psychic maturity, a truly missionary spirit, and ability to adapt and integrate fully. Finally, senders and receivers should work together to provide better training in language, and in knowledge of the history, culture, mentality, customs, social and economic situation, and religious condition of the country to which a missionary is sent.

Pironio's political sense was such as never to allow his enthusiasms to obscure the limits of the possible. He responded to the mood of caution emanating from the Vatican and taken up by the episcopal conferences of many Latin American countries in the early 1970s, a mood compounded of the inevitable swing of the pendulum back from the progressive currents that dominated Vatican II and of the fears of many that the left-leaning theologians prominent in the Theology of Liberation movement were rushing the church into alliances with Marxists. After his election to the presidency of CELAM in 1972, he left decision making progressively in the hands of the conservative Colombian bishop, Alfonso López Trujillo, who had succeeded him as secretary-general. López Trujillo during the following years moved nearly all the CELAM departments to Bogotá and placed them under the control of persons who shared his conservative views.

While López Trujillo was remodeling CELAM, Pironio was steadily expanding his contacts in Rome. He participated in the Synods of Bishops held in 1969, 1971, and 1974, as he had in that of 1967; and in 1974 he presented a report to the Synod on the state of the church in Latin America. In that same year he was named a member of the Council of the General Secretariat of the Synod, a continuing body between meetings of the Synod. Some months earlier, he had been made a member of the Vatican's Commission for Latin America, and also a member of the Congregation for the Doctrine of the Faith. As a further mark of the Vatican's growing regard for him, he was selected to lead the Lenten spiritual exercises for the pope and the curial officials.

During all these years, he continued to be active in the Argentine hierarchy, even though its evolution under domestic political pressures was not typical of what was happening generally in Latin America. Long a bastion of conservatism, it had during the late 1960s undergone a significant evolution that culminated in a kind of public conversion in April 1969. Gathered at San Miguel, a suburb of Buenos Aires, to read over together—as they had done the previous year at Medellín—the documents of Vatican Council II, they came up with a statement of their own that contrasted sharply, especially in its treatment of justice and peace, with the former mentality, style and language. They openly attacked capitalism, following the lead of the Medellín Documents, insisted on the urgent need of change, and placed the institutional church in the forefront of the struggle for justice.

During the following years, and particularly as Argentina tottered on the brink of civil war when Juan Perón's widow, Isabelita, assumed the presidency in 1974, the challenge to the church intensified. Attacks were made on various church institutions by the Argentine Anti-Communist Alliance (AAA) and other extreme rightwing terrorist groups. Among the dioceses singled out by the extremists was Mar del Plata, of which Pironio had become bishop in 1972, and Pironio responded with a vigorous denunciation of the bombings, kidnappings, threats of death, and other injustices in a public statement in June 1975. Three months later, Pope Paul named him an archbishop and called him to Rome to the Congregation for Religious. No public explanation was given, but the move was interpreted as inspired by the Vatican's fear for the safety of Pironio if left in Argentina.

The Congregation for Religious and Secular Institutes is a curial department charged with the supervision of some 300,000 men members of religious orders, congregations and similar institutions, and about a million nuns. Vatican Council II had decided that radical change in the understanding of religious life and in the rules governing religious was needed, and it wrote a document, the Decree on the Appropriate Renewal of Religious Life, to serve as a justification and guide for updating. But when Cardinal Valerio Valeri (then head of the Congregation) died in 1963, Pope Paul made the mistake of naming Cardinal Ildebrando Antoniutti to replace him. Antoniutti during the Council ranged himself consistently with Cardinal Alfredo Ottaviani as a leader of the intransigent minority. When named Prefect of the Congregation for Religious, he insisted that all instances of unquiet in religious congregations resulted from a spirit of rebellion against authority. "He was a Turk," to quote one who had inside knowledge of his manner of operating as prefect, "you couldn't talk to him at all." His idea of reform was to measure the height of the hems of nuns' skirts, and he gave full backing to Cardinal James Francis McIntyre of Los Angeles in his vindictive campaign against the Sacred Heart Sisters in their efforts to conform to the spirit of the Vatican II directives. He was equally supportive of other bishops who wanted to keep the nuns in their traditional function of underpaid and unappreciated servants of the clergy.

Pironio went to work right away to clean up the mess made by Antoniutti. And the reactions from informed leaders of religious orders of both men and women are very positive. Meanwhile, his experience at CELAM has prepared him for the politics of the Curia, so that he knows how to get things done without making too many enemies. In addition to his primary job as Prefect of the Congregation for Religious, he has become a member of the Council for the Public Affairs of the Church; of the Congregations for Bishops, for the Sacraments and Divine Worship, and for Catholic Education; and of the Commissions for the Laity and for the Reform of the Code of Canon Law.

At the same time, he retains contact with his home base. According to the extremely well informed London newsletter *Latin America*, it was he who persuaded the pope to write a personal letter to the Argentine bishops urging them to protest the violence instigated or condoned by the military dictatorship that has held power in Argentina since Isabelita Perón was ousted in 1976. The result was a strong statement from the meeting of the Argentine bishops in May 1977. The bishops indicated their serious preoccupation, in particular, at numerous disappearances and kidnappings for which the authorities refuse to be answerable; the fact that many prisoners have been subjected to tortures, "which are unacceptable to any Christian conscience and which degrade not only those who suffer them, but also those who apply them," and the detention of people for lengthy periods without being able to defend themselves or even know the cause of their imprisonment. The bishops stressed several times in their statement that those detained, tortured and murdered during the previous year included priests and nuns.

Born in 1920, Pironio at fifty-eight is still somewhat below what cardinals usually regard as the minimum age for election to the papacy. But he is coming close to what is called the "age window," put by some at sixty-three to sixty-seven while others would widen it to sixty to seventy. He must therefore be regarded as a serious possibility. The recent emphasis in Roman rumor mills on the generally admitted fact that his reputation as an administrator is higher than his delivery may indicate a campaign by reactionary curialists to eliminate him as a candidate. Nevertheless, he has a lot going for him; and the fact that he is of Italian descent would soften for Italians the break with centuries of Italian monopoly of the papacy, as would his current good standing as head of a curial congregation.

Cardinal Raúl Francisco Primatesta

Born in Capilla del Señor, La Plata, Argentina, 14 April 1919, Cardinal Primatesta studied in the minor and major seminaries of La Plata, then went to Rome in 1937 and obtained a laureate in theology at the Gregorian and in Scripture at the Biblical Institute. After ordination at age twenty-three, he returned to Argentina, spent a short time in parish work, then taught Latin and Greek at the La Plata seminary, later became assistant rector of the seminary and professor of dogmatic theology and Scripture, and finally rector. During these years he contributed studies to several theological and biblical reviews. In addition to Spanish, Latin, and Greek, he knows French, Italian, and Hebrew. He was for a time president of the Argentine Society of Professors of Sacred Scripture.

In 1957 he was named auxiliary to the archbishop of La Plata, and in 1961 he went to San Rafael as its first bishop. In 1965 he was promoted to Córdoba as archbishop, and in 1973 received the cardinal's hat. He is a member of the curial Congregations for Religious and Secular Institutes, for the Sacraments and Divine Cult, for the Bishops, and for Catholic Education.

Primatesta has maintained a low profile in the complicated political and social upheavals that have characterized Argentine life for many years. He would seem to be a moderate reformer, likely to join the progressive Latin American cardinals in a papal conclave.

Cardinal José Humberto Quintero

Born in Mucuchies, Mérida, Venezuela, the third child of a family of modest means, 22 September 1902, Cardinal Quintero entered the minor seminary at Mérida aged eleven. Nine years later he was sent to Rome to complete theology and study canon law at the Gregorian. Ordained a priest in 1926, he worked as assistant pastor in Mérida, then taught philosophy in the same city. In 1929 he was named secretary of the diocesan chancery, and five years later, vicar-general of the archdiocese. Meanwhile, he published various literary and historical works which merited him a corresponding membership in the Academy of History and the Academy of Language of Venezuela. He also devoted himself to painting, specializing in portraits of former bishops and university figures.

In 1953 he was named coadjutor with right of succession to the archbishop of Mérida, and in 1959 he was moved to Caracas as archbishop. A year later he was made cardinal.

During Vatican II, Quintero made several important interventions. In the debate on ecumenism, he insisted that a precondition for church reunion was an interior renewal of the Catholic church and holiness of life, without which the church could never hope to appeal to others. Stressing Catholic responsibility for the Protestant Reformation, he said that "Luther fought against the pagan and dissolute morals" of Catholic prelates of the time. "Ever since the Reformation, we have failed in charity toward the Protestants. . . . Let the Council issue a statement asking pardon."

A year later, he was one of seventeen cardinals who signed a petition to Pope Paul that was one of the turning points of the Council. Reactionary elements in the Curia had decided to emasculate the statement on the Jews, which they could do only by violating the procedures of the Council. The vigorous reaction of these seventeen cardinals won the day.

In his diocese, Quintero has sought to be a mediator in the unrest that has disturbed Venezuelan society for more than a decade. When a Christian Democrat government came to power in 1968, he supported its efforts to negotiate an end to the guerrilla activities that had been a source of major trouble for the previous five years. Agreeing to head a mediating committee, he said in reference to the guerrillas: "If a mountain won't come to us, we'll go to the mountain."

Quintero has maintained a generally low profile in the Latin American church, but there is no reason to doubt that he would work with its more progressive cardinals in a papal conclave.

Cardinal Agnelo Rossi

Although very successful as the bishop of a small diocese, Cardinal Rossi was unable to cope with the job entrusted to him in October 1964, seven months after the military seizure of power in Brazil and a moment of major crisis for the church, as archbishop of Brazil's biggest city and one of the most populous Catholic dioceses in the world. After six years of hesitant leadership in São Paulo, he was moved upstairs to a job in the Curia at the Vatican, and he has now effectively reached the end of the line in his sinecure as Chamberlain to the Sacred College. He is also a member of several other curial Congregations and Commissions.

Born at Joaquim Egidio, near Campinas, state of São Paulo, 4 May 1913, Rossi entered the seminary at Campinas at age twelve. After secondary, pedagogical, and philosophical studies, he was one of the first Brazilians to go to the Brazilian College in Rome and study at the Gregorian for a laureate in theology. Ordained at twenty-four, he returned to Campinas as personal secretary to the bishop. He taught ethics, theodicy, and moral theology at the central seminary in São Paulo from 1940 to 1944, then returned to Campinas as a professor and dean of the Faculty of Philosophy. In 1956 he became vice-rector of the University of Campinas, but within a few months was named bishop of Barra do Piraí, state of Rio de Janeiro. Two years later, he was named Brazilian representative to CELAM, and in 1962 he was promoted archbishop of Ribeirão Preto in the state of São Paulo, and from there to the city of São Paulo two years later.

During Vatican II, he pursued the generally progressive line of the majority of Brazil's bishops. During the discussion on religious liberty, for example, he proposed in the name of eighty-three Brazilian bishops that a statement be included acknowledging the historical errors committed by the church in regard to freedom of religion. And in the discussion of the document on the church in today's world, he noted that Latin America had undergone a political revolution but had yet to experience the necessary social revolution.

The Brazilian bishops, meeting in Rome in 1964 during the third session of Vatican Council II, elected Rossi to a 5-year term as president of their national conference. Faced with the major upheaval of Brazilian society as the military dictatorship that had seized power some months earlier set out to destroy labor, student and other civic institutions, he proved unequal to his task. His term of office was marked by vacillation, attempts to reconcile the unreconcilable, gestures in favor of the generals in the hope that they would give more freedom to the church in its activities. A close friend of Medici, the general picked by his colleagues for the office of President, he appeared frequently at military functions, an action interpreted as giving legitimacy to the dictatorship. He also backed a proposal by a group of businessmen who sought to exploit religious sentiment for financial gain by making the shrine of Our Lady of Aparecida, the national patroness, into a paying affair, when neither the cardinal archbishop of Aparecida nor the religious order in charge of the shrine favored the project.

Rossi's transfer to Rome in 1970 and his replacement in São Paulo by his most dynamic auxiliary bishop (now Cardinal Arns) was generally interpreted in Brazil as papal support for a more progressive policy and a stronger stand by the bishops against the excesses of the dictatorship, something that has in fact occurred. Rossi's friends describe him as a good man, but naive, moved by sentiment and lacking political vision. A loyal servant of the Holy See, he is also happy with the Curia's power and opposed to the trend to give more autonomy to national hierarchies. His life-style is upper-class, his personality domineering and authoritarian, yet ready to compromise if challenged. He maintains little active interest in theological developments. He is insensitive to the views of his fellow bishops and even more distant from priests and laity. All in all, he must be ranked as a member of the most conservative faction in the Curia.

Cardinal José Salazar López

As the retired cardinal-archbishop of Mexico City (Miguel Miranda y Gómez) is over 80, Cardinal Salazar is Mexico's only papal elector. The church in Mexico differs in important respects from other Latin American churches. Thanks to the strong anti-clerical influences in the Mexican Revolution in the early part of this century, the clergy is entirely indigenous. Having lost its wealth and power, the church has identified with the poor and tends to be socially aware and progressive. Although Salazar has maintained a rather low profile, he is definitely in tune with this general attitude.

Born into a middle-class family in Ameca, archdiocese of Guadalajara, 12 January 1910, Salazar entered the local minor seminary at thirteen, went to Rome at the end of his secondary studies for philosophy and theology at the Gregorian. After ordination to the priesthood in 1934 he taught for ten years at the seminary at Guadalajara, then moved into administrative posts at the seminary, becoming rector in 1950. Eleven years later he was made coadjutor bishop of Zamora, and in 1967 he succeeded as bishop. In 1970 he was promoted to Guadalajara, and in 1973 he was made a cardinal. As cardinal, he is a member of the curial Congregation for the Sacraments and divine Worship.

When Pope Paul published *Humanae Vitae*, Salazar joined with his fellow bishops in minimizing the significance of the statement, and the conflict with Rome became even more acute when the Mexican bishops expressed their approval of the government's policy on population control. The Vatican sent down an instruction that called on them to correct their statement, but they revised the Roman statement to take some of the force out of it, before they published it.

Salazar has always been supportive of Bishop Sergio Méndez Arceo of Cuernavaca, who takes in Mexico an evangelical-prophetic line similar to that of Dom Helder Camara in Brazil. In a Holy Week radio program in Bogotá, Colombia, in 1967, Salazar called for peace and Christianity in Latin America, insisting that these are possible "only when justice is done to the brother today nailed to the cross of misery, and when liberation is brought to every place in which repression has limited human fulfillment."

Cardinal Eugenio de Araújo Sales

One of the most deep-seated traditions of the church administrators in Latin America is to adjust their pastoral activities and public stands to suit the policies or whims of the government in power. Today there are notable exceptions, but the tradition survives and is perfectly exemplified in the career of Cardinal Sales, since 1971 archbishop of Rio de Janeiro.

Sales was born at Acarí, diocese of Caicó, in the State of Rio Grande do Norte on the Atlantic coast of Brazil's Northeast, 8 November 1920. His parents operated a small sea-transport service. He studied in the local minor and major seminaries and was ordained a priest at age twenty-three. After eleven years of pastoral and administrative duties, he was named auxiliary to the archbishop of Natal in 1954. In 1962, because the archbishop was gravely ill, he was placed in complete charge of the archdiocese as apostolic administrator. The Brazilian government of the time was socially progressive, and Sales took his cue by interrupting the building of a cathedral in order to provide homes for workers, and by campaigning vigorously in favor of land reform.

He was at that time a supporter of Dom Helder Camara, who as an auxiliary of the very traditional archbishop of Rio de Janeiro, since deceased, was beginning to be identified as the most dynamic and committed defender of the poor in the Brazilian church. While in Natal, Sales was the first to experiment with nuns as "vicars" in parishes that had no priests, a program he continued when moved to Salvador as archbishop in 1968. Brazil then had eighty-five million people, most of them nominal Catholics, served by 12,000 priests and 40,000 nuns. Soon a third of all nuns in the Salvador archdiocese were acting pastors, performing all pastoral functions—except celebrating the Eucharist and giving sacramental absolution—preaching, the Service of the Word, religious instruction, preparation for the sacraments, baptizing, presiding at marriages and funerals. This initiative of Sales was quickly adopted by many Brazilian dioceses.

Up to 1964, he was a strong supporter of the Conference of Brazilian Bishops, functioning as an officer of the Conference until both Dom Helder and he were ousted in elections in October 1964, some months after the military takeover, and replaced by conservatives who paralyzed it for five years. The ousting of Sales proved unnecessary. He immediately adopted a more "prudent" stand and called for church cooperation with the military government and the local elites who were given a free hand by the military to dismantle the reforms of previous administrations and return the peasants to their former destitution and powerlessness. Seeking to compromise on all issues, he avoided delegation of authority and forbade the establishment of any controversial programs in his diocese. His careful cultivation of the president and leaders of the regime was rewarded in 1967 when the government-controlled Association of Political Writers of Bahia voted him "personality of the year," and when he was made cardinal in 1969 and moved two years later to Rio de Janeiro, church honors obtainable only through the support of the government. By this time, he had become the church leader in whom the government had confidence, an able diplomat, always ready to compromise.

In theology he is traditionally Scholastic, has absolutely no interest in theological developments other than to condemn such aberrations as the theology of liberation and Teilhardian fantasies. His interest in the ecumenical movement is slight, as is his support of Vatican II, an event he has grown steadily to regard with greater mistrust. He is insensitive to the views of his fellow bishops and ignores those of his clergy and the laity. His life-style is upper-class; his personality, aloof and authoritarian. He feels no need for a change in the style of the papacy or the power of the Curia, feels threatened by the change in the world around him, shows little concern for violations of human rights, is equally opposed to married priests and to the ordination of women. Failing a change of the regime in Brazil, a rather unlikely eventuality for several years, he can be expected to back a conservative candidate in a papal election.

Sales is a member of the curial Congregations for Bishops and for the Clergy, and of the papal Commission for Social Communications.

Cardinal Alfredo Vicente Scherer

Less reactionary than his Brazilian colleague, Cardinal Agnelo Rossi, Cardinal Scherer is close to the conservative Cardinal Eugenio Sales in his general outlook and particularly in his ability to keep a low profile in the church-state conflict which has dominated Brazil's life since the military dictatorship was inaugurated in 1964.

Scherer was born 5 February 1903 in Bom Princípio, archdiocese of Porto Alegre, in Brazil's southernmost state bordering on the Atlantic and on Uruguay, Rio Grande do Sul. He entered the local minor seminary at age eleven and continued to the major seminary for philosophy and theology, then went to Rome for graduate work in theology at the Gregorian. Ordained a priest at age twenty-three, he returned to Porto Alegre to become secretary to the archbishop. Subsequently he worked in various parishes until made an auxiliary bishop in 1946 and later the same year archbishop of Porto Alegre.

Adjusting to the concerns of the socially progressive Brazilian governments of the 1950s and early 1960s, Scherer became heavily engaged in promoting social activities, establishing a diocesan secretariat for social action and encouraging the Agrarian Front, a movement of Christians in support of the small farmers of the region. He also expressed himself strongly in favor of land reform. He helped to draft strong episcopal statements in 1962 and 1963 in support of the social reforms being proposed by the government.

All this changed with the advent of the military dictatorship in 1964. As part of the effort to emasculate the progressive national conference of Brazilian bishops, Scherer—then the most important archbishop in the south of Brazil—was in 1965 named national secretary of Lay Concerns. The principal program of the Conference at that time was the lay movement, Brazilian Catholic Action. To ensure its continuance, Dom Helder Camara and his supporters tried to get the 1965 meeting to link this program to the recent decisions of the Vatican Council on the laity, so that lay militants would be free as individuals to adopt positions on temporal matters. Scherer joined the opposing group in blocking this proposal and tightening the hold of the Conference over Catholic

Action to such an extent as to emasculate the movement. Two sections, the university youth and the high school youth, declared their independence of the hierarchy, and Scherer responded by "eliminating" them. The priest who was secretary of the Conference section dealing with the laity resigned, saying that under Scherer "there is no plan for lay people."

In 1969, he supported the regime's reintroduction of the death peanlty, as did Rossi, while other bishops and influential lay groups denounced the proposal. However, he did support the almost unanimous condemnation by the hierarchy of the Death Squads who at that time were being allowed to pillage and murder the peasants and suspected progressives with impunity. Pope Paul named him a cardinal in 1969.

During the 1970s he consistently supported the dictatorship, even as the vast majority of his fellow bishops took a progressively more hostile attitude toward it. He places little stress on social justice, land reform, or human rights, is even less concerned about the status of women, and is rigidly opposed to the idea of married priests or the ordination of women. Traditionally Scholastic in theology, he makes no effort to keep himself informed on theological developments. He was never enthusiastic about the updating of the church ushered in by Vatican II, and he remains insensitive to the views of his fellow bishops, his priests, and the laity. His life-style is upper-class, his manner aloof, even though he is personally kind and honest.

Cardinal Raúl Silva Henríquez

Few cardinals have been more in the limelight since 1970, when Salvador Allende became president of Chile and committed the country to establishing a socialist system by constitutional methods, than Cardinal Silva. He was criticized then by many for being unduly sympathetic to Allende, later criticized by others after Allende's overthrow in 1973 for delaying so long before he took a strong stand against the excesses and violations of human rights of the military dictatorship. But the general consensus is that he acted with propriety in both situations, and in recent years he has really struggled to bring food and hope to the masses of children and adults who are literally starving.

Born at Talca in central Chile 27 September 1907, the sixteenth of nineteen children of a landowner and industrialist whose family was established in that area for several centuries, Silva went to the primary school of the Brothers of the Christian Schools in Talca, and the secondary school of the Fathers of the Divine Word in Santiago. At sixteen, he enrolled in the Catholic University of Chile and five years later in 1929 graduated as a lawyer.

In 1930 he entered the Salesian novitiate in Santiago, where he studied philosophy, then went to the Salesian Academy in Turin, Italy, for theology. Ordained a priest in 1938, he returned to Chile to teach canon law, church history, and moral theology at the International Salesian Theologate in Santiago. He continued in a variety of teaching and administrative activities until the early 1950s, when he was assigned to set up Caritas Chile, an agency of the Chilean bishops for emergency aid to the poor. He continued with the agency even after he was named bishop of Valparaiso in 1959. In 1961 he was promoted to be archbishop of Santiago, and the next year made a cardinal. He is a member of the curial Congregations for the Clergy and for Catholic Education, and of the Pontifical Commission for the Revision of the Code of Canon Law.

At Vatican II, he followed the lead of Bishop Manuel Larraín of Talca, Chile's pioneer social-action bishop. In answering those who said Christ had preached poverty, he distinguished poverty from misery and insisted that the church must work to eliminate misery. "Let us have faith in the possibility that Christians can organize the world so differently that misery will disappear." The problems of the church in Chile, he added, were caused by the attitudes of Catholics toward human misery and the social injustices committed by the rich. Supporting religious freedom, he said, "Throughout the world we must dissipate the opinion that Catholics are opportunists who apply a double standard, depending on whether they are strong or weak." In the discussion of contemporary humanism, he affirmed the intrinsic worth of temporal values. "The church must love the world as Christ loved it. . . . Let the Council offer a Christian cosmology and anthropology. . . . Contemporary atheism draws its strength from an affirmation of temporal values. The church must also affirm them."

Openness to many viewpoints characterized the church in Chile, with Silva's approval, in the years that followed the Council. Various research institutes were created, and their researches led many priests, nuns, and lay people to recognize the need for deep reform of the social structures. Silva strongly supported the land reform programs of the Christian Democrat government in power from 1964 to 1970. He adopted a more reserved but basically supportive role when the Allende regime came to power in 1970, although it was committed publicly to prepare the way for the establishment of a socialist state. When Allende nationalized copper, Silva had high praise for the way he did it. "The process of nationalization has been constitutionally impeccable," he said. "It is not proper that this matter be presented in unfriendly terms between two governments and much less between two peoples."

When the military, egged on by the Chilean oligarchs, the CIA, and the transnational corporations, overthrew the Allende regime in 1973, Silva tried to remain neutral. For many months, he deplored specific acts of violence, of torture, of violation of human rights, but stopping short of challenging the official policies of the Junta, and thus by implication legitimating it. Coming from the same upper-class Chilean tradition as Allende, he was confident that the rules of the game would be observed and that political differences could be worked out by negotiation "entre caballeros" (between gentlemen). What he failed to realize is that neither the computers of the transnational corporations nor the training methods for total warfare taught Latin American generals by their Pentagon military missions leave room for gentlemen. It took the killing of thousands and the torture and exile of tens of thousands, the imposition of thought control on the universities—including the universities hitherto directed by the church—and the introduction of an economic system that condemns a third of Chileans to a destitution far greater than Chile had ever known, to disillusion him.

The result has been the building up of the Solidarity Vicariate of Silva's diocese into the only institution able to channel aid to the starving and to go to the courts to demand action for "disappeared" persons. In a series of statements of growing harshness, the cardinal and the conference of bishops have protested the violations of basic rights. The standing committee of the conference of bishops said early in 1977: "Today it is no longer appropriate to speak of the apostolate, or of saving souls, but rather of solidarity, of support. . . . The church must make itself a presence, a witness, and a service. That may weaken it as an institution. but it will make its action more efficacious. Formerly the pastors stayed in their rectories all day; now they go out to help the people." This was followed by sermons of encouragement to union leaders on May Day by Silva and by several bishops. The Junta was so enraged that it had its secret police in the following days arrest many of the union leaders who had attended the cardinal's Mass, and their unions were declared illegal and dissolved.

Also in 1977, Tradition, Family and Property, an extreme rightwing vigilante organization now coordinated in Brazil, Chile, Argentina, and Uruguay, singled out Silva in its major campaign to smear progressive Christians. He is, it said, "an ally of communist subversion." But Silva refused to be intimidated. A little later he said that the poor, the oppressed, are "the privileged ones" of the church. "It is very easy to accuse us of playing politics. . . . Injustice and oppression exist. The church is independent. . . . It is the critical conscience, free and liberating, that has the duty of denouncing situations of injustice and of violence."

The total impact of the traumatic experiences he has been through under the Junta would seem to be a strengthening of Silva's moral fiber and commitment, He is deeply concerned about human rights in the broadest sense, including the right of the laborer to work and a living wage, the need to protect intellectuals from improper pressures, the need for radical land reform. He is opposed to racism and anti-Semitism, the latter important because of anti-Semitic overtones in much of the rightwing propaganda in Chile and neighboring Argentina. He has some concern about the status of women, would mildly support a married clergy, and has not closed his mind to the possibility of ordaining women. He is theologically flexible, maintaining some considerable interest in theological developments. He supported change at Vatican II and has since become more at home with the reforms the Council promoted. His life-style is middle-class, his personality open. He is strongly in favor of more autonomy for national hierarchies, and he would support moderate efforts to strengthen the Synod of Bishops—with consequent reduction in the power of the Curia. In a papal conclave, Silva will undoubtedly form part of the bloc of progressive Latin Americans.

Europe

For the first time in the eight hundred years since the College of Cardinals established itself as enjoying the exclusive right to elect a pope, the College has ceased to have a European majority. Of the 118 electors, 26 are Italians, 24 from other countries of Western Europe, and 6 from Eastern Europe, a total of 57. Of the Italians, 17 are employed at the Roman Curia and 9 are bishops of residential dioceses. Of the other Europeans, 23 are residential and 7 curial. When Pope Paul was elected in 1963, Europeans numbered 57, as now, but the total number of electors was only 80.

There is the widest possible range of theological and pastoral interests among the European cardinals, even among those belonging to the same country and faced with similar political and socioeconomic environments. It is convenient, nevertheless, to look at three distinct parts of Europe in turn, because of historical or contemporary patterns in each: Western Europe (excluding Italy); Eastern European countries with socialist governments; Italy.

Western Europe

At the Second Vatican Council (1962–65), the bishops of Europe north of the Alps and the Pyrenees formed a nearly homogeneous progressive bloc and played a determining part in keeping the Council on the path planned by Pope John. The bishops of Spain and Portugal, on the contrary, were mostly in the same conservative molds as almost all the Italians.

The line-up of cardinals for a papal conclave today would depart significantly from this pattern. The secret selection processes by which certain bishops are added to the College of Cardinals have tended under Pope Paul to produce papal electors who are middle-of-the-roaders. In addition, it turned out after the Council that some of the staunchest advocates of updating the church while in Rome were reluctant to yield any part of their authority within their own dioceses, a syndrome particularly noticeable in Germany but also present to some extent in one of the greatest leaders of the aggiornamento at the Council, Cardinal Suenens. In addition, Vatican policy makers are quick to provide a balance if a particular cardinal turns out to be too far either to the right or to the left in a given country. Thus, Archbishop Joseph Ratzinger of Munich was made a cardinal in 1977 as a moderate progressive to balance the extremely conservative archbishop of Cologne, Cardinal Joseph Höffner.

Spain and Portugal have changed radically since the Council, with the ending of the Franco and Salazar regimes and a considerable opening of the formerly repressive political climate. Of Spain's four cardinals, two are classifiable as moderate progressives, Jubany in Barcelona, and Tarancón in Madrid, while only González Martín in Toledo is in the old highly conservative channel. The Portuguese cardinal is a middle-of-the-roader, but not a strong personality. One other factor that must be recognized, though difficult to measure, is the influence of Opus Dei, which since its foundation in Spain in 1928 has grown to be a worldwide power and reputedly commands the allegiance of several cardinals. Cardinal König went out of his way in 1977 to stress that he was not opposed to Opus Dei, an action interpreted as signifying that he feared its opposition might block a candidature for the papacy. A further indication of König's interest in becoming pope was a surprising volte-face in an interview on the Austrian radio in 1977. Formerly a strong supporter of better Vatican relations with the socialist regimes of Eastern Europe, he said he is now pessimistic about the possibility, a statement seen as a move to placate rightwing cardinal electors.

In the still unlikely eventuality that the next papal conclave will look for a candidate other than an Italian, while at this time the front-runner is Cardinal Pironio (the Argentine of immediate Italian ancestry), several Europeans would be considered. In addition to König, there is Cardinal Willebrands, now Dutch primate but still president of the Secretariat for Christian Unity and curialized from many years in Rome to the point of having a favorable image with the Italians. Another possible candidate is Cardinal Enrique y Tarancón of Madrid, while Cardinal Hume of England cannot be excluded.

Cardinal Suenens, the front-runner in the early 1970s, has ceased to express concern in structural church reform and currently concentrates on neopentecostalism. Although no longer a potential candidate, he will have a major impact on colleagues not only from Europe but from all parts of the world. Other important opinion makers among the West European cardinals include Alfrink (Holland), Marty and Villot (France), and Ratzinger (Germany).

Vaticanologist Giancarlo Zizola (see Introduction, above) estimates that twelve European cardinals are radical-evangelists; seventeen, progressives; and twenty-seven, conservatives. This evaluation is for the whole of Europe, including Italy and the socialist states. The evaluations of the European cardinals offered in this book are less sanguine. If Pellegrino is the only progressive Italian cardinal, we already have twenty-six conservatives in Italy. Add to them Gray in Scotland, González Martín in Spain, Höffner in Germany, and four curial cardinals: De Furstenberg (Belgium), Philippe (France), Filipiak (Poland), and Šeper (Yugoslavia). That gives 33 conservatives, well over half the total European cardinals—an indication of how unrepresentative of the church in Europe is its representation in the ranks of the cardinal electors. The reader can judge from the records of the others as presented in this book how many of them are radical-evangelists:

perhaps Alfrink (Holland), Garonne, Guyot and Marty (France), Hume (England), Jubany (Spain), and König (Austria). Even if all are included, that adds up only to seven. The others are spread out on a broad center band of the spectrum.

Some elements likely to have major impact on the collective attitude of the cardinals of Western Europe emerged in the formal and informal discussions at the fifth Synod of Bishops, Rome, October 1977. The dominant theme in the formal discussions, one recognized by the delegates from all parts of the world but with particular urgency by the West Europeans, was the need for radical updating of catechetic methods if the church is to avoid major losses within a generation. This would involve, not only new ways of instructing the young, but a significant transfer of emphasis toward a more solid Christian formation—an emphasis on personal conversion—of parents. It was particularly stressed that young people in their upper teens and early twenties will retain interest only in a religion that challenges their generosity by an active call to them to engage in social action. In the informal discussions, on the other hand, many took note of the wide appeal of such conservative movements as that headed by dissident Archbishop Lefebvre. These apparently contradictory phenomena would suggest the desirability of a pope who is strongly committed to internal reform of the church, a decentralization of power and authority, and a major commitment to the social Gospel, while firm and moderately conservative on theological issues. For their own reasons, these specifications would also suit the cardinal electors living under socialist regimes.

Cardinal Bernard Jan Alfrink

Although retired and in his seventy-eighth year, Cardinal Alfrink is one of the most influential of today's papal electors, trusted by most of his fellow cardinals, recognized as one of the great church leaders of the twentieth century and a main architect of Vatican Council II.

Born at Nijkerk, Utrecht, Holland, 5 July 1900, Alfrink was a brilliant student at the Utrecht seminary, then studied Scripture at the Biblical Institute in Rome. The Biblicum was far more advanced and open than other Roman universities, and the laureate Alfrink won there represented a significant level of scholarship. This experience laid the basis for his later progressive stands. He was ordained a priest in 1924.

Returning to Holland, he engaged in parish work until 1933 when he became Scripture professor in the Utrecht seminary, from where he moved in 1945 to the chair of biblical exegesis at the Catholic University of Nijmegen. About the same time he was appointed a consultor to the Pontifical Biblical Commission. In 1951 he was named coadjutor to the archbishop of Utrecht, and he succeeded as archbishop in 1955. Pope John made him a cardinal in 1960. He is a member of the curial Congregations for the Evangelization of Peoples (Propaganda Fide) and for Catholic Education, and of the Commission for the Revision of the Code of Canon Law. His published works include translations of and commentaries on several books of the Old Testament, and he took a leading role in the preparation of a new edition of the Bible in Dutch.

At the very start of Vatican II, he was one of the leaders of the group who blocked the curial attempt to have a vote on proposed members of the key Council Commissions before the Fathers had time to caucus and draw up their own lists. The original lists were all heavily loaded in favor of the Curia and its reactionary friends. The other leaders with Alfrink were Cardinals Liénart, Frings and König. Were it not for this initiative, the Council might never have achieved its objectives. Alfrink continued to take action at critical moments during the Council. Later in the first session he joined the three just mentioned cardinals, plus Léger and Suenens, in rejecting the curial draft proclaiming two distinct sources of revelation, Scripture and tradition, a draft which if approved would have seriously damaged the then budding ecumenical movement. He was similarly incisive in his criticism of the curial draft on "The Church," especially its silence or negativeness regarding the Episcopal College. The overall result was to establish the legitimacy of theological views that challenged the traditional Roman theology, deeply legalistic, triumphalistic and polemical. In addition, the vast majority of the Fathers were won over to support moves to end the Curia's stranglehold on input, and to set up commissions, on which the various viewpoints would be represented, to redraft the documents.

Other highlights of Alfrink's action at the Council included his part in the successful effort to prevent the Council's secretary-general (now cardinal) Felici from scuttling the statement on the Jews; his backing of Léger and Suenens for their openness on the birth control issue; his insistence that there should be no "sterile condemnation of communism." Some characteristic statements: "The human and Christian education of children is possible only when genuine conjugal love exists, a love that is normally nourished by sexual intercourse. When there is a conflict, the only solution is to make the sex act possible without procreation." On communism: "Many join the communist party not because of its philosophic doctrine but because of despair and for reasons of social justice. Let us not make a new condemnation of communism. It is useless, whereas dialogue can be profitable. Let us insist that all should enjoy religious liberty. Let us try to understand our own Christian faith better. Let us bring about social justice wherever there is need, instead of limiting ourselves to principles."

At a talk in Rome to a number of his fellow bishops during the final Council session in 1965, he described with a frankness and directness seldom found in the statements of churchmen what were the motives that had underlain his input to the Council. "If the term *anti-Roman* means 'anti-papal,' then I can in all good conscience deny the charge categorically. Quite the contrary. But if it means that some members of the Catholic community of the Netherlands object—and sometimes vehemently—to certain methods of the Roman government apparatus and to the way certain persons use these methods, then I could not and would not deny it. . . . But it would be a heartbreaking error to think that this anti-Roman spirit is found only in the Netherlands. It is found just about everywhere, even in Rome."

Since the Council, he has not deviated from this line. At the 1967 Synod of Bishops, he defended theologians against the criticisms of curial spokesmen, saying a document expressing thanks to the theologians would be more useful than a catalogue of errors or even a list of the truths of the faith. On marriage of a Catholic and a Protestant, he urged that the canonical form imposed by the Council of Trent should be abandoned or else required only for liceity, with power to the bishop to dispense. He urged flexibility in the training of seminarians: "We are in an era of uncertainty and research. The classical methods of information have ceased to be viable. What works today is experimentation."

In 1969, he named as vicars in parishes of his diocese five deacons and one layman, all of whom had completed theology but had indicated that they did not want to be bound by celibacy and would not be ordained priests. In 1973, speaking in London as president of the pacifist Pax Christi movement on the tenth anniversary of Pope John's *Pacem in Terris*, he said, "It would be overoptimistic to regard a few advances achieved in creating peace as a confirmation of the 'signs of the times' of which John spoke. The facts show that the armaments race continues with the same savagery, that violence continues to determine the relations between the superpowers, and that the chasm between rich countries and poor countries continues to grow."

In 1975, when 140 immigrants to Holland who were being sought by the authorities because their papers were not in order, took refuge in churches in Amsterdam, Alfrink wrote to all members of the Dutch parliament to stress the need to help "those who have often worked long years here for low wages, without social security and in poor housing. They are now in danger of becoming the victims of a situation caused by the unacceptable practices of those who profited from their services. . . . The decisions made by Parliament to resolve such situations in many cases worked injustice."

Perhaps the greatest of all Alfrink's achievements was to maintain dialogue between the very conservative and very advanced sectors of the church in Holland, and to maintain dialogue between the Dutch hierarchy and the Roman Curia which time and again pushed the Dutch to the brink of schism by attempts to interfere in the internal affairs of the church in Holland. By resigning when he reached age 75 in favor of Cardinal Johannes Willebrands, a Dutch member of the Roman Curia, he ensured the continuation of his policies. While in the same line as Alfrink, Willebrands had kept a lower profile. He would not have been the choice of either group in Holland, yet both groups accepted his appointment with relief as the best compromise in the circumstances. Although retired, Alfrink is in reasonably good health and mentally fully alert. He can be expected to be a major influence on a papal conclave, even possibly promoting the candidacy of Willebrands if it should appear that a substantial number of electors was ready to consider a non-Italian pope.

Alfrink is a member of the curial Congregations for the Evangelization of Peoples (Propaganda Fide), and for Catholic Education, as well as of the Commission for the Revision of the Code of Canon Law.

Cardinal Alfred Bengsch

Having made a major contribution to the preparation of the Second Vatican Council, and having intervened more than once in the Council discussions in favor of progressive initiatives, Cardinal Bengsch now finds himself as archbishop of a divided Berlin cast in a more conservative holding pattern. Some observers think he has become very comfortable in this changed role.

Bengsch was born in Berlin, 10 September 1921, the son of a postal employee. From the parish primary school he went to a Jesuit secondary school, then in 1940 to Fulda to study philosophy, a study that was soon interrupted when he was inducted into the German army. He saw active service on several fronts until in August 1944 he was gravely wounded and taken prisoner by the American forces in Normandy. On his discharge from hospital, he returned to Fulda, completed his philosophy and theology studies, and was ordained a priest in Berlin in 1950.

After four years in parish work, including the post of chaplain to a youth group, in Berlin, he went to teach at the seminary of Erfurt, East Germany. Simultaneously, he did advanced study at the University of Munich and received a doctorate in theology in 1956. There followed teaching and administrative posts in several seminaries until 1959, when he was made auxiliary to the bishop of Berlin. He succeeded as bishop of Berlin in 1961, with the personal rank of archbishop. The cardinalate followed in 1967. He is a member of the curial Congregations for the Sacraments and Divine Worship, and for Religious and Secular Institutes, and of the Commission for the Revision of the Code of Canon Law.

One of Bengsch's stronger interventions at Vatican II was to condemn the curial draft proposing the Scriptures and tradition as two separate sources of revelation. He was aware how harmful such a statement would be to the cause of ecumenism in Germany, and his exposure to contemporary theological thinking in German universities had taught him that no such separation was needed. He similarly supported Archbishop (now Cardinal) François Marty of Paris in his call for open dialogue with atheists, stressing in particular the need for deeper analysis of atheistic ideologies.

His political situation has undoubtedly influenced his gradual withdrawal to more conservative positions over the years. He is aware that church survival in Eastern Germany requires the avoidance of divisive issues that could be exploited by the regime, and his overriding concern is to maintain a united front of Christians against the pressures of the Marxist regime. Because the communists pride themselves on upholding primitive moral values, banning prostitution and punishing social and political corruption, he insists on the observance of a strict moral code in order not to be outflanked by his opponents. The result is that he reacts to the moves of the other side, rather than taking his own initiatives. One who knows him says that he has so internalized his new role as to be today "a truly malign presence in the College of Cardinals." If this is correct, he would in a conclave support a theologically ultraconservative candidate. At the same time, his circumstances would tend to range him with the other cardinals living under socialist regimes to the extent that they would best be served by a pope who is identified as socially progressive and willing to continue dialogue with Marxists governments.

Cardinal José M. Bueno y Monreal

Born in Saragossa in northcentral Spain 11 September 1904, Cardinal Bueno y Monreal entered the junior seminary at Madrid at age ten. Seven years later he went to Rome to complete his studies at the Gregorian and the Pontifical Academy of St. Thomas Aquinas, obtaining laureates in philosophy, theology and canon law. He was ordained a priest at age twenty-three.

Returning to Spain, he taught dogmatic theology at the Madrid seminary for seven years, and subsequently canon law and moral theology. With the foundation of the Center for Higher Religious Culture, he moved there to teach the Public Law of the Church, a post in which he remained until made bishop of Jaca in 1945. He was transferred to Victoria in 1950, and to Seville as coadjutor with right of succession and apostolic administrator in 1954. He became archbishop of Seville on the death of the incumbent in 1957, and was made a cardinal a year later. He is a member of the curial Congregation for Religious and Secular Institutes.

His interventions at Vatican II were mixed. He revealed a basic hostility to the ecumenical movement, said that "liberty for false religions harms the one true religion," and urged that the wording of the draft text should be made more cautious, lest it appear to sanction a kind of "Pan-Christianity" or religious syncretism with the corresponding danger of indifferentism. As the Council progressed, however, he grew with it. In the discussion on seminaries, for example, he questioned the need for minor seminaries in which youngsters from the age of twelve or earlier were withdrawn from family influences into a closed ecclesiastical atmosphere. Boys, he said, "have a more natural and perfect seminary in their own homes." And at the final session in the discussion of the draft document on the church in today's world, he pointed out that the doctrine of the absolute inviolability of private property was not the teaching of the church. The draft, he said, was "too much imbued with a mentality of individualistic liberalism and capitalism," failing to take adequate note of "the mentality of collectivism existing in a large part of the world." After the Council ended, he urged his priests and people to cooperate faithfully in implementing its decisions. "It's perfectly fine to die for Christianity, but it's much harder to live as Christians."

The authoritative French Catholic publication, *Informations Catholiques Internationales*, described him in 1976 as in much the same line as Cardinal Enrique y Tarancón, archbishop of Madrid and key figure in the Spanish church. Bueno y Monreal, it said, is "very human, very intelligent, with a good knowledge of current problems and a desire to solve them, but very prudent." While still basically conservative, he is not a reactionary. In a papal conclave, he would undoubtedly follow the leadership of Tarancón, who is committed to the conciliar church but with the same cautious approach to implementation as Pope Paul.

Cardinal Vicente Enrique y Tarancón

Today the key figure in the Spanish church, Cardinal Tarancón was born at Burriana, diocese of Tortosa, on the Mediterranean coast of northcentral Spain, 14 May 1907. At the age of ten, he entered the Tortosa seminary and there completed his studies with a laureate in theology. He was ordained a priest at age twenty-two. His first assignment was as assistant pastor and organist in a local parish. In 1933, he moved to Madrid to work in Catholic Action. To guide him in his work, he made an intensive study of the methods in use in Italy, France and Belgium. At this time, he also developed a close friendship with Angel Herrera Oria, the future cardinal bishop of Málaga.

When the Civil War broke out in 1936, Tarancón was at Tuy in the extreme west of Spain, just north of the border with Portugal. In 1938, at the end of the war, he returned to Tortosa and worked in various parishes until made bishop of Solsona in 1945. Seven years later, he was elected secretary of the conference of Spanish bishops and in 1964 he moved to Oviedo as archbishop. Having been promoted to the primatial see of Toledo in 1969, he received the cardinal's hat two months later. He is a member of the curial Congregation for Bishops, and of the Commission for the Revision of the Code of Canon Law.

From Vatican II to the effective ending of the Franco regime with the series of constitutional changes introduced by Juan Carlos when he became king on Franco's death in 1975, the Spanish church was deeply divided between those traditionalists who supported Franco and the "conciliars" who wanted to have the Concordat modified, eliminating state controls over the church, including the decisive voice it enjoyed in the naming of bishops. Tarancón was a leader of the "conciliars," and when it became apparent in 1970 that the archbishop of Madrid was near death, Pope Paul moved him to Madrid as administrator. He succeeded as archbishop in 1971. The reason for this maneuver was that, while Toledo is the primatial see, Madrid as the capital is the center of power, and the Vatican wanted to forestall pressures by the regime to give it to Bishop José Guerra Campos of Cuenca, a fervent supporter of Franco.

Already at Vatican II, Tarancón had exhibited an openness that was then unusual among Spanish bishops. He stressed the need for a greater participation of the laity in decision making, recalling Pius XII's affirmation that public opinion is an essential dimension of the life of the church as of all societies. He expanded these views in three long declarations (a pastoral letter, an interview, and a sermon) when he took office in Toledo in 1969. They called for a "daring conciliar reform, dialogue in the church, church autonomy vis-à-vis the state, and a renewal of the social apostolate." The world, he said is moving fast, so that not only immobilism but a too slow aggiornamento of the church is inacceptable. We must move prudently but daringly, learning as best we can the global evolution of which the Council spoke. Pluralism in the church follows inescapably from the Council's orientations, and the worst thing now would be a spirit of conformism on the part of the people, a failure to listen to the calls of the Spirit. The church further has to regain the confidence of the workers by actions and attitudes that make sense to them, not just Catholic Action, but a real presence of the church in the world of the workers. Referring to the Concordat, he said that it should be revised to produce a new kind of relationship, because "the old church-state relationship weighs heavily on the national conscience."

Pluralism today definitely marks the church in Spain. One can distinguish three trends among militant Catholics, that is, those who play an active role as leaders: the preconciliar, the conciliar, and the postconciliar. For the first group, everything is clear. The church is in disarray because Marxists, Freemasons, and pseudo-Christians have infiltrated its structures. The church can be restored only by the tactics of the Guerrillas of Christ the King, an extreme-right vigilante movement. Less aggressive but basically in the same line is the powerful Opus Dei. For long this tendency had the backing of a majority of Spain's bishops, but episcopal support is now down to 16 or 17. At the opposite end of the spectrum is the less organized but growing force supported by the base communities whose greatest strength is in the worker quarters of Madrid and Barcelona. Their political choices run from center left to extreme left, with many claiming the right to be simultaneously Christians and socialists. Their support includes many Catholic Action worker movements. They agree with the bishops on one key point: the ending of the government's right to present bishops for Vatican confirmation. They would also abolish compulsory religious instruction in the public schools, end state salaries to priests, and separate religious and civil marriage. They have the sympathy of some twenty bishops but the open support of only one, Bishop Alberto Iniesta Jiménez, an auxiliary of Madrid in charge of a worker district with 400,000 inhabitants.

Between these groups are some twenty conciliars led by Tarancón. Intelligent and open to dialogue, he is more a pastor than a theologian. A diplomat, he has succeeded in avoiding a rupture either with the regime or with the Left, and he works particularly hard to maintain dialogue between the bishops of opposing views. While no revolutionary, he is by temperament a liberal. He is strongly opposed to a Catholic political party, especially in the present transitional period when the parliament falls far short of being fully representative, because the rural conservative vote has significantly more weight than the urban progressive vote. Thus, Soria has a vote in a joint assembly of the two houses of parliament for every 14,000 inhabitants, while Madrid has one per 140,000. At the 1977 plenary meeting of the Spanish bishops, Tarancón said, "Everyone knows that the hierarchy has neither inspired nor does it encourage any particular political party."

The limits to Tarancón's openness were also set out by him in November 1977 when the draft text of a new constitution for Spain was issued. It stated in Article 3: "The Spanish state is nonconfessional." Tarancón protested this radical abandonment of Spain's traditional support of the church. Speaking for the eighty bishops and auxiliary bishops of the bishops' conference, he said, "We are not asking for privilege, but we have to keep in mind that we are in Spain, and in Spain we Catholics are in the majority."

In a papal conclave, Tarancón can be expected to support a moderate progressive. Bueno y Monreal and Jubany will go along with him, but not González Martín, acknowledged leader of the preconciliar faction in the hierarchy.

Cardinal Maximilien de Furstenberg

A member of a diplomatic and wealthy family, Cardinal de Furstenberg was born in the Castle of Ter Worm, Heerlen, diocese of Roermond, Holland, 23 October 1904. Although born in Holland, he was of Belgian nationality, and shortly after his tenth birthday he was sent to the school attached to the Abbey of Mardesous near Namur, Belgium. Five years later he went to the College of Saint Louis, Brussels, for classics and philosophy. From 1922 to 1925, he traveled extensively on several continents and did his military service, then went to the University of Louvain for advanced studies of philosophy, graduating with a licentiate. In 1928 he went to Rome for four years of theology at the Gregorian, which gave him a laureate.

Ordained a priest in 1931, he began to teach in the diocesan college of Antwerp, two years later transferred to the major seminary of Malines. In 1946 he returned to Rome as rector of the Belgian College. Ordained a titular archbishop in 1949, he was sent to Japan as delegate apostolic, and when in 1952 Japan established diplomatic relations with the Vatican, he became internuncio. In 1960 he was transferred to Australia as apostolic delegate, his territory extending also to New Zealand and Oceania. From there he went to Portugal as nuncio in 1962, and in 1967 he was recalled to Rome to be awarded for his successful diplomatic career with the cardinalate and the post of prefect of the Congregation for the Oriental Churches. He retired from this post, in which he was little more than a figurehead—the secretary (Archbishop Mario Brini) making the decisions—in 1973. He continues as a member of the Council for the Public Affairs of the Church; of the Congregations for the Bishops, for Religious and Secular Institutes, and for the Evangelization of Peoples (Propaganda Fide); of the Segnatura Apostolica, the highest Vatican tribunal; of the Commissions for the Revision of the Code of Canon Law, for the Interpretation of the Decrees of Vatican II; for Vatican City State; and for Oversight of the Institute for the Works of Religion, a major financial institution.

Like most Vatican diplomats, de Furstenberg has avoided expressing personal substantive views on theology or anything else, and those close to him regard him as a docile servant of the Curia. There is no reason to doubt that he will follow the Curia's lead in a papal conclave.

Cardinal Gabriel-Marie Garrone

A reforming head of a Congregation of the Roman Curia gradually worn down to resigned impotence by his reactionary associates, Cardinal Garrone was born at Aix-les-Bains, archdiocese of Chambéry, in eastern France not far from the frontiers of Switzerland and Italy, 12 October 1901. He entered the local minor seminary at age ten, then went to the French seminary in Rome for his ecclesiastical studies, obtaining laureates in philosophy and theology at the Gregorian. Having performed his military service, he was ordained a priest in 1925.

His first assignment was as a professor in the minor seminary in which he had studied earlier, and while there he continued his university studies and obtained a laureate in literature and a diploma for graduate work in philosophy. In 1926 he became professor of philosophy, and later of dogmatic theology and church history, at the Chambéry major seminary. In World War II he was mobilized with the rank of captain and was cited by his regimental superiors as "the officer with the highest sense of duty and of honor." Taken prisoner, he maintained his leadership role in the prison camp, organizing classes for all, particularly for seminarians.

Released in 1945, he became rector of the Chambéry major seminary until 1947 when he was named coadjutor to the archbishop of Toulouse, whom he succeeded as archbishop in 1956.

In Toulouse, he became known for his progressive positions, and at Vatican II he spoke his mind clearly on a variety of issues. He sought consistently to strengthen and clarify the statement on the church in today's world. He said, for example, that it had to deal with burning questions for which the church had no readymade or definitive answers. "We must not think the church has easy solutions for all problems. . . . The church's attitude to the world is one of open cooperation." Of the creation he said that many Christians reduce it to the origin of the world. "They do not understand that it implies the permanent essential dependence of all things on God. The believer who does understand this sees the creative presence of God in all terrestrial activities. This dependence on God is the profound reason for the spirit of poverty which we have so often stressed." On peace: "Peace for many is merely the absence of war. They confuse fear of war with love of peace. But the possibility of war will never disappear until every effort is made to establish justice."

The greatest sensation he created at the Council, however, was an attack on the Congregation of Seminaries and Universities, then a citadel of conservatism. It should take local needs more into account, no longer behind the times and negative in approach, should have members from all over the world, be open to progress and change in the sciences that pertain to seminary training, use the experience of true experts in every field of higher learning. The response to this challenge from the bishops around the world was so overwhelmingly positive that in early 1966 Pope Paul called him to Rome to reform the Congregation he had attacked, but giving him the second position, with the whole of the administration still intact, and the 88-year-old Cardinal Pizzardo still at his desk and insisting on signing everything.

When Garrone was made a cardinal in June 1967, he did gain effective control, even though Pizzardo remained the formal head until 1968 when Garrone became prefect. Garrone's report on his objectives to the 1967 Synod of Bishops was a masterpiece. He said Vatican II had given a mandate for true change in seminary training; that contemporary youth had qualities and activities that—even if they sometimes upset us—are signs of the times. Vatican II had ordered extensive decentralization of the regulation of seminary life and activities, and it was up to conferences of bishops in each country to work out the appropriate reforms. In addition, bishops should stop referring "the most trivial questions" to Rome for a decision. Students should play a major role in their own training, living as teams and following courses that would bring them into contact with the world outside the seminary. Seminary teaching staff should include lay people.

He set out to implement this program with his customary vigor. He refused, for example, to make a ruling for the rector of a seminary as to whether or not a particular candidate should be given or denied ordination, insisting that Rome could not know as much about the individual as the seminary authorities. As the Paris Catholic publication, *Informations Catholiques Internationales*, commented in September 1969, "He has shown absolute determination to reform the structures of higher education in spite of the violent campaigns of defamation waged against him by integrist circles." But by the early 1970s, advancing age and the persistence of his adversaries wore him down, so that he now lets his subordinates make rulings that are far more conservative than he would make. But there is no reason to think that he himself has changed. In a papal conclave, he can be counted on to stand firmly with the progressive French cardinals.

In addition to being prefect of the Congregation for Catholic Education, Garonne is a member of the Council for the Public Affairs of the Church; of the Congregations for the Doctrine of the Faith, for the Bishops; for the Eastern Churches; for Religious and Secular Institutes, for the Evangelization of Peoples (Propaganda Fide), and for the Causes of Saints; and of the Commission for the Revision of the Code of Canon Law.

Cardinal Marcelo González Martín

The recognized leader of the traditional segment of the Spanish hierarchy, Cardinal González was born at Villanubla, archdiocese of Valladolid, 16 January 1918. He studied first at the local seminary, then at the Pontifical University of Comillas, where he received a laureate in theology. After ordination to the priesthood in 1941, he taught theology for many years at the Valladolid seminary and in the Faculty of Medicine and Law of the state university. In 1960 he was made bishop of Astorga, from where he moved in 1966 to Barcelona as coadjutor, to become archbishop by succession the following year. Transferred to Toledo in 1971, he was made a cardinal in 1973. He is a member of the curial Congregation for the Evangelization of Peoples (Propaganda Fide).

At Vatican II, González had a mixed record. He spoke very positively of the need for church reform. He urged a sharing of wealth between rich and poor dioceses, asserting that the present disparity was scandalous and contrary to the social teaching of the church. In addition, it prevented others from taking the church seriously. "Before the church can hope to be heard by those outside, she must devote herself earnestly to internal reform." And suiting his action to his words, he moved out of his episcopal palace in Astorga into a more modest home. But in a discussion on the media, he showed his pro-Franco bias by criticizing the way in which segments of the Catholic press (notably in France, the Netherlands, Germany and the United States) stressed the pressures exerted by the Franco regime against religious minorities in Spain.

As the Spanish government has not recognized the conference of Spanish bishops, it regards González, as Primate of Spain, as the only spokesman for the hierarchy. He is far removed from the other three Spanish cardinals, Tarancón, Bueno y Monreal, and Jubany. For him, to be a good Christian, one must be a good patriot, by which he means a supporter of the sociopolitical philosophy that undergirded the Franco regime. He is often presented as the epitome of the "national Catholicism" bishop, an old Spanish concept going back to the Middle Ages when the popes gave the Spanish monarchs the control of the church which they later denied to Henry VIII of England. It was he who presided over the obsequies for Franco and delivered the eulogy. He is uncommunicative, rarely answering letters and receiving few visitors. This attitude of reserve was accentuated by his bad experience in Barcelona. As he spoke little Catalán, was unfamiliar with Catalán customs, and emotionally far removed from the separatist aspirations of most Cataláns, relations between him and the priests and people of Barcelona were always unsatisfactory.

Cardinal Paul Gouyon

Born at Bordeaux 24 October 1910, Cardinal Gouyon had an experience unlike that of almost all his fellow cardinals in that he completed his primary and secondary studies and a degree in literature at the University of Bordeaux, then fulfilled his military service before deciding at age twenty-two on an ecclesiastical career. He studied philosophy for two years at the Bordeaux seminary, then went to Paris for three years of theology. After ordination to the priesthood in 1937, he went to Rome for further study of theology and canon law at the Gregorian.

There followed some eighteen years of pastoral and administrative work in the Bordeaux diocese until 1957 when he was named bishop of Bayonne. In 1963 he moved to Rennes as coadjutor to the archbishop, whom he succeeded the following year. Named a cardinal in 1969, he is a member of the curial Secretariats for Christian Unity and for Non-Christians.

Although he has never emerged as a major leader in the French church, his contributions to the debates at Vatican II showed considerable erudition and sound, progressive judgment. In the discussion on collegiality, his knowledge of the history of the early church made a deep impression. Criticizing the first draft of what would become the powerful statement on the church in today's world, he said its preface lacked a broad cosmic view of the differences between light and darkness in the world: weak and anemic language; a text that seemed to have been written by men living in peace, not by those having a part in the world's anxieties. In a clearly Teilhardian perspective, he summed up: "We must clarify the theological foundations of technological progress, the means of communicating thought, the triumph of medicine. . . . All of this represents the fulfilment of the command given by God in Genesis to 'fill the earth and subdue it.' "

The French were pleased when he was made a cardinal, the characteristic comment being that he was open. He confirmed this view very shortly by having the first priest-bishop encounter ever held in France with the clergy of his diocese, a meeting which he described afterward to the press as "an honest but limited experience of coresponsibility."

In 1977, he joined with six other French bishops in a powerful declaration of solidarity with the church in Latin America. The statement, given wide publicity in the French press, said in part: "The peoples are being tested. . . . Liberty of expression and association are limited or eliminated. . . . Leaders of political and trade-union organizations are threatened, imprisoned, liquidated. Torture is systematically practiced. Suspects 'disappear.' . . . Bishops and priests are not spared, . . . because they have taken the side of the Gospel. They speak for those reduced to silence. . . . We support this church, . . . but we must be honest. . . . We in Europe who claim to belong to the most advanced nations on earth are among those who benefit from the exploitation of the poor nations. We fail to see the suffering that results for entire peoples, in their flesh and in their spirit. We contribute to reinforce the division of our world in which the rich dominate the poor; the powerful, the weak."

As a bishop in Brittany, the most Catholic but also the most traditional and one of the most backward parts of France, Gouyon maintains pastoral practices that give him a conservative image in France. But it is clear that he has an awareness of the signs of the times and sees the need for the church to move forward with the world. In a papal conclave he would favor a progressive candidate.

Cardinal Gordon Joseph Gray

An old-fashioned, kindly priest who loves the church as he knew it in the past and accepts change reluctantly, Cardinal Gray was born at Edinburgh, Scotland, 10 August 1910. He was seventeen when he entered the minor seminary, then continued to the major seminary of the diocese of Southwark, England, and was ordained a priest in Edinburgh in 1935. He engaged in parish work for twelve years, was then called by the bishops of Scotland to head the country's national minor seminary at Aberdeen. While in parish work in Edinburgh, he had continued his studies and obtained a master's at Saint Andrew's University. In 1951 he was named archbishop of Saint Andrews and Edinburgh. A cardinal since 1969, he is a member of the curial Congregations for the Sacraments and Divine Worship, and for the Evangelization of Peoples (Propaganda Fide), and of the Pontifical Commission for Social Communications.

He has always been interested in the media, and he was one of the first students—just after becoming a cardinal—in a center set up by the bishops of England, Wales and Scotland, to train priests, nuns and lay people in the techniques needed to participate in radio and TV religious programs. But in general he hews to the old ways, in tune with the Catholics of Scotland, a minority in a long hostile environment and only slowly opening to elementary ecumenical encounter. The authority of the church is for him primary, an authority understood in the traditional way. Along with the other Scottish bishops, he has always stood for the most literal interpretation of *Humanae Vitae* and unquestioning obedience to the papal directives. A faithful servant of the church, he is moved more by emotion than independent thinking. In a papal conclave, he would probably follow the leadership of the Roman Curia.

Cardinal Jean Guyot

Born at Bordeaux 7 July 1905, the son of a doctor, Cardinal Guyot did his secondary courses at the College of Saint-Genest, then went on to obtain a licentiate in jurisprudence at the Bordeaux Faculty of Law. In 1927, he entered the Bordeaux seminary and was ordained a priest in 1932. After a short period in parish work, he went to Rome and obtained a degree in theology at the Angelicum.

Returning to Bordeaux, he engaged in pastoral work, mostly with the young, introducing the Young Christian Workers and the Young Women Christian Workers to the diocese and acting as their chaplain for eight years. He then started a seminary for late vocations, and in 1944 he was named vicar-general and given as his specific work the fostering of vocations to the priesthood. In 1949, he was made coadjutor to the bishop of Coutances, succeeded to the incumbent the following year, and in 1966 was promoted to Toulouse as archbishop. He was made a cardinal in 1973 and is a member of the curial Congregations for the Clergy and for Catholic Education.

At Vatican II, he actively supported the generally progressive and open line of the French hierarchy. In a discussion on the priesthood, he made clear his desire to have the ban imposed by Rome on worker priests in France removed, an action taken not long afterward by the conference of French bishops. He also strongly supported the elimination of gold rings and other "signs of ostentation" from clerical garb, stressing that "poverty is the sign of the incarnation and should also be the sign of the church." In recent years, he has continued in the same line, speaking out most strongly against the armaments race and against sales abroad of French armaments. In 1973, he joined with Bishop Guy-Marie Riobé of Orleans and several other French bishops in a condemnation of France's program of nuclear testing. "I have been against these tests from 1970," he said. "They expose mankind to frightful dangers."

Cardinal Joseph Höffner

Probably the most qualified cardinal academically in a wide range of ecclesiastical and secular subjects, Cardinal Höffner is also the leader of the conservatives in the German church.

He was born at Horhausen, diocese of Trier, in the Rhineland near the border with Luxembourg, 24 December 1906, the eldest of nine children. After a short period in the local seminary, Höffner went to the German-Hungarian College in Rome, where from 1926 to 1934 he studied philosophy and theology at the Gregorian. He received a laureate in philosophy in 1929 and a licentiate in canon law in 1931. Having been ordained a priest in 1932, he added a laureate in theology in 1934.

On his return to Germany he continued his studies at the University of Freiburg in Breisgau and obtained another laureate in theology. He added a diploma in economics in 1940 and a doctorate in political sciences in 1941. In 1944, the theology faculty of the University of Freiburg gave him the license to teach, and he was called to the chairs of pastoral theology and social sciences in the Higher School of Theology at Trier. In 1951, at the special request of Pope Pius XII, he went to Münster where for nearly ten years he taught the Christian social sciences and established the Institute of Christian Social Sciences. He became a member of the scientific council of three ministries of the Federal Republic (West Germany).

In 1962 he was made bishop of Münster, and in 1969 he was moved to Germany's biggest diocese, Cologne, as coadjutor to Cardinal Joseph Frings, who resigned almost immediately and was replaced as archbishop by Höffner. Named a cardinal in 1969, Höffner is a member of the curial Congregations for Religious and Secular Institutes, for the Evangelization of Peoples (Propaganda Fide), and for Catholic Education; of the Secretariat for Non-Believers, and of the Prefecture for Economic Affairs of the Holy See.

A typical indication of Höffner's priorities was provided by his intervention in the discussion of ecumenism at Vatican II, when he indicated that he felt no great need for the aggiornamento of the church as proposed by Pope John, but rather a greater effort in its struggle with external enemies. "Our greatest cross," he said, "is not primarily the reform of the Curia or a change in the demarcation of dioceses; rather it is militant atheism spreading particularly in the great urban centers among the workers and the intellectuals. Let us address a separate chapter to our paganized brethren."

His subsequent career shows him to be rigidly orthodox, known in particular for his absolute backing of clerical celibacy in opposition to the widespread movement for optional celibacy among priests in Germany and elsewhere in Europe north of the Alps. At the 1977 Synod of Bishops, he warned that the creativity and enthusiasm for action of young people today, especially when confronted by injustice and oppression, constituted a danger because they could easily be misled. They should, he said, "be instructed in the social teachings of the church so as to be forewarned against the utopia of an earthly paradise." He is believed to be connected with Opus Dei, a conservative power in the church with strong influence on a significant number of cardinals. He is also a friend of the conservative German Christian Democrat leader, Joseph Strauss.

Cardinal George Basil Hume

"A man of profound spirituality and of great personal charm," in the words of the *Times* (London), Cardinal Hume was the first priest to jump directly to the metropolitan see of Westminster since Cardinal Manning in 1865. He is also the first Benedictine monk in this post, though there has always been a Benedictine in the British hierarchy since it was reestablished in 1850.

Born at Newcastle-on-Tyne on the North Sea coast of northern England, 2 March 1923, Hume is the son of Sir William Hume, a famous heart surgeon and an Anglican. His Catholic mother was French, and he speaks perfect French. At baptism he was given the name George, for which he substituted Basil when he became a Benedictine. From primary school he went to the Benedictine college at Ampleforth for secondary studies, then began monastic studies at eighteen in the Abbey of Saint Lawrence, Ampleforth. He read history at Oxford and has a doctorate in theology from Fribourg, Switzerland, where he also learned German. He took his final vows as a Benedictine in 1945 and was ordained a priest in 1950.

From 1953 he taught modern languages at the Ampleforth secondary school and dogmatic theology to the young monks in the attached abbey. In 1963, he became Abbott of Ampleforth, an abbey with 130 monks, of whom 53 work in parishes or study centers in seven dioceses. He has had considerable foreign travel, including a period in the United States where he helped set up a Benedictine community. Highly ecumenical, he was president for four years of the Benedictine Ecumenical Commission, and he is a former member of the Council of Churches of Rydale, Yorkshire. Examples of his ecumenism are his pioneer efforts to establish an Orthodox center at Ampleforth, and the organization of a residential center for young Russian, Greek, and Yugoslav Orthodox so that they could attend the local school. Named archbishop of Westminster in February 1976, he was made a cardinal the following May. He is a member of the curial Secretariat for Christian Unity.

Hume was completely unknown to the general public when appointed to Westminster. He was well received by the tiny minority of Catholics with influence in high society. Other newspapers

126

followed the lead of the *Times*. "His most obvious credentials are to be found in his unquestionable holiness," said the *Guardian*. He is "endowed with great wisdom," according to the *Tablet*. Some, nevertheless, asked why one with little pastoral experience and identified with the ruling classes should become head of a church composed preponderantly of workers. But within a short time he succeeded in projecting an image that impressed favorably the entire Catholic community, even those of Irish birth or immediate descent who constitute half of England's six million Catholics.

A typical statement was his condemnation of violations of human rights in an article in the *Guardian*. "It would be unacceptable if only a single person were involved, but there are tens of thousands throughout the world in prison for following the dictates of their consciences and who, with increasing regularity, are being subjected to the barbarous practice of physical and psychological tortures." The Irish read into this a condemnation of the interrogation techniques used by the British army in Northern Ireland, techniques for which Britain was found guilty of sanctioning the official use of torture by the European Court of Human Rights.

Interviewed by E. A. Ostro for Universal Press Syndicate, Hume showed himself very optimistic about the state of religion in England. While people are less interested in the church as an institution, there is "a desire for God, a desire to know and understand the kind of message which the Gospel brought." He finds widespread dissatisfaction with a materialistic society, with the consumer society that in England doesn't have goals and targets that are really worthwhile.

In Hume's opinion, one of the areas of conflict within the Catholic community in England is whether Catholic schools should be continued. Even though the state pays a large part of the cost, some feel that the church is concentrating too much of its effort in this area while neglecting adult education. Without committing himself on the issue, Hume indicated that his diocese has started a major program of adult education, and he thinks this is "absolutely right."

On one controversial issue, Hume stated his position very forthrightly. He is in favor of ordination to the priesthood of married men, and he believes that the decision should be in terms of the effectiveness of the individual as God's instrument. "I'm quite convinced as a result of my experience in the religious life over the years that the vocation to celibacy is one thing and the vocation to the priesthood is another. This is my firm conviction. . . . I think some are more effective celibate and some would be more effective as married men." However, he also noted, he does not think that the church is yet ready for this change, certainly not in England.

Hume is a strong advocate of a juster social order. His concern for human rights extends to the rights of women, and he has not closed his mind to the possibility of women priests. What he sees as the first order of business, however, is the divorce of celibacy and priesthood. He maintains an active interest in theological developments, although his approach to issues is pastoral rather than theological, in the Benedictine tradition. He is sensitive to the views of his fellow bishops and has quickly won their firm support, and he is also sensitive to the views of priests and people. He is less than enthusiastic about *Humanae Vitae*, and he resents the control exercised by the Roman Curia, anxious for more independence for national hierarchies and an increase of the powers of the Synod of Bishops. He is believed to favor the movement for the introduction of general absolution, a practice strongly condemned by top curialists when introduced in Memphis, Tennessee, by Bishop Carroll Dozier in 1976. Although his main concern in his first year in Westminster was to get to know his diocese and imprint his stamp on it, he is expected to play an increasingly big part in the life of the church internationally. Reportedly, he has already met with leading churchmen of Western Europe to discuss coordination of efforts for updating the church. He is still on the young side to be seen as a candidate for the papacy, but if the cardinal electors at the next conclave turn seriously to search for a non-Italian pope, Hume would undoubtedly figure prominently in a list of prospects.

Cardinal Narciso Jubany Arnau

An open and balanced Catalán, able to adjust himself to the extremely complicated pressures to which the archbishop of Barcelona was subjected under the Franco regime and in the subsequent transitional period, Cardinal Jubany was born at Santa Coloma de Farnés, diocese of Gerona, in the heartland of Catalonia and to Catalán-speaking parents, 12 August 1913. He studied for the priesthood at the Pontifical University of Comillas in Spain and the Gregorian in Rome, obtaining a laureate in canon law from the former and a laureate in theology from the latter. He was ordained in 1939.

There followed several years of pastoral and administrative work in Barcelona, including the post of counselor to Catholic Action Youth. In 1955 he was named an auxiliary to the archbishop of Barcelona, moved to Gerona as bishop in 1964, and returned to Barcelona as archbishop in 1971. He was made a cardinal two years later.

At Vatican II in 1963, when the question of married deacons and permanent deacons had started to be discussed and was met with violent opposition from many prominent Fathers, Jubany made an impressive intervention in the name of twelve Spanish bishops, asking the assembly not to close the door on either of these issues without first exploring the theological and pastoral implications. In the end, the Council approved both innovations.

At home, he always maintained his distance from the Franco regime. The United States National Catholic news service reported in 1969 that a pastoral letter in which he had criticized the state of siege had been suppressed by the Franco regime. In 1973, with Franco still in power and the regime hostile to Catalán movements, he made a relatively strong statement on behalf of striking workers, one of whom had been killed and several wounded in a clash with the authorities. "These are serious events," he said, "and they show clearly that social relations, especially in the world of labor, are not adequately based on truth, justice, love, and liberty." The following year he published an open letter to the government in which—without naming them directly—he gave full support to the position and demands of

129

13,654 strikers at the SEAT automobile factory. The right to strike should be written into law, he said. The time has come when those who enjoy certain positions of privilege should agree to abandon them.

He maintains an active interest in theological developments, and while continuing to think in Scholastic categories, is open and flexible. He gave full support to the Vatican II changes and has since the Council become more attuned to its spirit. He is sensitive to the views of his fellow bishops and his priests, and—to a somewhat lesser degree—to those of the laity. He is not significantly influenced in his decisions by government pressures or fear of offending influential vested interests. He is moderately concerned about human rights, including women's rights, but is opposed to married priests or the ordination of women. Though tending to legalism, he is tolerant with his priests and easy to deal with. His support of *Humanae Vitae* was unenthusiastic. He would like to see a less powerful Roman Curia, a more powerful Synod of Bishops, a more modern style of church government, but his prudence counsels patience on all these issues. In a papal conclave, he would figure as a moderate progressive.

Cardinal John Carberry, archbishop of St. Louis, provides music and song as he visits aged and infirm residents of the Little Sisters of the Poor Home for the Elderly in St. Louis. The cardinal, an accomplished amateur violinist, occasionally performs when visiting institutions and residences in the archdiocese. (United States)

Cardinal Humberto Medeiros, archbishop of Boston, admires the family snapshots of a prisoner while on a pre-Christmas visit to the Massachusetts Correctional Institution at Walpole, Mass. The prelate wears a scrimshaw (hand carving on whalebone) pectoral cross which he was given in the prison. (United States)

Above, *Cardinal William Wakefield Baum, archbishop of Washington. (United States)*

Below, *Cardinal John Patrick Cody, archbishop of Chicago. (United States)*

Above, *Cardinal Terence J. Cooke, archbishop of New York.* Below, *Cardinal John Joseph Wright, prefect of the Sacred Congregation for the Clergy. (United States)*

Above, *Cardinal John Francis Dearden, archbishop of Detroit, one of the leading Catholic ecumenists and first president of the United States National Conference of Catholic Bishops. Below, Cardinal Timothy Manning, archbishop of Los Angeles. (United States)*

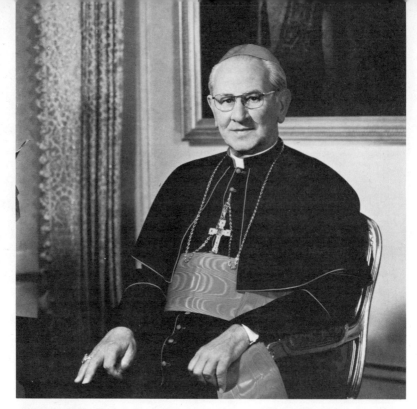

Above, *Cardinal John Joseph Krol, archbishop of Philadelphia.* Below, *Cardinal Lawrence Joseph Shehan, retired archbishop of Baltimore. (United States)*

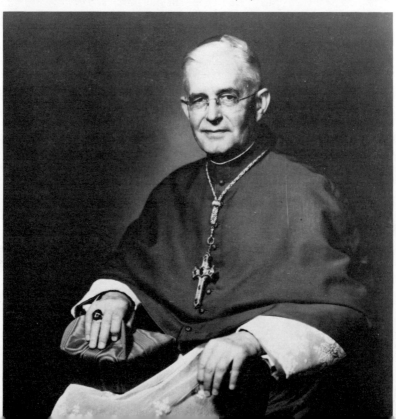

Cardinal Paul Emile Leger (right), former archbishop of Montreal, with the late Pope John XXIII, following a private audience in the pontiff's private studio. (Canada)

Cardinal Maurice Roy, archbishop of Quebec, addressing a biennial convention of the National Council of Catholic Men in St. Louis. (Canada)

Above, *Cardinal George Flahiff, archbishop of Winnipeg. (Canada)*

Below, *Cardinal Aloisio Lorscheider, archbishop of Portaleza. (Brazil)*

Above, *A man kisses the episcopal ring of Cardinal George Basil Hume. The Benedictine Abbot of Ampleforth Abbey, Hume was the first monk to become archbishop of Westminster since the restoration of the Catholic hierarchy in 1850. (England)* Below, *Cardinal Franz König of Vienna is shown explaining to reporters at the Vatican Press Office the guidelines drawn up by the Secretariat for Non-Believers. (Austria)*

Above, *Cardinal Johannes Willebrands, president of the Vatican Secretariat for the Union of Christians and archbishop of Utrecht. (Holland)* Below, *Cardinal Leo Jozef Suenens, archbishop of Malines Brussels. (Belgium)*

Above, Cardinal Giovanni Benelli (right) with Pope Paul shortly after Benelli was named archbishop of Florence. (Italy)

Above, *Cardinal Sergio Pignedoli, president of the Vatican's Secretariat for Non-Christians. Below, Cardinal Sebastiano Baggio, prefect of the Sacred Congregations for the Bishops. (Italy)*

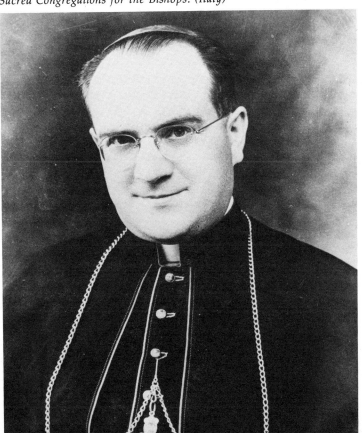

Above, Cardinal Pericle Felici, president of the Pontifical Commission for the Revision of the Code of Canon Law. (Italy) Below, Cardinal Jaime L. Sin of Manila. (Philippines)

Cardinal Bernardin Gantin, archbishop of Cotonou, Dahomey, with Pope Pius XII, shortly after Gantin was named auxiliary bishop of the African diocese. (French West Africa)

The Conclave takes place in the Sistine Chapel, shown here with the canopied stalls of the Cardinals placed around the sides. The one canopy still erected (right) signifies the stall of the newly-elected pontiff. The voting takes place in this chapel with the ballots being inserted into a chalice on the altar.

Cardinal Franz König

Born 3 August 1905, in Rabenstein, Austria, Cardinal König has passed the age generally regarded as making a cardinal eligible for consideration as a papal candidate. He is, however, considerably younger than was Pope John when elected in 1958; and if the cardinals are looking for a change of pace and a so-called transitional pope after Paul's relatively long reign, König could not automatically be eliminated. And in any case, he is a man of high culture, broad experience, and respected by his colleagues. In a conclave, he would have a significant influence on the decision.

After classical studies in a Benedictine school in Austria, he went to Rome for philosophy and theology at the Gregorian. He studied simultaneously at the Biblical Institute, a pontifical graduate school whose standards and methods distinguish it from the typical ecclesiastical institutions of Rome. His specialization at the Biblicum was in the religious history of Iran. From Rome, he went to the University of Lille (France) for a degree in social sciences, then to the University of Vienna for yet another degree, this in the law of the Eastern Churches. There followed several years of teaching, first as a professor of religion, then of the Old Testament, and finally of moral theology at the University of Salzburg.

In 1952, Pius XII named him coadjutor bishop, and four years later he became archbishop of Vienna. This is a diocese normally headed by a cardinal, and König received the red hat in 1958. Since World War II, Austria has been a key location in church affairs as well as in international politics, and the church could hardly have found a better choice than König to handle its affairs there. He is a universal man, of tremendous ability, fluent in many languages, at home in philosophy, anthropology and politics. He had the tough assignment for years of dealing with Cardinal Josef Mindszenty, whose presence as a political refugee in the American Embassy in Hungary prevented any normalization of Vatican relations with Hungary, and who refused to leave the country until finally given a formal order by the pope.

In the development of its opening to Eastern Europe, the Vatican relied heavily on him. Meanwhile, he had constant problems to meet in Austria, where deep divisions developed within the church as a result of Vatican II, with many pressing for radical change while others wanted to stay in the old ruts. One of his practices that has brought universal approval is that he has office hours every morning when in Vienna. No appointment is needed. One may have to wait in line for an hour or two, but nobody fails to be welcomed and listened to by the cardinal in person.

While maintaining a delicate balance between the conflicting groups in his diocese, König is very much on the progressive side, and he has lost none of his enthusiasm for the work of the Council. Actually, he was one of the people who thwarted the plans of the curialists at the opening session of the Council, joining with Cardinals Achille Liénart (France), Joseph Frings (Germany), and Bernard Alfrink (Holland) in insisting on an adjournment so that the Council Fathers could caucus and draw up their own lists of candidates for membership of the Council's commissions. Later in the first session of the Council, when the curial draft of a statement on the church was introduced, he singled out for attack its presentation of the church almost exclusively as a condition for individual salvation, whereas it has—he insisted—irreplaceable tasks to perform in relation to the entire human race. When the document on religious liberty was introduced and met with violent opposition from the conservatives, he sprang to its defense. This document, he said, is "a sincere defense of liberty." At the same time, he urged that the church should also speak about those who are not free to live and practice their religion: "This world sins against tolerance, against pluralism, and even against scientific principles."

He quickly gained the reputation in Rome of being the patron of progressive theologians, especially Karl Rahner and Hans Küng, the bêtes noires of the Curia. As primate of Austria, he is also patron of the University of Innsbruck, a Jesuit institution, the cradle before World War II of kerygmatic theology, forerunner of the "new theology." It was this university that gave the Council such theologians as the Rahner brothers and the liturgist J. A. Jungmann. When Karl Rahner at the Council prepared a counterdraft on the source of revelation as an alternative to the draft prepared by the Curia which insisted on distinguishing the Bible and tradition as distinct sources of revelation, König strongly supported Rahner; and in the end Rahner's draft provided the basis for the Council's statement.

His optimism about the survival of religion in the Soviet Union and its satellites seems to have lessened recently. Back in 1965, he said in an interview with *Corriere della Sera* (Milan), "There is a growing Christian ferment in the Soviet Union today. Perhaps the communists themselves are beginning to understand that religion is not a superstructure but a spiritual need of man in every society." Subsequent comments tended to follow the same view, but in a surprising volte-face, he said in an interview on Austrian radio in August 1977 that he is now pessimistic regarding the attitude of the Eastern European governments toward religion. Commenting on the visit of the first secretary of Hungary's Communist Party, Janos Kadar, to Pope Paul, he said: "So far no fall-out beneficial to the faithful in Hungary can be observed; at least, I have no knowledge of such." He went on to cite Istvan Szarnos, secretary general of the Hungarian Patriotic Front, as insisting that all children— including those of religious parents—must be raised in the spirit of socialism, "that is to say, in the spirit of atheism." His conclusion was that these governments keep negotiations in progress with the Vatican in order to make world opinion believe that everything is going fine, but "the reality is that the words are never translated into deeds."

Some commentators have suggested that this surprising change may have been a political one on König's part in the anticipation in the not too distant future of a conclave to elect a pope. In this interpretation, König would be mending his fences with conservatively minded cardinals, either to promote his own candidacy or simply to widen his area of influence within the conclave. If the former, it would be a bad sign, for one of the few hard-and-fast rules of Vatican watchers is that no cardinal who lobbies before a conclave emerges from it as pope. But if his purpose is to increase his influence so as to gain support for someone else in his own general intellectual and spiritual channel, he may make some new friends without risking the loss of those he already has.

Cardinal François Marty

A man who as head of the vast diocese of Paris puts daily into practice his belief that the pastoral mission of the priest is intrinsically universal, the same concern for the fallen-away, the atheists, the Moslems, and migrant workers, as for regular church-goers, Cardinal Marty was born at Pachins, diocese of Rodez, southcentral France, 18 May 1904. His father was a farmer. He studied at the local seminary and at the Catholic Institute of Toulouse, where he received a laureate in theology with a dissertation on Modernism.

Ordained a priest in 1930, he worked in various parishes of the diocese until made vicar-general in 1951, and bishop of Saint-Flour eight months later. In 1959 he moved to Reims as coadjutor and succeeded as archbishop of Reims in 1960. From Reims he went to Paris as archbishop in 1969 and was made a cardinal the following year. He is a member of the curial Congregations for the Sacraments and Divine Worship, for the Eastern Churches, and for the Clergy, and of the Commission for the Revision of the Code of Canon Law.

Marty was long connected with the Mission de France, the worker-priest movement that was forced by the Roman Curia in 1959 to limit its activities drastically but was revived in its original form by the French Bishops' Conference as a result of additional autonomy it obtained at Vatican II, and he was superior of this work for several years. "In Archbishop Marty," to quote *Le Monde*'s Henri Fesquet, "the spirituality of the Mission de France, founded by Cardinal Suhard, makes its entrance into the aula," that is to the meetingplace of the Council Fathers in St. Peter's. Marty's contributions to the Council were vast and always progressive. He was tireless in urging the church to recognize both the universality of its mission and its failure to adapt, to adjust, to read the signs of the times.

Thus, on atheism he said, "Whether they are positivist, Marxist, existentialist, or formed in the school of psychoanalysis, atheists do not deny God systematically. They refuse to believe in God because, in their eyes, belief is an illusion that diminishes man.... When a Christian encounters an atheist in the flesh, he must always strive for greater honesty. To be real, such an encounter demands a purification of one's own faith and a deeper understanding of its contents. The natural and supernatural must be better distinguished in order to be better united. The same is true of sacred history and profane history, theological hope and terrestrial hope."

Among the signs of the times Marty includes the contemporary techniques of business organization, to the point that some see him as primarily a clerical executive. He has taken the enormous diocese of Paris and broken it down into separate sections, with an auxiliary bishop responsible for each, and all working together with him as a team. He views his task realistically. "The Paris region is no longer a land of Christianity," he said in Rome in September 1977. "The 'living forces' of the church, religious, priests and laity, should learn better to live in coresponsibility. The present church teaching on marriage, for example, is often based on an outdated anthropology. I hope there can be found an attitude that will be a sign of mercy for some divorced and remarried people."

Coresponsibility is one of his key concepts. "Coresponsibility? An 'in' word that I hope won't become just a slogan, because the reality it expresses is important, indispensable. We have not yet found ways to collaborate with the Holy See, to be present in Rome. But even at that point, one must be realistic. The bishops cannot exercise their universal charge unless they too respect the principle of subsidiarity, that is, the sharing of their responsibilities."

The executive has not suppressed the human in Marty. Asked during a radio interview in 1969 if he was embarrassed to have his photograph appear in the mass-circulation *France-Soir* sitting in a Paris café chatting with the barman, he answered, "The great sorrow of the archbishop of Paris is to have to spend most of his time in an office, handling problems, answering questions, reading reports. . . . At times, the pressure is such that I get up and walk the streets, just as Christ did. . . . The other day, on such a walk, I passed the home of a man who came from the same village. Does the archbishop of Paris not have the right to shake a neighbor's hand and have a few words with him? What would my father have said if he knew I walked past without stopping?"

In 1973, after five years in Paris, he summed up his conclusions for the press. He questioned if "preventive detention," as practiced in the French police and judicial system, respects human dignity. He reaffirmed his belief that immigrant workers are not given their rightful place in society. Of the Palestinians, he said they have a right to life and to a territory. On the doctrinal responsibility of bishops: "The church must get outside itself to speak the Message. A church that refuses to be open to all challenges is a dying church." But faith and generosity are not enough to guarantee the transmission of an authentic evangelical message. Having discovered the lack of belief during the Council, bishops today "have ten years to transmit in truth the deposit confided to them." Salvation is neither merely an earthly liberation nor a simple sanctification.

Since his term as head of the French Bishops' Conference ended in late 1975, he has felt freer to express his personal views. Thus in early 1976, in a sermon at Notre-Dame de Paris, he formulated as his first priority—in which he invited all French Catholics to join him—the search for peace. He denounced "the collective hypocrisy," presented as based on "an ill-conceived economic need," by which France allows itself "to achieve a balance of payments by developing arms sales. . . . Very few dare raise a voice of protest. But Christians should raise their voices. . . . We cannot resign ourselves to making money by placing instruments of death in the hands of others." In a subsequent TV interview, he agreed that the problem was complicated, but "I believe that within a reasonable time the armaments industry can be made over for peaceful purposes." Government spokesmen responded negatively and bitterly, the prime minister saying that small countries seeking to defend themselves have France to turn to. But that did not stop Marty. Again in June 1976, at Notre-Dame, he insisted that France had to get out of the arms race, a position reaffirmed in a general condemnation of the arms race shortly afterwards by the Vatican in a vigorous note to the UN secretary-general.

The document on sex ethics issued by the Vatican in January 1976 brought a very negative response in France, many church leaders openly criticizing "the tone" of the statement. Here Marty was among the most outspoken. In a press interview, he said that national episcopates had not been adequately consulted. While agreeing that the Congregation for the Doctrine of the Faith (ex-

Holy Office) was right in claiming that morality is not a popularity contest, he summed up: "It is my hope to be able to present this document under its positive aspects, to speak of the way of life. Without tossing overboard the necessary protections, there is room to move a long way beyond catalogues and prohibitions."

Marty is highly ecumenical. Typical of his attitude was the signing of a joint appeal with the head of the Protestant Federation of France and the head of the Orthodox Church in France for funds to save the prestigious Protestant weekly *Réforme*, which deals primarily with political, social and cultural issues.

At a papal conclave, Marty's will be a strong and highly influential voice in favor of a candidate committed to guiding the church into the mainstream of the world's search for justice and dignity.

Cardinal Paul Philippe

For more than half a century, the French church has been generally progressive, even to the point of conflict with the Roman Curia, as in the case of the worker priests. But there always remained a conservative element, exemplified by Action Française, and more recently by the significant support for Archbishop Lefebvre. Cardinal Philippe, a Romanized Frenchman, belongs to this conservative wing. Born in Paris 18 April 1905, he studied in Paris and Versailles, joined the Dominican Order in 1926, and was ordained a priest in 1932. After further study for a laureate in theology, he went to the Dominican student house in Lvov, Poland, to teach philosophy; but almost immediately he was called to Rome to teach the history of spirituality and mystical theology at the Angelicum. In 1950 he established at the Angelicum the Institute of Spirituality to train spiritual directors of seminaries and novice masters. In 1953 he set up, also in Rome, a school for novice mistresses, and he headed it to 1967. In 1954 he was given a post in the Holy Office (now, Congregation for the Doctrine of the Faith), and in the following years he became a member of or consultor to several curial commissions and congregations.

In 1959 he was appointed secretary of the Congregation of Religious, and three years later was made a titular archbishop. In 1967 he moved to the Congregation for the Doctrine of the Faith as secretary. He had ambitions to succeed as prefect and continue the reactionary policies of the outgoing Cardinal Alfredo Ottaviani but was disappointed when Pope Paul picked Cardinal Franjo Šeper for that post in 1968. Instead he had to settle for the less important assignment of prefect of the Congregation for the Oriental Churches when he was made a cardinal in 1973. He is also a member of the Congregations for Religious and Secular Institutes, and for the Evangelization of Peoples (Propaganda Fide); of the Secretariat for Christian Unity; and of the Commissions for the Revision of the Code of Canon Law, and for the Revision of the Code of Eastern Canon Law.

In his entire career in the Curia he has had the reputation of being rigid and difficult to deal with. His theology is strictly preconciliar and Roman. There is no doubt that in a papal conclave he would be a solid element in the reactionary curial bloc.

Cardinal Joseph Ratzinger

A theologian of international repute and all his life a university professor until named in 1977 archbishop of Munich and a cardinal, Joseph Ratzinger, descended from an old Bavarian family, was born 16 April 1927, at Marktl on the Inn. His father was a police officer and member of a farming family of lower Bavaria; his mother, a daughter of artisans of Rimsting on Lake Chiem.

Near the end of World War II he was drafted into the auxiliary antiaircraft services. He was ordained a priest in 1951 after five years of philosophy and theology at Freising and at the University of Munich. In 1952 he began to teach at Freising's Superior School of Philosophy and Theology. In 1953 he obtained a doctorate in theology with a dissertation on "People and House of God in Saint Augustine's Doctrine of the Church." In 1957 he qualified as a university lecturer under a famous professor of the University of Munich with his work on "Saint Bonaventure's Theology of History." Having taught dogmatic and fundamental theology at Freising, he went on to teach similar subjects from 1959 to 1969 at Bonn, Münster and Tubingen. From 1969 until named archbishop, he was professor of dogmatic theology and the history of dogmas at the University of Regensburg, of which he was also vice-president. He is a member of the Commission for the Faith of the German Bishops' Conference, and a member of the International Theological Commission. He has lectured in many countries, including France, Ireland and Colombia.

At Vatican II, Ratzinger was peritus (theological adviser) to Cardinal Joseph Frings whom he has now succeeded as archbishop of Munich. Father Ralph Wiltgen, whose book *The Rhine Flows into the Tiber* develops the theme that the Germans took over the Council and distorted it, says in his conclusion that nobody—after the pope—was more influential in passing Council legislation than Cardinal Frings, and that Frings leant heavily on Karl Rahner, a former teacher of Ratzinger. As the Council progressed, Wiltgen says, Frings became more cautious in accepting Rahner's proposals; and Ratzinger, who had seemed to give almost unquestioning approval to Rahner's views, came to disagree with him on various points, and "would begin to assert himself more after the Council was over."

Subsequent events would seem to confirm Wiltgen's evaluation of Ratzinger, who was indeed an enthusiastic supporter of the movement led by German, French, Belgian, and Dutch bishops to end the monopoly of the so-called Roman theology, but who subsequently had withdrawn somewhat to a more conciliatory and middle-of-the-road position. At the end of the first session of the Council, Ratzinger said that the failure of the Fathers to approve a single draft text was "the great, astonishing, and genuinely positive result of the session." It demonstrated "the strong reaction against the (curial) spirit behind the preparatory work," and this for him was the truly epoch-making character of the session.

At the second session, Cardinal Ottaviani, then head of the Holy Office, took the floor to attack three periti—unnamed but assumed to be Rahner, Ratzinger and the Jesuit Gustave Martelet—accusing them of going outside their role by soliciting groups of bishops in favor of a married diaconate. About the same time, Cardinal Ildebrand Antoniutti, Prefect of the Congregation of Religious, was reported to have sent a letter to superior generals of religious orders with houses in Rome warning them against twelve periti, including Rahner, Ratzinger, Hans Küng and Yves Congar. Antoniutti issued a formal denial, generally regarded as based on the casuistic distinction between a lie and a mental reservation.

Among Ratzinger's contributions to the Council was a criticism of the draft document on the Virgin Mary as "a source of greatest concern," calculated to do great harm ecumenically, with both Protestants and Orthodox. He also helped to redraft a statement on mission that had lacked a theological perspective and betrayed little knowledge of modern missiology problems.

Since the Council, Ratzinger has not only maintained the Council's spirit but has advanced slightly beyond its stands. However, he has established a clear distance between himself and such ultraprogressives as Hans Küng. While perhaps slightly to the right of the middle in Germany, he is definitely still in the progressive camp in Roman terms. His choice as cardinal in 1977 has been interpreted as a gesture to the progressive Germans who resented the naming of the very conservative Cardinal Höffner. Ratzinger will function as a counterweight to him, one whose reputation as a theologian ensures that he will be heard with respect by all parties.

Cardinal Alexandre Charles Renard

One of the more conservative of French cardinals, but sharing the overriding French concern for pastoral innovation to revive the faith that is dead or dying among the many nominally Catholic French who retain an emotional identification with the church, Cardinal Renard was born at Avelin in the extreme north of France close to the Belgian frontier, 7 July 1906. His father was a university professor. He completed his studies at the Catholic University of Lille, obtaining a diploma in philosophy and a laureate in literature.

After ordination to the priesthood in 1931, Renard taught at the Catholic Institute of Lille and filled administrative posts in the Lille diocese. In 1953 he was named bishop of Versailles, promoted to Lyons as archbishop in May 1967, and made a cardinal the following month. He is a member of the curial Congregations for Religious and Secular Institutes, and for the Evangelization of Peoples (Propaganda Fide).

At the first session of Vatican II, Renard came out clearly for renovation and renewal. At the second session, he insisted that it is an ancient teaching of the church that the priests constitute, together with and under their bishop, a presybterium, a senate or counseling body for the bishop. But his major concern then and now was marriage, and specifically whether to allow religious marriages for two baptized persons who no longer have faith and regard the ceremony as a desirable social formality. The practice of different bishops in France, where the problem is endemic, then varied and continues to vary. Renard proposed at the Council that a possible solution would be to allow such persons to pronounce their vows before the pastor and witnesses without any religious ceremony.

He returned to the issue at the first Synod of Bishops in 1967. He said he had heard much comment on the problems raised by marriage of a Catholic to a non-Catholic, but little about the dangers involved in a marriage of a practicing Catholic and a Catholic who had lost the faith, or of two baptized Catholics who have no intention of raising their children as Catholics. He said there was a theological question as to whether the marriage of such is a sacrament. He now offered three alternative solutions: marriage in the presence of a priest without any religious ceremony; marriage in the presence of witnesses known to the priest, with dispensation from the canonical form; and a civil marriage, with the permission of the bishop and a clear notification to the parties of the indissoluble nature of marriage.

Underlying Renard's concerns there seems to be a sense of being threatened by the changes in the church and the world. Already at the Council he criticized the statement on the church in today's world as playing down original sin and failing to bring out "the existential ambiguity of human values." His concern about marriage reflects a kind of traditionalist French attitude that marriage has to be maintained as a basic cultural value, even for those for whom it lacks religious meaning. He does maintain theological concerns, right of center but not reactionary, and his articles are published in the conservative *Osservatore Romano*. On *Humanae Vitae*, which he has supported wholeheartedly, he is far out of tune with the great majority of French bishops and with the reality of the practice of French Catholics. In a papal conclave, nevertheless, he would tend to a centrist rather than a far rightist position, recognizing that his pastoral problems would be aggravated by an archconservative in the Vatican.

Cardinal Antonio Ribeiro

Born in Gandarela di Basta, archdiocese of Braga, Portugal, 21 May 1928, Cardinal Ribeiro studied at the local seminary and at the Gregorian in Rome. He was ordained a priest in 1953 and received his laureate in theology in 1958. Later, he taught social philosophy, moral philosophy and social psychology at the Overseas Center of Social and Political Sciences in Lisbon. In 1965 he became director of the Institute of Higher Catholic Culture in Lisbon, and there he also taught introduction to theology, the methodology of the social sciences, and the social teaching of the church.

Named auxiliary to the bishop of Braga in 1967, he moved to the same position in Lisbon in 1969 and succeeded as Patriarch of Lisbon in 1971. He was made a cardinal in 1973. He is a member of the curial Congregation for Catholic Education, and of the Commission for Social Communications.

Ribeiro maintained a low profile during the Salazar regime, but when protests against the war in the Portuguese colonies in Africa surged up during the transitional Caetano regime that followed Salazar, he came out in favor of the protesters. Specifically, when a group of students in December 1972 began a 48-hour fast in the church of Rato, Lisbon, to protest the war in Africa and do penance for the crimes the Portuguese had committed there during the previous twelve years, he expressed his approval of their stand.

Later, when civil war threatened and there was a prospect of a Marxist faction seizing power, he sided with the more moderate socialist Soares who in fact succeeded in his efforts to gain power. Ribeiro had to use all his persuasive talents to calm down the bishops of the north of Portugal who wanted a much more conservative solution that would not threaten their longstanding power.

Ribeiro is basically a conservative establishment man, a good politician, more concerned with maintaining the institution than with theology. In a papal conclave he would probably support a moderately conservative candidate.

Cardinal Joseph Schröffer

Formerly a bishop in Germany and a member of the Roman Curia since 1967, open as curial cardinals go, Schröffer was born at Ingolstadt on the Danube, diocese of Eichstätt, Bavaria, 20 February 1903. His father having died in battle in World War I, he entered the diocesan seminary at age fourteen. Having received his teaching license, he went to the German-Hungarian college in Rome for nine years of study at the Gregorian, emerging with laureates in philosophy and theology, and the advanced degree of Magister Aggregatus in theology. He was ordained in 1926.

Back in Germany, he spent two years in pastoral activity before becoming professor of moral theology and later also of pastoral theology in the Superior School of Philosophy and Theology at Eichstätt. In 1941, a time of intense Nazi pressures on the church, he became vicar-general of the diocese, and in 1948 the bishop. He played an active part in the postwar material and spiritual reconstruction, and as German president of the pacifist Pax Christi movement, promoted French-German rapprochement.

At Vatican II he was elected to the Theological Commission with the highest number of votes received by any candidate. His contribution to the Council was substantial. Speaking on behalf of sixty-nine German bishops on the draft document on the laity, he said he was happy that it stressed the "universal priesthood" of the laity. "This is an idea that had been largely forgotten, and for that reason lay people were inclined to define themselves in relation to the secular world, while in fact they are religious people charged with the responsibility of bearing witness to Christ in the world."

He headed the subcommission on Peace and the International Community, one of nine working groups named to redraft the statement on the church in today's world. In this office, he prepared a point-by-point rebuttal of the thesis of Archbishop Philip Hannon of New Orleans, a former paratrooper, who said the text insulted the United States by its reference to "have" and "have-not" nations, and its condemnation of nuclear weapons. His rebuttal swung the votes of most of the United States bishops to support of the text.

In 1967, Schröffer was called to Rome to become secretary to the curial Congregation for Catholic Education, then known as the Congregation for Seminaries and Universities. He left this post in 1976 at age seventy-three. He remains a member of the Council for the Public Affairs of the Church, the Congregation for the Bishops, and the Commissions for the Laity, and for the Revision of the Code of Canon Law. In a papal conclave he would probably go along with the progressive majority of the German cardinals.

Cardinal Leo Jozef Suenens

No longer regarded as a serious candidate for the papacy but still likely to wield enormous influence on the selection of the next pope, Suenens was born at Ixelles, diocese of Brussels-Malines, 16 July 1904. After primary schooling with the Marianist Brothers and high school in the diocesan minor seminary, he went to the Belgian College in Rome and obtained laureates in philosophy and theology and a baccalaureate in canon law at the Gregorian.

After ordination to the priesthood in 1927, he taught briefly in the diocesan minor seminary, then became professor of moral philosophy and pedagogy in the seminary of Malines, and in 1940 vice-rector of the University of Louvain. The university came under extreme pressures during the Nazi occupation of Belgium, the rector being jailed in 1943. Suenens took his place for eighteen months until the liberation came at a moment when the Nazi commander had listed Suenens as one of thirty hostages to be shot.

Named auxiliary in 1945 to the archbishop of Malines and vicar-general of this diocese (to which Brussels was joined in 1961), Suenens became responsible for censorship of books, problems concerning the administration of the sacraments, and a number of sodalities. He devoted major effort to promoting devotion to the Virgin Mary, becoming president of the Belgian branch of the Legion of Mary, recently introduced from Ireland. He was also liaison between the Belgian bishops and the superiors of religious orders and congregations, national president of the pacifist Pax Christi movement, president of the Catholic Center for Radio and Television, president of the Interdiocesan Press Commission, national assistant of Catholic Action, and national director of the Catholic Rail Workers. Books published at this time and translated into many languages include *Theology of the Apostolate of the Legion of Mary*; *What to Think of Moral Rearmament*; *The School Question*; *Love and Self-Control*; *Daily Life, Christian Life*.

Named archbishop of Brussels-Malines in 1961, Suenens received the red hat the following year. He is a member of the curial Congregations for the Evangelization of Peoples (Propaganda Fide), and for the Causes of the Saints; and of the Commission for the Revision of the Code of Canon Law. Continuing to write, he produced books that made a wide impact during Vatican II and later: *The Church in the State of Mission*; *Theology of the Apostolate*; *Apostolic Advancement of Nuns*; *Coresponsibility in Today's Church*.

His personal contribution to the success of Vatican II was perhaps greater than that of any other single individual. Combining traditional piety and a gentle manner with a progressive and optimistic vision, he made full use of his membership of the Secretariat for Extraordinary Affairs to achieve Pope John's objective in establishing it, namely, to end-run the curial obstructionists at the Council. He was one of seventeen signatories of a letter to the pope in 1964, drafted in strong language and expressing great concern regarding Archbishop (now Cardinal) Pericle Felici's maneuvers against the declaration on religious liberty, maneuvers that seemed to be "apparent violations of the Council's regulations." This letter produced action that saved the declaration. He also came out strongly for a change in the church's rules regarding contraception. "There is another goal of marriage besides procreation," he said. "There is interpersonal communion. Let us develop and encourage it."

At the first Synod of Bishops in 1967 he proposed the creation of an international commission of theologians to advise the Congregation for the Doctrine of the Faith (ex-Holy Office). Approved overwhelmingly by the Synod, the commission was created by Pope Paul in 1969. The members he appointed were strongly conciliar, but the postconciliar theologians, concerned with secularism, atheism, earthly realities, renewal of Christology, and the formulation of the message of salvation, were strikingly absent. At this Synod, Suenens also urged a radical revision of seminary training. "It should produce specialists," he said. "We must rethink the role of the priest radically, and stop envisaging him as a kind of monk. On the other hand, the day of the priest who turns his hand to any kind of work is gone. We must go for top qualifications, specialization, and 'shared responsibility' with the bishop."

Frustrated with the slow and inadequate implementation of Vatican II, and laying the principal blame on the Roman Curia, he gave an interview in 1969 to José de Broucker of *Informations Catholiques Internationales* of Paris, an interview quickly reprinted in all parts of the world. In it he said that "the church is a family or it is nothing; and in the family one should be able to dialogue freely in order to resolve misunderstandings and clear the air." Tension on the issue of coresponsibility since Vatican II, he said, resulted from a conflict of theologies. A formalist, juridic view, seeing the church as a "perfect" society, insists on centralization. Those who see the church primarily as an evangelical reality in its spiritual and deeply sacramental mystery, are less concerned with legalities and center on the realities of the church of God in each place, Paris, London, New York, or Bombay.

Following a section on primacy and collegiality, which stressed that for both ecumenical and theological reasons, the pope should never be presented in isolation from the college of bishops he heads, Suenens turned to relations between bishop and people. Bishops, he said, should recognize in theory and practice that many problems can no longer be solved by a decree of authority without the backing of priests and laity. All have to be involved—if not in decision-taking—at least in decision-making. This is true of the head of a family, of a business manager, of a college president. Today we are dealing with a modern person with a different anthropology, a different scale of values, a different mentality, one conscious of personal dignity, of human rights, of the inalienable rights of conscience, of the right to be judged by one's peers in open court. In all these respects, he concluded, the Roman Curia is an anachronism. It is not the pope's authority that is being challenged by the faithful, but the "system" that keeps him prisoner, that makes him responsible for the smallest decision of any Roman Congregation, a decision the pope had not signed or even seen. Change, he admitted, involves risk, but that is in the nature of life. "If you let the air blow through, you risk a cold; if you keep the windows closed, you run greater risk of asphyxiation."

The Curia's disapproving response, though deafening, was not nearly as deafening as the worldwide response of approval. Agreeing that the principle of collegiality proclaimed by Vatican II had not been properly implemented, Cardinal Michele Pellegrino of Turin praised Suenens for insisting, and added that "participation of the Christian community in the election of bishops should be in the very nature of things." The *Times* (London) said the Suenens manifesto gave new hope to the many Catholics in favor of reform and renewal who had lost faith in the hierarchy. "Suenens is no extremist," said Bishop Basil Butler of Westminster. "He stands in the 'extreme center' openly and prudently." To which *Le Figaro*'s theologian René Laurentin added: "This is the jet age, yet the church still slogs along on foot."

In spite of the overwhelming public support, the Curia limited itself to some cosmetic changes, relying as always on time as its sure ally. Suenens carried his campaign to the United States and other countries, speaking both to influential audiences and on general television. But gradually he tired, and by 1975 he was concentrating his energies on the suddenly popular neopentecostal movement. In that year he participated in an international meeting in Rome with a number of strange bed-fellows. They included United States Jesuit Francis Sullivan, professor of theology at the Gregorian; John McTernan, founder of the International Protestant Church for which he claims 200,000 members and two million friends, and who plays golf Wednesdays with Illinois-born Bishop Paul Marcinkus, the Vatican financier who lost a pile of Vatican money in the Sindona bankruptcy; David DuPlessis, white South African and pastor of the Assembly of God; and Fred Laderius, Italian citizen of Dutch origin, founder of the—reportedly CIA-funded—Silent Church which channels substantial sums to "fight communism" in Latin American and other countries ruled by rightwing military dictatorships. Joseph H. Fichter in his sociological study of Catholic pentecostalists in the United States, *The Catholic Cult of the Paraclete* (Sheed & Ward, 1975), observes that "the charismatic renewal movement tends to withdraw its members from the struggle for social justice and to blunt their zeal for social reform." That seemed to be its initial impact on Suenens, but the end result may be different. After talks with Dom Helder Camara of Brazil, leader of the evangelical social activists among the world's bishops, Suenens in 1978 called on all charismatics in a major article in *Magnificat*, organ of the charismatic movement, for a commitment to social justice. The response among charismatics was mixed, but certainly not all negative.

Critics of Suenens say he has projected a very liberal image abroad but has been consistently rigid at home. They point to his decision to remove Abbé Jean Camp as teacher of religion at the teacher-training college of the Dames-de-Marie in Brussels, a decision that caused a strike both of the trainees and of the nuns who taught them. Kamp was removed following publication of a book entitled *Credo sans foi, foi sans credo* ("A creed without faith, faith without a creed"), a Hegelian interpretation of God which Suenens said made of God "the immanent sense of evolution and of human history." According to Kamp's supporters, Suenens had acted without consulting the school authorities, and with the advice of only very few theologians.

In 1976, at the end of its 3-year term in office, the Council of French-speaking Priests of Brussels criticized Suenens harshly. What, they asked, are the real powers of an organism that officially represents the priests of the archdiocese but is in fact very rarely consulted by their bishop. A further complaint was that during the frequent absences of Suenens, "the power to make decisions is not effectively delegated to the vicars-general."

Even if his halo has been somewhat tarnished, Suenens still enjoys great prestige and influence with many cardinals around the world. At one time, his chances of succeeding Pope Paul on the papal throne were rated high, but his public challenge to the Roman system in his interview with José de Broucker was regarded by many as violating the conventions of the "cardinals' club." He was, of course, well aware of this when he gave the interview, considering the good of the church more important than his career. Even though more than a third of the electors would oppose him because of that interview and his overall progressive views, many respect him for his honesty and commitment. If not himself papabile, he will have great influence on the outcome of a conclave.

Cardinal Jean Villot

"French, sixty-six years old, 6' 4" tall, bespectacled, with a full head of hair, exasperatingly courteous in the French manner, insistingly righteous, efficient, with his own lines of communication to France, progressive, tolerant of weakness, humanistic." Such was the description given in 1971 by Malachi Martin, a longtime member of the Roman Curia, of the man who in principle exercises the greatest power—after the pope—over the internal and foreign affairs of the church.

Born at Saint-Amant-Tallende, close to the Auvergne mountains in central France, 11 October 1905, he went, after classical studies with the Brothers of the Christian Schools and the Marist Fathers, to the Catholic Institute of Paris for philosophy and theology. After ordination as a priest in 1930, he worked for four years at the Vatican Library researching a doctoral dissertation in theology, and simultaneously studying canon law at the Angelicum. From 1934 to 1939 he taught at the major seminary of Clermont-Ferrand, his diocese of origin. He was also assistant to the Young Christian Student movement. He next went to the theology faculty of the Catholic University of Lyons as professor of moral theology, and later as vice-rector.

From 1950 to 1959 he was secretary of the French Bishops' Conference, and from 1954, when he was made a bishop, he also worked as auxiliary to the archbishop of Paris. In December 1959, he was made coadjutor with right of succession to the archbishop of Lyons, and became archbishop in 1965. The cardinal's hat followed the same year. Two years later, Pope Paul called him to Rome to head what is now the Congregation for the Clergy, then moved him up to the key curial post as Secretary of State and Prefect of the Council for the External Affairs of the Church in 1969. He is also a member of the Congregations for the Doctrine of the Faith, for the Bishops, for the Evangelization of Peoples (Propaganda Fide), for the Causes of Saints; of the Commissions for the Revision of the Code of Canon Law, for the Revision of the Code of Eastern Canon Law, and of the Cardinal Overseers of the Institute for Works of Religion (one of the major financial institutions of the Vatican). He is also president of the Office for Administration of the Patrimony of the Apostolic See, and of the Commissions for the State of Vatican City and of the Council "Cor Unum" established in 1971 to promote human and Christian progress.

The first non-Italian Secretary of State since Pius X picked the Anglo-Spaniard Cardinal Merry del Val, Villot is approachable, widely traveled, listens well, and reads all papers placed on his desk. A commentator noted when he was named that previously the pope picked a Vatican diplomat because the job mainly involved dealing with governments, but he had now picked one with pastoral experience because the principal contacts are with bishops' conferences and individual bishops. He established the personal practice, when he came to Rome, of taking a bus each Saturday, dressed as an ordinary priest, to go to confession in a workingclass district of Rome.

In practice, his power was less than in theory. He has felt himself an outsider in the Curia and never learned how to circumvent the techniques by which his subordinate, Benelli, was able to impose his preferences. Although he never complained in public, because of his sense of loyalty to the pope, he reportedly was close to resigning several times when his diplomacy was torpedoed by officials who had the pope's ear. When he warned that a referendum on divorce in Italy would result in a major defeat for the church, he was told he didn't understand Italians. And though he was right, he got no credit.

Villot is definitely not a member of the reactionary bloc at the Curia. In a papal conclave, he would probably support a moderate progressive, but certainly someone moderate and open.

Cardinal Hermann Volk

Born at Steinheim, in the Rhineland diocese of Mainz, 27 December 1903, Cardinal Volk was ordained a priest in 1927, after which he received laureates in philosophy and theology at the University of Fribourg (Switzerland) and the University of Münster, respectively. He was named professor of theology at the University of Münster in 1943, bishop of Mainz in 1962, and cardinal in 1973. He is a member of the curial Congregation for the Doctrine of the Faith and of the Secretariat for Christian Union.

A theologian in the German tradition, conservative in a good sense, stressing the importance of biblical foundations for theological speculation, he played an important part at the Vatican Council in raising theological issues missed by the drafters of various documents. He had long been active in ecumenical affairs in Germany, and at the Council he stressed the need to be open to everything that is authentically Christian in the Orthodox and Protestant churches. "It is a grave obligation. Let us distinguish clearly between what can be changed in the Catholic church and what is essential. The episcopal college, for example, is something essential. This has always been recognized by the Eastern churches but has been forgotten in the West."

His interests are those of the professional theologian, and he has kept a low profile as head of a diocese. He would be a man in the middle in a papal conclave, studying the character of the candidate and his record, little influenced by labels.

Cardinal Johannes Willebrands

Known as "the Flying Dutchman" because of his incessant travel for twenty years in his work as secretary and later as president of the Vatican Secretariat for Christian Unity, Cardinal Willebrands is an interesting combination of Dutch progressivism and the caution acquired by long membership of the Roman Curia.

Born at Bovenkarspel, diocese of Haarlem, 4 September 1909, Willebrands completed the usual studies of philosophy and theology in the Warmond seminary, and was ordained a priest in 1934. He then went to Rome for further study of philosophy at the Angelicum and was awarded a laureate for a dissertation on the thought of John Henry Newman. After three years in parish work in Holland, he returned to Warmond seminary in 1940 as professor of philosophy and later as rector.

Thanks to the common sufferings of Catholics and Protestants in Holland under Nazi occupation during World War II, the ecumenical movement had become a living reality in that country while still a matter of abstract discussion nearly everywhere else. An ardent supporter, Willebrands was named president in 1946 of the Association of St. Willibrord, the national promoter of ecumenism, and shortly afterwards the Dutch bishops named him as their official delegate for ecumenical activities. In 1951, he organized the Catholic Conference on Ecumenical Questions, an unofficial group of Catholic theologians, most of them from Europe, who met once a year to exchange reflections and determine orientations. Willebrands became its secretary.

In 1960, Pope John named Willebrands secretary of the newly created Secretariat for Christian Unity. Its president was the 79-year-old but vigorous and progressive German Jesuit, Cardinal Augustin Bea, and Willebrands and he became a team with a single mind that for the first time in centuries showed that a curial office could be run for the benefit of the church. The fact that Willebrands was a compatriot and personal friend of Dr. Visser 'tHooft of the World Council of Churches was an added positive factor as Rome hesitantly offered its hand to the separated brethren who it was finally willing to concede shared the spirit of Christ.

A major work of Willebrands in the years that followed was the preparation of three documents for submission to the Vatican Council: on ecumenism, on religious liberty, and on relations between the church and non-Christian religions. Over fierce curial opposition, all three documents were finally approved by the Council without substantial alteration. He was simultaneously negotiating with the Anglican, Protestant and Orthodox churches to arrange for their observers to be present at the Council. The negotiations were fully successful with the Anglicans and Protestants, but only partly so with the Orthodox. The only Orthodox church to send observers was the Russian.

The refusal by Patriarch Athenagoras, however, was not from ill will but because of problems of protocol and a cumbersome machinery of decision making. What more than compensated for the absence of observers from the Patriarchate was the meeting of Pope Paul and Athenagoras in the Holy Land in January 1964. This was a great triumph for Bea, Willebrands and their associate, Father Pierre Duprey, their top specialist on Orthodoxy and a longtime friend of Athenagoras. After the Patriarch had given pectoral chains to the pope and accompanying cardinals, he gave Willebrands and Duprey the Cross of Saint Andrew, an Orthodox order awarded for special services on behalf of the Orthodox Church. Willebrands had a further major success in November 1965 when he headed the Vatican delegation to the Phanar in Istanbul to arrange with the Orthodox authorities for the removal of the reciprocal excommunications which in 1054 formalized the division of the church into Roman and Orthodox.

When Willebrands was made cardinal in 1969 and succeeded Bea as head of the Secretariat for Unity, he continued the dynamic line set by Bea, with the result that by now many of the major theological issues developed since the Reformation regarding the nature of the sacraments, the nature of the priesthood, the apostolic succession and the papal primacy have either been resolved or seen in a more positive and less divisive perspective.

When Alfrink submitted his resignation in 1975, the pastoral council of Utrecht decided not to submit to Rome a "profile" of the kind of man they would like to succeed him. Such action proved counter-productive on two previous occasions in Holland, when Rotterdam in 1970 and Roermond in 1972 presented very progressive profiles and the Curia imposed on them two reactionaries,

Bishops Adrianus Simonis and Joannes Gijsen. As already noted, Willebrands was received with relief by most in both camps. Only a few grumbles were heard. The Catholic daily *De Volkskrant* said the Dutch people had again been treated like "a gang of irresponsible children." It added, nevertheless, that the choice reflected a church policy based on realism and providing an appropriate solution for the Dutch situation. Protestants were pleased because of Willebrands' ecumenical openness as head of the Secretariat for Unity. Albert van den Heuvel, secretary general of the Dutch Reformed church praised him as a tenacious fighter of the highest intelligence, and said his removal from Rome was a loss to the ecumenical movement. Actually, he has not been removed from the Roman scene, for he remains president of the Secretariat for Unity and commutes to Rome from Utrecht for meetings.

His Roman training will, however, slow down the pace of ecumenical progress in Holland. He caused widespread disappointment by not allowing the Old-Catholic Archbishop Kok, and the president of the Netherlands Council of Churches, Berkofs, to receive the Eucharist at his installation, although they were guests of honor. The only authorized intercommunion is at the marriage of a Catholic and a Protestant, but the practice is widespread on other occasions in Holland. What Willebrands has made clear is that ecumenism in Holland must proceed according to the Roman model and at the Roman pace, which means that the Dutch must now mark time while others catch up. The problem of intercommunion as raised in Holland is new for Willebrands. Most of his work has been with churches that have an episcopal structure, whereas in Holland the main churches have neither an episcopal nor a sacerdotal ministry. This cautious adherence to his Roman training and experience would be more of an asset than a liability to him in a papal conclave. Progressives recognize him as one of their own. Conservatives are assured that he will stick to the rules. In the not very likely event of a search by the conclave for a non-Italian candidate, Willebrands would be definitely in the running. And in any case, he will—like Alfrink and in agreement with him—be a strong influence for an open and dynamic pope.

In addition to being president of the Secretariat for Christian Unity, Willebrands is a member of the Congregations for the Doctrine of the Faith, for the Eastern Churches, for the Sacraments and Divine Worship, for the Evangelization of Peoples (Propaganda Fide), and for Catholic Education. He is also a member of the Commission for the Reform of the Code of Canon Law and the Commission for the Reform of the Code of Eastern Canon Law.

Archbishop Roger Etchegaray

Born at Espelette, diocese of Bayonne, France, 13 July 1947, Etchegaray was ordained a priest in 1947 and a bishop in 1969. He was made Archbishop of Marseilles in 1970. He has been a consistent advocate of progressive pastoral initiatives in the French hierarchy, and in 1975 he was elected president of the Conference of French Bishops.

Marseilles has a large population of Algerian Moslems, many of them living in slums. Etchegaray has shown particular concern for their needs. The Moslems have great devotion to the Virgin Mary and in Marseilles they flock to a noted Marian shrine. Conservative French Catholics were shocked when Etchegaray decided to provide a building at the shrine for them to worship, but he refused to be swayed. The general reaction in France was one of approval for his ecumenical gesture.

Archbishop Tomás O Fiaich

Tomás O Fiaich, the Gaelic version which he prefers to the English Thomas Fee, was born in 1924 at Crossmaglen, Co. Armagh, Northern Ireland. He studied at the minor seminary in Armagh, at the National University of Ireland, and at the University of Louvain. A historian, he has specialized in the history of the first centuries of Christianity in Ireland. He was appointed professor of modern history at St. Patrick's College, Maynooth, in 1953, and president of the college in 1974. Saint Patrick's is both Ireland's national major seminary and a college of the National University.

Armagh, which by tradition Saint Patrick chose as his See in the fifth century, is the primatial See of all Ireland, and its territory lies partly in the Republic and partly in Northern Ireland. The British government resented the naming of O Fiaich as its archbishop in 1976 without it having been consulted. Its anger increased when in his first public statement as archbishop—an interview with Northern Ireland's biggest Protestant newspaper, the *Belfast Telegraph*—he called on the British to make a firm statement of intent to withdraw from Northern Ireland. While he believes a long-term solution of the "Irish question" must be found in an all-Ireland context, he says he is prepared to trust the sense of fair play of Northern Protestants if sovereignty over Northern Ireland is transferred to them from Britain. O Fiaich has condemned the violence of the Provisional IRA, while stressing his parallel condemnation of those identified as "representatives of law and order."

O Fiaich's expression of readiness to accept a Protestant-dominated regime in Northern Ireland is an indication of new openness in Irish Catholic leadership. It would suggest that he will also withdraw from the traditional church practice of imposing its preferences on the government of the Republic. At Maynooth he had a reputation for fairness and allowed wide theological pluralism. He is approachable and diplomatic, while direct in expressing his views. As a cardinal, he would belong with the moderate progressives.

Eastern Europe

Two of the six cardinals from the socialist countries of Eastern Europe, Filipiak of Poland and Šeper of Yugoslavia, are longtime members of the Roman Curia, totally Romanized, and no longer of influence in their respective countries. Resident cardinals are four, Wojtyla and Wyszyński in Poland, Lékai in Hungary, and Tomášek in Czechoslovakia. For all of them, the overriding concern is to maintain the widest possible area of activity for the church within regimes committed to the militant propagation of atheism and to the progressive diminution of church influence.

All have accepted the fact of coexistence and the likelihood that the socialist regimes will retain power for the indefinite future. They are thus committed to the widest possible cooperation with the regimes in socially progressive policies as evidence that the church, no less than the communists, is in practice as well as in theory supportive of social justice. At the same time, they live in a state of constant tension as political circumstances make possible a tactical gain by one side or the other in the unending struggle for the allegiance of the people.

The techniques of the struggle vary with the individuals and the situations. Wyszyński in Poland can be daring and aggressive, knowing the solid commitment of the vast majority of Poles to the church. Wojtyla, a younger man more concerned with longterm trends that victories that may prove Pyrrhic, is more flexible. But he agrees with Wyszyński on basic policy, and does not hesitate to take the initiative when he judges the time right, as in his support of worker demands in 1977 for higher wages without a balancing increase in prices.

Lékai in Hungary does not have the same base support and consequently has to maintain a lower profile, and the situation of Tomášek in Czechoslavakia is even weaker than Lékai's. But they and the Polish cardinals would be at one in a papal conclave. They will want a pope who will maintain the "Opening to the East" initiated by Pope John and continued vigorously by Pope Paul, a policy now being challenged in Italy and to some extent in France as tending to strengthen the communist parties that in those countries are within reach of coming to power by constitutional means. He should also be concerned for social progress and committed to the cause of the poor and downtrodden, thus evidencing that the church is working for the betterment of mankind. At the same time, he should be theologically conservative, because all these cardinals believe that change in the traditional practices of the church disturbs their people and provides opportunity to the socialist regimes to sow confusion and encourage the formation of dissident groups. Their "profile" is not easy to find in the College of Cardinals, yet it is not far removed from that of the Western Europeans and many in the Third World countries.

Cardinal Boleslaw Filipiak

A Pole who emigrated in 1948 as the communist regime consolidated its power in Poland, and who has since lived in Rome and become totally curialized, Cardinal Filipiak was born at Ośniszczewko, a village in a part of Poland known in the local dialect as Kujawy, of an old farming family located there for many centuries, 1 September 1901. He studied for nine years in Inowroclaw, in a part of Poland then ruled by Prussia. By 1920, when Poland was reunited, he had finished his legal studies at Poznań University. He then entered the archdiocesan seminary, whose rector—Stanislao Ianasik—would be his predecessor as auditor of the Roman Rota, the Vatican's marriage court. Ordained a priest in 1926, he worked in various parishes until sent to Rome by Cardinal Augusto Hlond in 1930 to obtain a laureate in utroque iure (canon and civil law) at the Apollinare.

Returning to Poland, he was secretary to Hlond for eleven years, sharing his fate when arrested by the Gestapo in February 1944 and sent first to the Benedictine Abbey of Altacomba, then to secret Gestapo prisons in Paris, Baric-Duc, and finally Wiedenbrueck (Germany). Liberated by United States troops on Easter Day 1945, the two flew via Paris to Rome, then returned to Poland. Filipiak became president of the tribunal of the Archdiocese of Gnesna and held other posts in which he similarly utilized his legal knowledge. In 1946 he was brought to Rome as auditor of the Rota. He became the dean (head) of the Rota in 1967, and was ordained an archbishop and made a cardinal on his retirement in 1976. He is a member of the Congregation for the Causes of Saints; and of the Commission for the Revision of the Code of Canon Law. He continues to reside in Rome, and in a papal conclave would be a member of the conservative curial bloc.

Cardinal László Lékai

The naming of Cardinal Lékai as primate of Hungary with the approval of the Marxist regime, after a 27-year deadlock, marks the most significant event to date in the Vatican diplomatic initiative for an opening to the East undertaken by Pope John and pursued aggressively by Pope Paul.

Born at Zalalövő 12 March 1910, the son of an artisan, Lékai started high school at Nagykanizsa, then transferred to the minor seminary at Veszprém. From there he went for ecclesiastical studies to the German-Hungarian College in Rome, obtaining a laureate from the Gregorian in philosophy, in 1931. He was ordained a priest in 1934.

Back in Veszprém, he combined parish work with teaching, being professor of philosophy in the major seminary of Veszprém from 1936 to 1940, and of dogmatic theology from 1940 to 1944. In 1943, he had become consultor to Bishop (later Cardinal) J. Mindszenty, and he became his secretary in 1944. Those were the years of Nazi occupation, and both Lékai and Mindszenty were arrested by the Nazis in November 1944 but were released when Hungary was liberated the following February. Lékai resumed parish work until named to head the diocese of Vezprém as apostolic administrator and titular bishop of Giro di Tarasio. The difficulties between the Vatican and the Marxist regime prevented the naming of bishops to vacant Hungarian dioceses.

From the outset, he made it clear that it was his policy to ensure a frank and loyal cooperation of Catholics with the socialist regime to the extent that both sought the betterment of society. He was consequently the logical choice to become apostolic administrator in 1974 of the metropolitan see of Esztergom, when Pope Paul finally forced Mindszenty to resign and leave the country after many years in the United States embassy in Budapest.

After protracted negotiations that involved several trips of special papal envoy, Archbishop Luigi Poggi, from Rome to Budapest, a modus vivendi was worked out which not only enabled Lékai to be named archbishop of Esztergom and accept the cardinal's hat, but to permit the naming of bishops to all vacant dioceses in Hungary. In a statement to the press, Lékai said he would not use the traditional title of prince-primate. "It is my duty," he

163

explained, "to face reality, not to turn back, but rather promote the search for progress. Reality calls on believers and nonbelievers to live together in a socialist society. . . . As faithful Catholics, we can respect the ideological convictions of others, and expect like response from them. Sincere dialogue, while retaining our ideological stand, helps to develop the understanding and cooperation demanded by the good of the country."

That Lékai was succeeding in obtaining cooperation to the satisfaction of the regime from the deeply divided church to which two of every three Hungarians give allegiance was confirmed in June 1967. For the first time Pope Paul received the head of a communist party, Janos Kadar, First Secretary of the Hungarian Communist Party. Recalling that the Vatican's "Opening to the East" policy had begun in 1963 when Pope John sent Archbishop Agostino Casaroli to Budapest to "open a dialogue," Paul commented: "Today, fourteen years later, experience has confirmed the validity of the road chosen." This road, Paul continued, is "a dialogue on issues, careful to protect the rights and legitimate interests of the church, but open at the same time to understand the concerns and actions of the state in the areas that are its proper field."

Another significant step took place the same month in Hungary. Austrian President Rudolf Kirchschlaeger, on an official visit to Budapest, asked to call on Lékai at Esztergom. Not only was there no official objection, but the Hungarian Head of State Pal Losonczi accompanied him. It was the first visit of a foreign head of state officially to the Catholic primate of communist Hungary, and also the first official visit of the President of the People's Republic to the primate's residence.

As Kadar left the Vatican, he remarked: "I am full of biblical memories. I remember in particular the story of Lot's wife changed into a statue because she looked back. We must not look back."

The requirements of peaceful coexistence in a Marxist state and socialist society will be a dominant concern for Lékai in a papal conclave. He will want a pope who will maintain the "Opening to the East," one who by his concern for social progress and commitment to improving the lot of the world's downtrodden will persuade the leaders of Hungary and the other communist countries that the church is also working for the betterment of mankind.

Cardinal Franjo Šeper

A cardinal who started out in the Curia as open and progressive but has withdrawn to archconservative stands, Šeper was born at Osijek, diocese of Djakovo, in what is now Yugoslavia, 2 October 1905. His parents were tailors, and they moved for business reasons to Zagreb, where Šeper completed his primary and secondary studies. In 1924 he entered the German-Hungarian College in Rome, and obtained laureates at the Gregorian in philosophy and theology. He was ordained a priest in 1930, in company with Aloysius Stepinac whom he would later succeed as archbishop of Zagreb.

On his return to Zagreb he taught religion in a high school until Stepinac made him his secretary in 1934. He became rector of the major seminary in 1941 and administrator of the parish of Christ the King in Zagreb in 1951. In 1954, when Stepinac had come into open conflict with the Tito regime and was confined to his home region of Krasic, Šeper was made bishop coadjutor in charge of Zagreb, and he became archbishop of the diocese which has 390 parishes and more than two million Catholics when Stepinac died in 1960.

At Vatican II Šeper spoke in the discussions on the liturgy, on relations with Jews, on the diaconate as a special state, on the laity, on ecumenism, on concelebration and the Eucharist under two kinds, and on the rights of emigrants. His contributions tended to be positive and progressive. On the liturgy he said that as Christians are so obviously a minority in the world, every help should be given them to live their faith as well as possible, and that included opening the whole treasury of the liturgy in the language each understood. On the diaconate, he disagreed with his fellow Yugoslav, Franjo Franić, who had argued that a married diaconate would be harmful to a celibate priesthood. On the laity he criticized the draft document for drawing too sharp distinctions between priests and lay people. Ordination, he said, did not cause the priest to lose any of his functions as part of the people of God. Christian activity in the world was the responsibility of all, with common involvement of all in making decisions.

In a discussion of atheism, Šeper spoke from the viewpoint of a

pastor living in a Marxist society. "We have to discuss atheism.
But let us speak about it in terms of the atheistic mind. Many look
upon atheism as progress. Let us try to understand this psychology. Many of our contemporaries were born atheists. It is not
therefore their fault. . . . Christians are much too often partisans of
a past order and are themselves thus the cause of atheism. Many
Christians are opposed to the progress of the world, yet it is God's
explicit will that there be more justice in the world."

In a similar framework at the first Synod of Bishops in 1967, he
urged that the reform of canon law should include a profound
decentralization of the law-making processes, citing as one reason
"the exceptional circumstances in which the church can find itself
in some countries in times of persecution."

When the Synod came to elect a commission to establish
guidelines for the Congregation for the Doctrine of the Faith (ex-
Holy Office), Šeper received the highest number of votes and was
named chairman of the commission. Responding to the clear desire
of the elected representatives of all the bishops of the world who
constituted that Synod, Pope Paul in January 1968 summoned
Šeper to Rome to replace Cardinal Alfredo Ottaviani as head of the
Congregation for the Doctrine of the Faith. He had already been
made a cardinal in 1965. Today, in addition to heading this Con-
gregation, he is a member of the Congregations for the Bishops, for
the Sacraments and Divine Worship, for the Clergy, and for
Catholic Education; of the Council for the Public Affairs of the
Church; of the Commissions for the Revision of the Code of Canon
Law and for the Interpretation of the Decrees of Vatican II; and of
the Office for the Administration of the Patrimony of the Holy See.
He is also president of the Theological Commission and of the
Biblical Commission.

Šeper's appointment to replace Ottaviani was hailed by progressives everywhere as a major victory, and for some years, he lived up
to expectations. But Šeper is basically a politician, as he established in Yugoslavia, where he managed to keep in the good graces
of Tito when his friend Stepinac tried a frontal fight and lost.
Before long, he began to adjust himself to the mentality of the
people who had surrounded Ottaviani and who now literally be-
sieged him. The conventions of the Curia made it effectively impossible for him to clean house and build his own staff. So he gave

up the fight and let them go their traditional way. In this, he may also have been influenced by his own experience and that of other churchmen from Eastern Europe. They had come to the conclusion that the changes demanded by Vatican II tended to loosen the tight controls that they felt necessary to maintain church structures under the pressures of the communist regimes, and a structured and fixed theology is a necessary scaffolding for that kind of church.

An indication of how radically Šeper has changed is provided in an analysis of the Catholic and Protestant pentecostal movements in the Rome ecumenical weekly, COM-Nuovi Tempi, in 1974. Having noted that the impact of these movements is to "depoliticize" religion and thus ease pressures for social reform among Christians, and that they enjoy heavy subsidization from international business and finance for that reason, it added that the movements had the support of high-ranking curial cardinals, one of them being Šeper, "who consider Pope Paul VI and Bishop [now Cardinal] Benelli, [then] Substitute Secretary of State, as following a dangerous communist line."

Šeper provided another instance of his regression when sent from Rome in 1977 to participate in ceremonies in Yugoslavia for the first anniversary of the beatification of Leopold Bogdan Mandic. He caused extreme offense to the Orthodox when, in the presence of a dozen Catholic bishops and Orthodox and Moslem observers, he recalled in a sermon that the Blessed Leopold had been sent to Padua to study, but was desperately anxious to return home so that "he might acquire merit by converting Eastern Christians to Catholicism." The Catholic bishops of Split openly rejected his statement. "Our brothers not in union with Rome," they said in a public statement, "often show more love toward Catholics than some Catholics themselves. It is idle to think of church unity if we don't start by converting ourselves."

In a papal conclave, Šeper would form part of the hardcore curial conservative bloc.

Cardinal František Tomášek

Long years of patient and complicated maneuvering with Czecho-slovak communist regimes preceded Tomášek's success in establishing a relative détente between church and state, an event marked by the disclosure in 1977 that Pope Paul more than a year earlier had named him cardinal in petto (secretly). Tomášek was born at Studénka, Moravia, 30 June 1899, the son of the principal in the local school. When Tomášek was seven, his father died at the age of forty, and his mother moved to the city of Olomouc in order to provide better educational facilities for her six young children. After secondary school, junior college, and brief military service, Tomášek entered the major seminary in 1918 and was ordained a priest four years later.

His first assignment was to teach religion, and this was to become the main interest of his apostolate. In 1934, he went to the theological faculty of Olomouc as assistant professor of pedagogy and catechetics. With the Nazi occupation of Czechoslovakia, all universities were closed from 1939 to 1945. Tomášek in 1946 qualified as a university lecturer, and by decree of the president of the republic he was named extraordinary professor of catechetics and pedagogy, a post he held until it was abolished by the communist regime in 1950. He had been made an auxiliary bishop the previous year, and in 1950 the Government Office for Church Affairs authorized him to engage in parish work; but in 1951 he was interned for three years, then sent to a small rural parish. His experience was part of a major effort by the regime to destroy the power of the church, with the arrest, expulsion or imprisonment of many bishops, including Archbishop Josef Beran, the primate.

The Vatican's official yearbook for 1963 lists Tomášek as still impeditus, that is, prevented from performing his duties as bishop. Actually, during 1963, thanks to the initiatives of Pope John, Archbishop Beran was released from prison, and Tomášek was allowed to attend the second session of Vatican II, His most striking intervention echoed a comment made at a talk given by Dr. Kristen Skysdsgaard, a Protestant observer, who had said Catholics should not be under the illusion that many Protestants looked to the Roman church with "nostalgia" and desired to return to the bosom of a church they still judged defective; that reunion could come only when the churches sat down as "equals," and as such were reunited. Tomášek urged specifically that the major Orthodox churches should sit down at a "round table" with Catholics, without any presidency, and discuss their differences as equals. For this initiative he later received a commendation from the Russian Patriarch Alexei.

Although released, Beran had not been allowed to resume his duties, and Tomášek was apostolic administrator of Prague at the time of the "Prague Spring" of 1968. He took the lead in rebuilding bridges, speaking in laudatory terms of the Dubcek regime. In a message published in *Katolicke Noviny*, a former Catholic newspaper earlier transferred by the regime to renegade Catholics and then on the Vatican's *Index of Prohibited Publications*, he said: "We have borne heavy burdens, known mockery, defamation, intimidation, exclusion from public life, internments, jailings. . . . But the church has continued to live its interior life. . . . Today we wait for the new situation to give us the possibility to prove the force and greatness of Christianity in its authentic evangelical form, which is characterized by service to the world. Our purpose is not merely the good of the church but the good of the world." The regime responded by approving the reestablishment of the Greek Catholic church, earlier forced to join the Orthodox, and allowed three bishops to return to their dioceses. In an interview, Tomášek said the regime had recognized the Vatican's right to propose candidates to fill the other five vacant dioceses.

Before new bishops had been named, an invasion of Soviet, Hungarian, Polish, Bulgarian and East German troops overthrew Dubcek's liberalizing regime, and the church was driven back into the catacombs. In 1969 Beran died in Rome. By 1973, eleven of the twelve Czechoslovak dioceses were without bishops. Pressures against the church continued to mount, facilitated by the fact that—unlike Poland—the regime did not find itself faced by a strong episcopate or a majority of deeply believing Christians. Josef Plojar, the excommunicated priest who headed the organization of dissident priests (Pax) and who had been ousted during the 1968 "Spring" was back with a new organization, Pacem in Terris. He engaged in violent attacks on the Catholic press and specifically on Tomášek as apostolic administrator of Prague.

Tension was still high in 1976, with some Catholics demanding a stronger stand. A French Catholic magazine published a long unsigned article sent by a group of Czechoslovak Christians, highly critical of the Vatican's pussyfooting with the regime and calling on the church not to yield to communism. By 1977, the challenge to the regime's progressive methods had come into the open. Some 300 persons, mostly intellectuals and including several Protestants, issued a manifesto calling for the observance of human rights. Intellectuals in many countries sent messages of support, as did the Communist Party of Great Britain.

It is against this background that must be seen the regime's decision to allow Tomášek to go to Rome to receive the cardinal's hat. In an obvious effort to reduce the challenge to its policies, the Czechoslovak embassy to Italy was instructed to give a reception for Tomášek and high Vatican dignitaries, the first such event since World War II. Diplomats from all the socialist countries except Albania and Vietnam attended. Even more striking, on Tomášek's return to Prague, he gave a reception in honor of the head of state and the government. Gustav Husak, president of the Republic and secretary-general of the Communist Party, wrote him: "We are interested in a positive development of the negotiations with the Holy See. I take note of your desire to exercise a positive influence on these negotiations."

Through all this tangled history, Tomášek has shown himself a consummate politician, and in a papal conclave the overriding concern for him would be the attitude of candidates to his situation. He would welcome a pope committed to social progress while theologically conservative, at least to the extent that he would maintain a strong central government in Rome as a support for himself in his struggles to survive.

Cardinal Karol Wojtyla

A contrast in style to the better-known and hard-hitting Cardinal Stefan Wyszyński in his dealings with the Polish communist regime, yet in full agreement with him in substance, Wojtyla was born at Wadowice, archdiocese of Kraków, 18 May 1920, the son of working-class parents. While in high school and college, he worked in a factory producing chemicals, thus acquiring a firsthand awareness of the concerns and problems of workers. Having studied the ecclesiastical sciences at the Kraków major seminary, he was ordained a priest in 1946. Two years followed at the Angelicum in Rome, where he obtained a laureate in philosophy, then returned to Kraków for a laureate in theology at the State University. After some years of work with university students and graduates, he became professor of ethics at the Catholic University of Lublin and at the theology faculty of the University of Kraków.

Named auxiliary bishop of Kraków in 1958, he succeeded as archbishop in 1964. The cardinalate followed in 1967. He is a member of the curial Congregations for the Sacraments and Divine Worship, for the Clergy, and for Catholic Education.

At Vatican II, Wojtyla exhibited consistently open attitudes, often influenced by his own existential situation under a socialist regime. On the discussion on the church, he urged that the statement should speak of the "people of God" before dealing with the hierarchy, that is, to deal with the whole before a part. At a moment when it seemed that the conservatives could rally enough opposition to have a statement on religious liberty dropped, Wojtyla and several other bishops from Eastern Europe took the lead in insisting that a firm statement would be of great help to them in their struggle with communist regimes. At the same time, he opposed the demands from some émigré groups for a strong condemnation of atheism, arguing that it would be at best counterproductive. Speaking on the church in today's world in the name of all the Polish bishops, he said: "It is not the church's place to teach unbelievers. She must seek in common with the world. . . . Let us avoid any spirit of monopolizing and moralizing. One of the major faults of this schema is that the church appears authoritarian in it."

At the 1959 Synod of Bishops, he joined in Cardinal François Marty's criticism of the draft statement on collegiality as falling far short of Pope Paul's stated desire for a concrete development of episcopal collegiality and even farther from the concepts of Vatican II.

In Poland, he has consistently taken a more conciliatory approach to the regime than Wyszyński, but never breaking ranks with him. He speaks out strongly on social and economic issues, encouraging the workers to demand higher wages while seeing that prices are kept under control. Similarly, he is the reconciler within the church. In 1969, Wyszyński reacted publicly and violently against an article by Jerzy Turowicz of Znak, a progressive Catholic publishing house, in which Turowicz said it was time to face the fact that there was a crisis in the church. Wojtyla publicly supported Wyszyński, then went to Rome to explain the objectives of Znak as seeking to maintain dialogue between the church and the regime. On his return, he said Paul—in keeping with his policy of the "Opening to the East"—had praised the Znak position as "very courageous." He then had a long meeting with Turowicz and the tension eased.

At the 1977 Synod of Bishops, Wojtyla took a stronger position that was his wont earlier against the communists, in this reflecting his personal theological conservatism, and possibly also the strong influence exercised over him by Opus Dei. The Marxist offensive against the teachings of the church he described as "the anticatechism of the secular world." For East European Christians, he added, "to catechize means above all to arm the Christian against the dangers of the environmental society, to form subjects of the church where the state seeks to create a type of man subordinated to its own specific ends."

At a papal conclave, Wojtyla would still probably agree with other East European cardinals that they would best be served by a pope who would be socially progressive enough to continue the dialogue with the socialist regimes, a man who at the same time would be conservative theologically and committed to maintain a strong institution capable of bringing influence to bear in moments of crisis.

Cardinal Stefan Wyszyński

The only churchman in East Europe to have maintained active and vocal resistance for many years to a socialist regime without being silenced, jailed or exiled, Cardinal Wyszyński was born at Zuzela, diocese of Lomza, northeastern Poland, 3 August 1901. After study at the seminary of Wloclawek, he was ordained a priest at age twenty-three. He did graduate study at the University of Lublin, obtaining laureates in the social sciences and in canon law. In 1929–30, he did research in Belgium, France and Italy, including several months in Rome.

On his return, he became professor of social sciences in the seminary of Wloclawek, and began a major output of popular and scientific articles and books, one book reporting on the various kinds of Catholic Action he had observed while traveling. In 1938 he took on the additional task of editing a scholarly review for priests. In 1939, when German and Russian troops invaded and partitioned Poland, Wyszyński went underground and managed to survive without being captured. He continued to provide what pastoral services he could, giving conferences and retreats mostly for nuns and intellectuals.

At war end, he returned to Wloclawek, reopened the seminary, restarted the review for priests, and became editor of a diocesan weekly newspaper. In March 1946 he became bishop of Lublin, throwing himself with his enormous vigor into reconstruction of a city and diocese ravaged by war and occupation, with special attention to restoring the Catholic University of Lublin, where earlier he had studied. In 1948 he was promoted to archbishop of Gniezno and Warsaw, Poland's primatial see. The red hat followed in 1953. Wyszyński is a member of the curial Congregation for the Eastern Churches, and of the Commission for the Revision of the Code of Canon Law.

Wyszyński's interventions at Vatican II were all conditioned by the struggle in which he had been long engaged with the socialist regime. Most of them tended to be on the conservative side, stressing the need for maintaining a strong institution and a united front of Christians to contain communism. He protested against progressives who "furnish ammunition to the communists when they say the church has forgotten the poor. . . . The church must speak of erroneous systems that sacrifice people to economic objectives." He urged that the Virgin Mary be called "mother of the church," "mediatrix," and "coredemptress," reflecting the correlation that usually exists between Traditional Mariology and the anticommunist complex. But the logic of his stand caused him on occasion to support the progressives. He rated radio and television highly as ways of reaching those indifferent to religious values, mindful of the restrictions on the Catholic press in Poland and hopeful of input from outside the country by the electronic media. And at a critical moment, he led the East European bishops in insisting that the Council not drop its plan to make a strong statement on freedom of conscience.

The same rationale governed subsequent implementation of the Council decisions. Just as there is "a Polish way" of implementing socialism, he said, so there is "a Polish way" of implementing the Council. It was for the bishops of each country, taking historic factors into account, to determine the character, the extent, and the rhythm of change. Germany, whose society has a rationalist base, must be different from Poland where sentimental elements take precedence over voluntarism. He bitterly opposed any Catholics who criticized the Polish church as moving too slow. For example, he violently rejected an article written in 1969 by Jerzy Turowicz, a member of the Znak group of intellectuals who sought dialogue between the church and the regime. Cardinal Wojtyla of Kraków, Turowicz's home, publicly agreed with Wyszyński, but managed to effect a compromise and restore calm. Later, Wyszyński seems to have come to realize that less intransigence would produce more results.

A seesaw has continued throughout the 1970s. The regime has scored some points, such as its highhanded but successful action to split the Znak group into a moderate section supporting the hierarchy and a dissident group manipulated by the regime. But an acute economic situation, with high foreign debt and declining agricultural production, caused in part by 1974 and 1975 weather, but also in part by lack of enthusiasm of the peasant farmers, has strengthened the position of the church, the main voice of the workers affected adversely by rising prices. In June 1976, for example, Wyszyński openly defended strikers who had been punished because strikes are illegal, insisting that human rights must be respected. His statement was followed by a joint bishops' pastoral demanding release of the strikers, and Wyszyński in sermons in his cathedral protested that several of the imprisoned strikers had been tortured by the police and encouraged workers to demand higher wages. Workers and intellectuals responded by several public acts of support for the cardinal. Two hundred thousand attended a religious ceremony in the streets of Warsaw at which Wyszyński reaffirmed that there can be no social peace unless the rights of the person and of the citizen are respected.

In an address to religious in Warsaw, in April 1977, Wyszyński revealed that he had written the government to warn it that the revolution was in danger of backfiring, that the workers were ready to carry out a Marxist-style revolution against their own communist government if basic human needs were not satisfied. He said that present conditions in Poland were like those described by Marx a century ago, because "in proletarian regimes the system of labor is capitalistic." He criticized the government policy of exporting food and manufactures to Russia and other socialist countries before the needs of Polish consumers were met. This address was released in Rome by an office of the Polish Bishops' Conference and made headlines worldwide.

Wyszyński felt in the 1950s that he was not being adequately supported by Pope Pius XII and the Vatican Curia. He has had better relations with Pope John and Pope Paul, but his reservations about the Curia remain. He prefers to deal directly with the Polish government and has successfully resisted the naming of a nuncio, allowing only periodic visits of Archbishop Luigi Poggi, one of the Vatican's trouble-shooters. His entire career indicates that in a papal conclave he would look for a candidate who as pope would be supportive of his policies. He would undoubtedly join with the other East European cardinals, for all of whom it is important to have a pope who projects the image of being socially progressive (thus stealing the thunder of the communists), open to dialogue with the socialist regimes, yet conservative in that he would maintain a strong institution and use its power as needed.

Italy

With very few exceptions, the most recent a Dutchman who lived for only one year after his election in 1522, popes have been Italians from the earliest days of the church. The preponderance of Italians among the electors reinforced the tradition since the cardinals became the sole papal electors 900 years ago. That preponderance has ceased with the expansion of the college of cardinals by Pope John XXIII and Pope Paul VI. But tradition dies hard in the church. Besides, the Italians alone today have a major constituency, twenty-seven cardinals. The next biggest national group is that of the United States, with ten.

Several factors make the Italians more powerful than their numbers. With the remarkable exception of Cardinal Michele Pellegrino, archbishop of Milan until his retirement in 1977, they form an ideologically homogeneous bloc. This bloc has a series of specific characteristics. Almost without exception, the members were removed from their homes at a very early age to live in the monsastic seclusion of a traditional seminary, wore a distinctive clerical dress even when visiting their homes, were removed from the normal activities and relations of young people. They had drilled into them the theology of the so-called Roman school, a product of the Counter-Reformation, stressing papal prerogatives, demanding absolute obedience to strict rules of conduct formulated in legalistic terms, exalting the dignity and power of the ordained priest and the duty of the laity to obey. They have a strong esprit de corps, a sense of their calling to a higher state, a confidence that in the collective mind of the hierarchical church as expressed by the spokesmen of the Holy Father is to be found the purity of truth and the practical guidance that is needed to navigate the shoals and quicksands of life.

Inevitably, shades of difference exist within this group. Pignedoli and Baggio—especially Pignedoli—are more open than most of their colleagues. Pappalardo is suave with dissent, whereas Felici is ruthless and dictatorial. Ursi in Naples is sensitive to the many poor of his diocese who live without hope on the edge of destitution. But the differences fall within a narrow range of the spectrum. For his Italian colleagues Pignedoli is so progressive that it is doubtful that many of them would support his candidacy for the papacy. In France or Canada he would be well to the conservative side of center. Baggio, for his part, thinks it is the duty of every Catholic to vote for a Catholic party where one exists, even one as corrupt as Christian Democracy in Italy. And when it comes to human rights, he believe the rights and interests of the church properly take precedence over those of people.

Adding to the power of this solid Italian bloc is a considerable number of cardinals from other countries who live in Rome either as active or retired members of the Curia. They are Maximilien de Furstenberg (Holland), Boleslaw Filipiak (Poland), Gabriel-Marie Garrone (France), James Knox (Australia), Umberto Mozzoni (Argentina), Paul Philippe (France), Eduardo Pironio (Argentina), Agnelo Rossi (Brazil), Franjo Šeper (Yugoslavia), Jean Villot (France), John Wright (United States). A few of these have resisted assimilation, notably Garrone, Pironio and Villot, but the others fit the Italian thought patterns, Wright, Philippe and Šeper leading the pack.

Elsewhere around the world, individual cardinals stand out as forming part of the same school: Carberry, Krol, Manning, and Cody, in the United States; Rugambwa (Tanzania), Nsubuga (Uganda), Zoungrana (Upper Volta), and Sidarouss (Egypt), in Africa; Casariego (Guatemala) in Latin America; Yü Pin (China, living in Taiwan) in Asia. Several others, if less clearly identified with this conservative tendency, are close to it. It would bring together at least forty and probably closer to fifty cardinal electors in a conclave, enough to veto an unduly progressive candidate and to carry major weight in the decision-making process.

Outstanding among the Italians, in addition to Pellegrino, are Benelli, Felici, Pignedoli and Baggio. Of these four, only Felici can be ruled out as an unlikely choice for next pope. He has made himself too many enemies by his highhanded methods as general secretary of Vatican Council II and subsequently as head of the Commission for the Revision of the Code of Canon Law. Pignedoli, as just noted, is somewhat too progressive for most of his fellow Italians, yet cannot be excluded as a compromise. That leaves Benelli and Baggio as front runners among the Italians, with Benelli's prospects improving the longer the conclave is postponed. Others mentioned by the tipsters are Pappalardo, Poletti and Bertoli. In addition to these, influential Italians—unlikely to be considered for pope because of age or other considerations—are Poma, Ursi, Colombo, Carpino, Luciani. The profiles that follow will give major attention to those mentioned above. The rest of the Italian cardinals are undistinguished followers, all solidly conservative or reactionary. Their primary concern is to hold on to as many as possible of the privileges the church possesses in a society that is formally secular but in fact dominated by the mentality and many of the laws of the church of the nineteenth century. They are willing to tolerate in silence the injustices of the society, the stagnation in poverty of a great part of the country, the abuse of power by the Christian Democrat party that has dominated Italian coalition governments since World War II. They insist that it is the duty of all Catholics to vote for this party, and their remoteness from the reality of their situation is highlighted by the eight million votes the Communist Party received in the 1976 elections. If and when the Christian Democrats are forced into opposition, transferring power to a socialist-communist coalition, the Italian cardinals will almost without exception also go into opposition, raising all the questions of human rights and government injustices on which they are now silent.

One of the problems in evaluating Italian cardinals is that there is almost no way to judge their personal attitudes. They believe in the system so blindly that, even if there is some element they dislike, they will never say so. In public—and at least for some, internally also—they accept Vatican II, then apply its prescriptions in preconciliar terms. The extent of the gap between the hierarchy and the believers was brought out in October 1976 when 1,500 delegates from all over Italy met as the "Estates General of the Church" to express their needs and formulate policy. One of the organizers was Father Bartolomeo Sorge, editor of *Civiltà Cattolica*, the most prestigious and authoritative of all Jesuit intellectual magazines. Sixty percent of the delegates were lay, the others diocesan priests and men and women members of religious orders. They did not include any of the important left-wing grassroots communities, preferring to present a consensus of the moderate believers. The meeting was opposed to "the temptation of a spiritual religion" that tends to favor a conservative status quo and does not disturb dictators. There was near unanimity against the efforts of the overwhelming majority of the hierarchy to close ranks against the advance of leftist parties. Christians, they concluded, should "verify" their faith at a political level, expressing "a preferential choice for the poor, the first step of which would be to disassociate the church from complicity with political, economic, and all other powers." In spite of Sorge's warning of the danger of polarizing into "two parallel churches in Italy," the hierarchy has continued on it traditional path, confident that its power can crush all internal opposition. There is no reason to assume that similar power concerns will not dictate the attitude of the Italian bloc of electors in a papal conclave.

Cardinal Corrado Bafile

One of the few cardinals who had another career before entering the seminary, Bafile was born at L'Aquila northeast of Rome in the Apennines, 4 July 1903. He first studied chemistry at the University of Munich, Germany, then switched to jurisprudence at the University of Rome. Having obtained a laureate in 1926, he practiced law until 1932 when he started to study for the priesthood, taking philosophy at the Gregorian, then entered the Roman major seminary and studied theology at the Atheneum. After ordination to the priesthood in 1936, he entered the Pontifical Ecclesiastical Academy to prepare for the Vatican diplomatic service, simultaneously studying at the Lateran for a laureate in canon law. In 1939 he joined the Secretariat of State, from which he moved in 1958 to the papal household of Pope John XXIII. Two years later, he was made a titular archbishop and sent as nuncio to Germany. He was recalled to Rome in 1975 to become proprefect of the Congregation for the Causes of the Saints. The following year he was made a cardinal and elevated to the post of prefect. He is also a member of the Congregation for the Clergy, of the Segnatura Apostolica, the Vatican's highest tribunal, and the Commission for the Revision of the Code of Canon Law.

During his long years in Rome before going to Germany, he was known primarily for his interest in the Sodality of the Abruzzi, the remote mountain region stretching east from L'Aquila; and for his promotion of the Legion of Mary, of which he was national director for Italy. Personally affable, he is a typical Italian diplomat who carries out his orders without question. At least twice while in Germany, he ran afoul of the hierarchy. In December 1972, under instructions from Cardinal John Wright, prefect of the Congregation for the Clergy, he wrote to the late Cardinal Julius Döpfner, then head of the West German bishops' conference, warning him that the conference had not the authority to authorize lay persons to preach during Mass. This was a recommendation scheduled to come before the national synod the following week.

In 1973, Bafile wrote to Cardinal Jean Villot, Secretary of State, asking him to dismiss Bishop Wilhelm Kempf of Limburg because of his overprogressive attitudes. They threatened, Bafile wrote, to

introduce into Germany "an island of Catholicism, Dutch-style."
When the letter was made public through the "indiscretion" of a
Vatican official, a wave of protest against Bafile swept Germany,
and an extraordinary meeting of the bishops' conference went on
record as supporting Kempf. The German press joined in the condemnation. He had acted against collegiality, it charged, by going
to Rome without first consulting the bishops' conference; and he
had violated a basic principle of equity by not giving a copy of his
complaint to the accused. From that time onward, his effectiveness
as nuncio was minimal. The fact that Rome took eighteen months
to recall him and then awarded him with a cardinalate is a measure of the curial support for his intransigence. In a papal conclave,
he can be counted on to reciprocate by supporting the curial candidate.

Cardinal Sebastiano Baggio

As little known to the world public as was Angelo Roncalli before he emerged from the 1958 conclave as Pope John XXIII, Cardinal Baggio must nevertheless be included in the select list of those whose age, qualifications, and experience make them potential successors to Pope Paul VI.

Born in the small town of Rosà, between Mantua and Padua in the north of Italy 16 May 1913, he entered the diocesan seminary of Vicenza after completing his secondary studies, then transferred to Rome where he studied canon law at the Gregorian, receiving a laureate. Ordained a priest at age twenty-two, he was accepted into the Vatican diplomatic services as a trainee and was sent for a short time to the nunciature in Vienna before returning to Rome for courses in paleontology, librarianship, and diplomacy at the Pontifical Ecclesiastical Academy, the finishing school for Vatican diplomats.

From 1938 to 1946, he was assigned to three Latin American nunciatures in turn, El Salvador, Bolivia, and Venezuela. After two years at the Secretariat of State in Rome, he returned to Latin America, this time as chargé d'affaires in Colombia. In 1950, he was recalled to Rome as assistant head (*sostituto*) of the Congregation of the Consistory. This body, known today as the Congregation for the Bishops, is a key unit of the Curia. It handles the arrangements for the appointment of bishops and auxiliary bishops, the establishment of new dioceses and other ecclesiastical divisions. It examines the reports that every bishop must send to Rome at 5-year intervals and keeps itself informed about the personal and official activities of bishops, sending a special delegate to examine the state of a diocese at its discretion.

Named archbishop in 1953, he spent the following sixteen years in major diplomatic posts, as nuncio to Chile, apostolic delegate to Canada, and finally as nuncio to Brazil. In 1969 he was brought back once more to Rome and made a cardinal. Rumor then had it that he was being groomed to become next Secretary of State, a post he was well qualified to fill because of his broad diplomatic experience and genial, open personality. Pope Paul, however, brought Cardinal Jean Villot from France to head the Secretariat of State. Baggio was reassigned to the Congregation for the Bishops, succeeding Cardinal Carlo Confalonieri as its head in 1973.

As is common in the Curia, he has accumulated a number of ancillary activities which give him a voice in a wide range of decisions. He is a member of the Council for the Public Affairs of the Church, the department that deals with civil governments, a member of the Congregations for the Doctrine of the Faith, for Religious and Secular Institutes, for Spreading the Faith, and for Catholic Education. In addition, he is a member of the Commissions for the Revision of the Code of Canon Law and for the Pontifical Sanctuaries of Pompeii and Loreto, and president of the Commission for Latin America and of the Commission for Pastoral Concern for Migrants and Tourists. Finally, he is a member of the Administration of the Patrimony of the Holy See.

A typical product of the Curia, Baggio is totally devoted to Pope Paul, very political minded, very shrewd and very smooth. He favors the selection of moderately progressive bishops, not so much out of strong personal feelings, as from his belief that it best serves the interests of the church today to have bishops who are theologically open and strongly committed to pastoral activities. No doubt influenced by his long experience in Latin America, where the shortage of priests is acute, he would be willing to ordain married laymen to the priesthood, while retaining the law of celibacy as the general rule. But he is violently opposed to the idea of women priests.

People close to him believe that he would reveal his own personality more fully if he were elected pope. He is strongly in favor both of national conferences of bishops and of elected priests' councils to work closely with the bishop in each diocese, and he would be likely to give to these representative bodies more authority and autonomy. He is generally supportive of the decisions of the Vatican Council, so long as their implementation is kept clearly within institutional bounds. He has no enthusiasm for worker priests, for example, would be opposed to seeing the Vatican downgraded as an institution, and strongly supports the teaching of *Humanae Vitae* on contraception. Similarly, on the issue of abortion he refuses either publicly or privately to make the distinction—traditional in Catholic theology—between law and morality.

He also agrees with Pope Paul's policy of seeking accommodation with the East European regimes, but he does not want that policy to influence attitudes to left-wing parties in Western Europe. On the contrary, he believes that Catholics should vote for a Catholic party where one exists, and—like all or almost all Italian cardinals—would oppose a government of the Left in Italy if the Christian Democrats went into opposition. Similarly, while the Christian Democrats are in power, he shows little enthusiasm for social justice or land reform, but would undoubtedly be much more vocal about government injustices and the practice of concentrating benefits on supporters of the regime, if the Left should gain the majority that seems almost in its grasp. On these issues his stands are determined by the belief he shares with most Italian cardinals and indeed most Italian churchmen that the rights and interests of the church take precedence over the rights and interests of people.

Even though the level of his cultural preparation to face the contemporary world is at best no more than satisfactory, there are few members of the college of cardinals highly qualified in this respect. Born in 1913, he is right in the "age window" and will continue in it for several years. His extensive diplomatic experience, and still more his present position as head of the Congregation for the Bishops, have given him high visibility within the church structures. He is undoubtedly one cardinal that will come under the scrutiny of his fellow electors in a conclave.

Cardinal Giovanni Benelli

Giovanni Benelli, made Archbishop of Florence and named a cardinal in 1977, stands a good chance of becoming pope one day, but probably not for several years. Born 12 May 1921, he is still three years short of the sixty judged by Vaticanologists as the minimum age for election. In addition, it will take some years to soothe the feelings of powerful enemies he made as Substitute Secretary of State, the key Vatican post he held from 1967 to 1977. But even if not yet *papabile*, the term Italians employ to describe those few cardinals who possess all the qualifications needed to be seriously considered for election as pope, Benelli is already a pope-maker, a cardinal with the skills and contacts needed to attract a substantial number of votes to his candidate.

Benelli's career followed the line that statistically gives most promise of becoming a cardinal. He entered the seminary at Pistoia, the diocese just north of Florence in which he was born, moved to Rome where he was ordained priest at age twenty-two, then continued his studies for a further four years. By 1947, when he entered the Curia as secretary to Giovanni Battista Montini (now Pope Paul VI), he had a licentiate in theology and a laureate in canon law from the Gregorian University, plus specialized studies at the Pontifical Ecclesiastical Academy, the graduate school for candidates to the Vatican's diplomatic service.

An enormous capacity for work combined with a pragmatic commitment to doing what his superiors told him was beneficial to the church, whether progressive, conservative, or reactionary, ensured a rapid and reasonably smooth ascent on the curial ladder. He filled progressively more important posts in the nunciatures in Dublin (1950), Paris (1953), Rio de Janeiro (1960), and Madrid (1962). He was named Vatican Observer to UNESCO in 1965, participating in congresses in Teheran and Caracas. In 1966, he was made archbishop and named Pro-Nuncio to Senegal and Apostolic Delegate to West Africa. A year later, he was called back to Rome to become Substitute Secretary of State. In typical curial fashion, he gradually acquired a long list of ancillary jobs and sources of influence: member of the Pontifical Commission for Russia, consultor to the Congregation for the Doctrine of the Faith, consultor to the Congregation for Bishops, consultor to the Commission for the Revision of the Code of Canon Law, consultor to the Pontifical Commission for Latin America, member of the Pontifical Commission for Pastoral Care of Migrants and Tourists, member of the Pontifical Commission for the Ecclesiastical Archives of Italy, and member of the Papal Household.

As Substitute Secretary of State, Benelli was in effect the pope's executive officer, always willing to assume responsibility for whatever unpleasant task the pope might want done without being personally identified with it. Benelli was the ideal man for this, strictly prochurch, totally loyal to the pope, choosing the diplomatic approach when possible, but able to be ruthless when necessary. He was early nicknamed the "Gauleiter" and the "Berlin Wall" by his fellow Italians because of his direct approach to rooting out corruption and his personal combativeness.

He can be conciliatory, too, when that is what he feels the situation requires or what he knows the pope wants. He played this part admirably in the late 1960s when a clash between Cardinal Florit of Florence and the working-class parish of Isolotto in Florit's diocese threatened to become an international cause célèbre. While failing to achieve a reconciliation between Florit and the Isolotto community, he was able to downplay the incident so successfully that it soon disappeared from the news.

A similar role was responsible for preventing a far more serious conflict about two years ago, when the deep differences between progressive and conservative Jesuits were aired at a general chapter in Rome. There have always been two currents, often difficult to reconcile, within the Jesuits. From their founding, they have taken a special vow of obedience to the pope in addition to the regular vows of the religious life, and that was intended to commit them to accept blindly whatever directions the pope gave them. At the same time, there has been a concept of specialists, each with his own individual vocation and charisms, a sort of free-lance discretion that made it acceptable for a Jesuit to be an astronomer or a paleontologist, or whatever. In the spirit of Vatican Council II, the chapter set about rewriting the rules to stress more emphatically the second aspect, the need for involvement in the hurly-burly of our rapidly changing world.

When the traditionalists saw they were being defeated, they

rushed off to some of their friends in the Curia, people like Cardinal Šeper, and through them got the message to the pope that the overriding commitment of the Jesuits to the Holy See was being eliminated. Finally, the pope sent for the Jesuit General, Pedro Arrupe, and gave him a dressing down in the presence of Benelli. Arrupe just kept his eyes on the ground and never opened his mouth. But the pope and Benelli could see that he hadn't changed his mind. So afterwards, Benelli went to one of Arrupe's top advisers and they succeeded in working out a compromise. Arrupe didn't give in. He would not resign, he said, because he felt—just as much as the pope felt about his own job—that he had a call from God to stay with it. The pope could fire him, and he would accept that decision. But he would not resign. Neither would he agree to splitting the Jesuits into two separate institutions, as some of the traditionalists wanted. If the pope approved that, he insisted, within a few years every religious order and congregation in the world would be similarly split. So the compromise was that those who didn't approve of the changes—most of them were from Spain—could go and live in a house or houses by themselves, but still under the Superior General. And Benelli was given the primary credit for resolving one of the most serious crises the church has faced since Vatican II.

While generally conciliatory, Benelli can talk a very tough line that often confuses people as to his real intentions. Sources in the Chilean resistance in Rome, for example, claim that as far back as 1975 he was supporting the nuncio in Santiago, Chile, Archbishop Sotero Sanz Villalba, who exerted constant pressure on Cardinal Silva to be more conciliatory to Chile's military dictator, Augusto Pinochet. He reportedly took a similarly hard line on the issue of abortion in Italy at a strategy meeting with the pope and various curial officials in early 1976 in anticipation of the Italian elections.

Some who know him well claim that such stands do not match his normal flexibility and are intended for public consumption while behind the scenes he uses his influence in quite the opposite direction. On the abortion issue, for example, it was important to talk tough so as to retain the confidence of the vast intransigent majority of Italy's bishops. These sources point, for example, to the general belief within the Curia that Benelli disapproved of the Justice and Peace Commission of which Monsignor Joseph Gremillion was secretary, and he encouraged that misconception because he believed the serious enemies of the Commission in the Curia would hold back and wait for him to pounce when he judged the time ripe. Actually, he was a close personal friend of Gremillion, even going with him on vacation, and he presided at the banquet when Gremillion decided to retire.

When Pope Paul sent Benelli to Florence, some observers recalled Pius XII's exile of Montini to Milan in 1954, a clear indication of his displeasure. But the two situations are entirely different. Pius XII was in fact annoyed with Montini because of his involvement with DeGasperi, the Christian Democrat leader. And no cardinal's hat accompanied his departure. Benelli, on the contrary, was given the concomitant tribute of the cardinalate, so that it is now universally agreed that the pope's purpose was to open up further opportunities for Benelli to become pope one day.

What kind of pope would Benelli make? A profile compiled by people close to him would rank him at best as moderately in the line of Vatican Council II, but tending to interpret it according to pre-Vatican II concepts; and probably also feeling that implementation of the Council's recommendations has already gone far enough. His enthusiasm for national conferences of bishops, for official organizations of diocesan priests to participate with the bishop in running the diocese, or lay participation in activities traditionally reserved to priests, is slight. He is strongly against ordination of women. He is equally strong in his determination to maintain the power and privileges of the Vatican, and on almost all issues highly approves of Pope Paul's methods of ruling and governing. One point that does not excite him is Paul's policy of promoting better relations with the Eastern European regimes, here no doubt influenced by his fear—a justified fear—that the number of Italian Catholics who vote for the Communist Party (and they already number eight million) will grow steadily bigger as they see the Vatican make its peace with communist regimes elsewhere. His loyalty, however, is such that he has always supported Paul's decisions on this issue, working cooperatively with Archbishop Agostino Casaroli, secretary of the Council for the Public Affairs of the Church, the man entrusted by Paul with top-level negotiations with East European governments.

His position on *Humanae Vitae*, the encyclical in which Pope

Paul dashed hopes of some significant change in church attitudes to contraception, would be close to that of Paul, though his diplomatic instincts would be to downplay the subject. But he is a canonist rather than a theologian, so he would have no deep insight into the issues.

His concern for justice for the poor is slight, he is indifferent to land reform, and he is opposed to the grassroots communities now a feature of church life in Italy. Their April 1977 convention in Naples reported that they number more than 350 and are found in all parts of Italy. These communities, strongly left-leaning and committed to withdrawal of the church from support of existing unjust social structures, reject the Christian Democrats and the Vatican's involvement in keeping them in power. Benelli, on the contrary, maintains that it is the duty of Catholics to vote for the "Catholic" party.

Perhaps his biggest defect is that, even though he speaks French and English very well, his level of cultural preparation to face today's world is quite inadequate. This is unfortunately true of most cardinals, because of the narrow scope and didactic form of their education. But it is aggravated in Benelli's case by an obsession with the idea that European Christian civilization, understood as the culture developed in Europe under church influences before the seventeenth and eighteenth century Enlightenment, is so superior to all other cultures that it is the ideal vehicle for the propagation of the Christian message. This is basically the same mind-set as that which underpinned colonialism and subsequently Fascism and Nazism.

Benelli trots it out in most of his speeches. He could not get away from it even in his first encounter-sermon with the Catholics in Florence when he took possession of his diocese in August 1977. In a talk that otherwise was well received as an expression of his awareness of his lack of preparation for his new job and his desire to listen and learn, he repeated his well-worn monologue on the "Eurocentrism" of civilization. This civilization, he said, is a "humanistic" one that has been "fundamentally Christian and as such must remain." That attitude will not endear him to the cardinals of Asia and Africa, and even those of Latin America, who were successful at Vatican II in having all cultures declared noble and of equal human value, so that the church must incarnate herself in all of them without identifying with any.

Benelli not only talks Eurocentrism but is trying to make it a reality. He was the initiator of a "European Weekend" in Augsburg, West Germany 18–19 September 1977, to which he invited such prominent politicians as the French Gaullist Chirac, Spain's prime minister Suarez, Belgian prime minister Tindermans, German Christian Democrats Kohl and Strauss, and Italian Christian Democrats Colombo, De Carolis, Fanfani, and prime minister Andreotti. Benelli's secretary explained that these politicians were selected because the meeting is a demonstration in favor of a Christian Europe and these particular leaders "appear to be inspired by Christian ideals." In addition to speaking on the church's contribution in the construction of Europe, Benelli celebrated solemn high mass in Latin, with Gregorian chant.

Benelli has his concrete reasons for his Eurocentrism and in particular for his support of the European Economic Community. He believes that a strong EEC will strengthen the Italian Christian Democrats through the backing of the British Conservatives and the French "majority parties." He reaffirmed his opposition to Eurocommunism in November 1977, rejecting the dialogue offered by Community Party Secretary Enrico Berlinguer and stating that "Christians who vote communist either don't know Marxism or don't know Christianity."

Benelli, nevertheless, remains one to be reckoned with. As archbishop of Florence, he is expected to play immediately a major role in the Italian bishops' conference, particularly because its secretary-general, Bishop Luigi Bartoletti, has little experience in dealing with the leaders of the Christian Democrats. In addition, a new president of the conference will be picked in 1978, and all indications point to Benelli for this post. It would add to his influence over the Italian cardinals in a papal election. Though now only a quarter of the electors, the Italians are still by far the biggest bloc, cohesive by tradition and theological attitude, and agreeing with Benelli—almost without exception—that the rights and interests of the church always take precedence over other considerations.

Cardinal Paolo Bertoli

Born at Poggio Garfagnana, diocese of Apuania, northwest of Florence, 1 February 1908, Cardinal Bertoli studied at the local seminaries, then went to Rome to obtain laureates in theology and in canon and civil law. Ordained a priest at age twenty-two, he entered the Vatican diplomatic service. Over the years he worked in nunciatures and apostolic delegations in East and West Europe, the Near East, and Latin America. Stationed in Switzerland just after World War II ended, he participated in many conferences dealing with settlement of refugees and other postwar problems, including the conference to revise the Geneva Conventions. His final post was as nuncio to France from 1960 to 1969.

Named a cardinal in 1969, he was recalled to Rome to head the Congregation for the Causes of the Saints, a post from which he retired in 1976. He remains a member of the Council for the Public Affairs of the Church; of the Congregations for the Bishops, for the Eastern Churches, and for the Evangelization of Peoples; of the Segnatura Apostolica, the highest Vatican tribunal; and of the Commissions for the Revision of the Code of Canon Law, and for the Vatican City State.

He is remembered in France as having been sympathetic to the French bishops who at Vatican II were active in developing the spirit of that Council, and those close to him describe him as a very fair and strict person. This would locate him as a moderate among the curial cardinals, but in a papal conclave, he would be unlikely to break step with them. The esprit de corps of the curial professionals tends to be stronger than any personal attitudes of individual members.

Cardinal Francesco Carpino

A reserved person who keeps his conservative views very much to himself, Cardinal Carpino has had a varied career both as head of different dioceses and as a high curial official. He was born in Palazzolo Acreide, Syracuse, Sicily, 18 May 1905, entered the minor seminary of Noto near his home, then went to the Roman major seminary for further studies. He earned laureates in philosophy and theology and a licentiate in canon law, and was ordained a priest at age twenty-two. After two years as professor of philosophy and theology at the Noto seminary, he returned to Rome to teach sacramental theology at the Lateran for twelve years. During this time, he published treatises on the Eucharist and on Penance, as well as articles in theological reviews and encyclopedias. Simultaneously, he worked part time in the Curia, being connected with the Vicariate, the Congregation of the Sacraments, and the Holy Office.

In 1951, he was made coadjutor to the Archbishop of Monreale, Sicily, became archbishop shortly on the death of the incumbent. Ten years later, Pope John recalled him to Rome as assessor of the Consistorial Congregation (now Congregation for the Bishops), in which office he automatically became secretary of the conclave in which Paul VI was chosen in 1963 to succeed John. In April 1967, Paul named him Pro-Prefect of the Congregation of the Sacraments, then four months later made him a cardinal and sent him as archbishop to Palermo. After a stay of only three years, he resigned and returned to Rome. Since then, he has been largely inactive, performing minor functions in the Curia, such as presenting a cause for canonization. He is a member of the Council for the Public Affairs of the Church, of the Congregations for the Clergy and the Causes of Saints, and of the Segnatura Apostolica, the curial supreme court.

Carpino is strongly supportive of the Vatican as an institution, but he avoids public expression of his opinions, so that it is not possible to categorize him on specific matters. However, he is believed to share the general view of Italian cardinals that the rights and interests of the church take precedence over those of individuals. Unlike his colleagues, nevertheless, he does not draw the conclusion that a Catholic must vote for the Christian Democrats, and he has openly shown that he does not want to be identified with that party. It may well be that his pastoral experience in Sicily, his homeland and the most deprived part of the state, has made him realize that one cannot expect from the Christian Democrats the reforms necessary to create human living conditions there.

Cardinal Luigi Ciappi

The twentieth Theologian of the Papal Household (formerly known as Master of the Sacred Palace) to be made a cardinal, Ciappi was born at Florence, 6 October 1909. After secondary studies in the minor seminaries of Lucca and Arezzo, he joined the Dominican Order, studied philosophy in Dominican seminaries at Viterbo and Pistoia, then went to Rome to the Angelicum for theology. Ordained a priest in 1932, he obtained his laureate in theology a year later. He next went to Fribourg, Switzerland, and Louvain, Belgium, for graduate work, then returned to Rome to teach dogmatic and moral theology at the Angelicum until 1955, when Pope Pius XII named him Master of the Sacred Palace, a post in which he followed the ultraconservative Irish Dominican, Michael Browne. He also became a consultor to the Secretariat of State, giving philosophical and theological evaluations on papal documents and on books and writings sent to the Secretariat; consultor to the Holy Office (now the Congregation for the Doctrine of the Faith); consultor to the Biblical Commission; and an official of the Congregation of Rites.

At Vatican II, Ciappi played a major role as professional theologian for Cardinal Ottaviani of the Holy Office, with whose reactionary views he was in total sympathy. He helped, for example, to prepare the curial draft proposing two separate sources of revelation—Scripture and tradition—a draft that was quickly rejected by the Council as untheological and antiecumenical. He was a leading member of the oldstyle Mariologists, whose excesses were openly condemned by leading speakers at the Council, and he had ready access to the pages of the *Osservatore Romano* for his extravagant articles, until Pope Paul responded to the criticisms at the Council and took steps to tone down the effusions of Ciappi and his friends.

Notwithstanding his ultraconservatism, his choice as cardinal in 1977 was welcomed by progressives as effectively eliminating another front-running Dominican candidate for the cardinalate, Father Henri De Riedmatten, longtime Vatican representative in Geneva to the United Nations and its specialized agencies. De Riedmatten has been much more aggressive than Ciappi in pushing *Humanae Vitae* and generally giving the church a preconciliar image among international bodies.

In a papal conclave, Ciappi will be a solid element in the reactionary curial bloc.

Cardinal Giovanni Colombo

Now in his upper seventies and preparing to retire, Cardinal Colombo has long been one of the more influential members of the Italian hierarchy, one not easy to categorize because of progressive stands on some issues and extremely traditional stands on others.

Born in Caronno near the Swiss border in northcentral Italy 6 December 1902, he attended the minor and major seminaries in Milan, graduating with a laureate in theology in 1926, the same year he was ordained a priest. He taught literature and Italian at the seminary while studying at the Sacred Heart University, Milan, for a doctorate in literature which he received in 1932. In the following years he taught oratory at the seminary and Italian language and literature at the Sacred Heart University, then moved into administration in 1953 as general rector of Milan's seminaries. In 1960 he was made auxiliary to Giovanni Montini (now Paul VI), who had been archbishop of Milan since 1954. A little later, he was named to the preparatory commission on seminaries and universities of Vatican II.

At the Council, in which he played an important role, speaking at times in the name of considerable numbers of Italian bishops, he insisted strongly on the need for radical reform of seminary life, a subject with which he was particularly familiar. He listed two principal weaknesses: a lack of organic unity in the studies, with the spiritual, intellectual, pastoral and disciplinary formations mutually ignoring each other and remaining isolated; and a lack of human formation that inhibited the maturing of the seminarian because of an unduly passive and prophylactic training "exclusively concerned with protecting the seminarians from the contagion of the world and cutting them off from the society they will one day have to evangelize."

When the Council discussed marriage, however, his traditional theology reasserted itself. Speaking for thirty-two Italian bishops, he demanded a clear statement that the church was not modifying its firm stand against artificial methods of contraception. Later, when Pope Paul issued *Humanae Vitae*, he supported it strongly and warned the Jesuits at Sacred Heart University, Milan, that he would not tolerate any challenge of the papal teaching on the issue.

Named a cardinal in 1965, he is a member of the Congregations for Catholic Education, the Evangelization of People, and the Sacraments and Divine Worship. He is also a member of the Commission for the Revision of the Code of Canon Law.

As head of the Milan diocese, he made some significant innovations. For example, he decreed that as from Lent 1969, the only form of baptism authorized for the entire diocese was a community celebration once each month, preceded by a course of instruction for the parents and godparents. This ended the practice, widespread in Italy, of baptism at home by a priest friend of the family, a practice that failed to express a principal aspect of the ceremony: the entry of the child into the Christian community. On other points, he proved more conservative, strongly opposed to worker priests, cool toward grassroots communities in good standing and fiercely opposed to those that took the law into their own hands. He has not been very enthusiastic about the diocesan council of priests, has little to say on issues of social justice, and is strongly against the idea of women priests.

He retains, nevertheless, a sense of political realism. When Luis Corvalán, secretary of the Chilean Communist Party, visited Italy after the Russians has arranged his release from a Chilean jail in a swap deal, Colombo joined in the tumultous welcome given him by the workers of Milan, industrial center of Italy. "We are very moved to have you among us and to be able to meet you in person," he told Corvalán. "On many occasions we spoke about you, especially during the dramatic days of the Chilean people. We suffered and feared for you and your many conationals threatened with suffering and dangers, and we feared for your life." In a conclave, this kind of political sensitivity would serve as a brake on the more impetuous traditionalists among his Italian colleagues.

Cardinal Pericle Felici

Opening the new scholastic year at Rome's Lateran University a few years ago, Cardinal Felici gave a beautiful and inspiring 45-minute talk on the Law of Christ as enshrined in the Gospel teaching, praising it as the ideal toward which the Christian is committed to strive. Then, to the amazement of his audience, he added that here we have indeed a lofty ideal, but in the political and moral situation of today's world it is incapable of realization. Instead, he concluded, we have to go back to canon law to guide us, a law that is highly logical and basically a reflection and expression of natural law.

What gives special significance to this amazing statement is that Felici, both by reason of his dominating personality and the key posts he holds and has held in the Curia, has been a major influence on the direction in which the institutional church has been moving since Vatican Council II. As head of the Pontifical Commission for the Interpretation of the Decrees of Vatican II, and as head of the Pontifical Commission for the Revision of the Code of Canon Law, he has probably done more than any other individual to minimize the impact of the Council on church life and structures. In the words of one who has had many dealings with him, "he is the archdevil in the Vatican political regime, probably the shrewdest person in the Curia, determined that the old church in its theological and legalistic molds will survive and prevail."

Born at Segni near Rome 1 August 1911, Felici received his early schooling at the diocesan seminary of Segni, then moved on to Rome's minor and major Pontifical seminaries. Ordained priest at twenty-two, he continued his studies at the Lateran for a further five years, ending up with laureates in philosophy, theology and canon law. He was immediately named rector of the Roman Pontifical Seminary for Juridic Studies at the Apollinare University. After a period as assistant professor of canon law at the Pontifical Institute *Utriusque Iuris* ("canon and civil law"), he was named professor of legal theological studies at the Apollinare and subsequently moral theology at the Lateran. Simultaneously, he held a position as an ecclesiastical judge of the Vicariate of Rome, the church body responsible for running the diocese of Rome while the pope concentrates on world concerns. There followed various posts in the Roman Rota, the curial office that deals with marriage cases, and a simultaneous appointment as head of a Vatican City tribunal.

For the four years preceding the opening of Vatican II in 1963, he was a key person in various preparatory commissions, and during that time he was made an archbishop to give him the status needed for dealing with prelates from all parts of the world. His suavity, outstanding clarity of mind, and ability to keep on top of a vast variety of problems ensured a steady progress to positions of ever greater importance. When the Council opened, he was assigned the key post of secretary general.

Here he proved himself a man of many parts. As a rule, he was efficient and charming, but he was simultaneously a clever politician, totally curialistic, personalistic and dictatorial. A stickler for protocol, he was such an expert on the peculiarities of the clothing of the various ranks of clerics and prelates that it was said of him more than once that he would excel as director of an ecclesiastical fashion show. In general, he was extraordinarily skilled in keeping his personal views to himself, but he could be intransigent and pull rank if crossed, to the extent that he was frequently described by those who came out second best as Monsignore Torquemada.

During the Council, he saw the pope several times a week, an opportunity most narrowly limited and giving those who enjoy it incalculable influence. His complicated procedural moves at critical moments of the Council debates were always in favor of the conservative minority, yet he was adept at keeping on good terms with all the parties whose views on the Council counted, with one exception. His polish and finesse did not extend to the press. In November 1964 he gave the *Osservatore Romano* an interview in which he described the newsmen covering the Council as "parasites and fungus growths . . . promoting confusion, insubordination and error."

The complicated elements that combine to give Felici his character and distinctiveness are well brought out by one who, as an official of the Curia, observed his meteoric rise to power. Writing shortly after Pope John's death, Carlos Falconi had this to say of Felici in his extremely informed and sympathetic evaluation of John in *Pope John and the Ecumenical Council*:

"That massive prelate, placid but strong, courteous but self-assured, simple in manner but capable of inspiring respect for authority, cordial but on occasion brusque, ceremonious but careful in his choice of words, is also a poet. Up to 8 June 1960, he was a peaceful official in the Congregation of Rites, auditor of the Roman Rota, and consultant to a couple of departments. Today, many consider him the *éminence grise* of the Council, or rather of the Curia at the Council; and in this they may not be far wrong in view of his attitudes on various points as shown in the *Osservatore Romano*, such as the slashing review of Lombardi's book, the praise accorded to the wellnigh antiecumenical pastoral by a Spanish bishop, and so on. In addition to all this, he is also a poet, and a Latin poet into the bargain, who speaks the language of Cicero as he does the dialect of Segni, the hilltop village of Latium—not far from Rome—where he was born, has written an essay on the ablative absolute, and, according to malicious gossip, never moves without the *Regia Parnassi* (a Latin rhyming dictionary)—they say he even dislikes going by car, because he can make his hexameters and couplets scan better when walking. . . . According to gossips, he is said to have decided to write a poem with the far from recondite title of Vaticaneides* secunda, once it is all over."

In the light of his education and life experience, it is not surprising that Felici should be a legalist. What is surprising to some is that his commitment to his own notion of what the law should be overrides the clearly expressed instructions of Vatican II and of the first Synod of Bishops of 1967. On the need for reform of the canon law, there had emerged a clear consensus at the Council. Collections of church laws had been made at various times in the past, the most famous being the sixteenth century *Corpus Iuris Canonici*, but the only attempt at scientific codification in the church's history was the Code of Canon Law ordered by Pius X in 1904 and promulgated by Benedict IV in May 1917, to come into effect a year later. Drafted by a small group of canonists working in a legalistic atmosphere and within the emotional pressures for centralization that followed Vatican Council I and the self-imposed prison of the popes within the walls of the Vatican, it sought to realize the ideal

---

*A pun on Virgil's Aeneid.

of nineteenth-century jurisprudence, the formulation—in an apparently complete and perfect system—of interlocking, abstract rules. It would reduce the judge's function to selecting the right rule to apply to any problem presented to him. The signs of the times had no meaning for these jurists. They thought of the worldwide church as still European, of the increasingly urban, industrialized and mobile society as still static, of the laity—often more informed than their priests—as still unlettered. Still worse, its spirit tended to subordinate theology and even the Scriptures to law, so that the Code became the primary rule of Christian belief and practice.

Pope John, in the same 1959 speech in which he announced he was going to convene an ecumenical council, said he also intended to reform the Code. But, he added, the Council would have to come first, so that revision of the Code could take account of the Council's decisions. In March 1963, shortly before he died, John named a commission of cardinals to undertake the task, but action was slow until Felici was named head of an expanded commission in early 1967. In a few months, several hundred of the Code's 2,414 canons were rewritten. The result, however, was to make clear that the issues could not be dealt with by cosmetic approaches. An interim report submitted by Felici to the Synod of Bishops held in October 1967 showed a substantial majority of the prelates opposed to Felici's concept of a strictly legal formulation of ironclad rules, seeking instead to reduce law in the church to a rule of faith and morals based on the person and teachings of Christ.

What they did approve was Felici's proposal to distinguish clearly the legislative, administrative, and judicial functions of church power, and also the organs charged with administering each of these functions. This principle, established in civil society by the American and French revolutions, is unknown to the church. It continues to combine the three powers at all levels from the Vatican to the rural parish, clinging to medieval practice in which the king both made the laws and administered justice.

The Synod lacked not only decision-making powers but even established rules of procedure. Although it indicated clearly the thinking of the bishops from around the world, all it could do was return the report to Felici and hope he would act to implement their expressed wishes. But Felici resists the advice of bishops.

While he must formally accept the concept of collegial rule of the church by the bishops, headed by the pope, he expressed very clearly his minimalist view of collegiality in an article he published in the *Osservatore Romano* in July 1969, an article designed to influence the discussion of that subject scheduled for the second Synod of Bishops some months later. Also in the *Osservatore* and during that same year, he criticized Cardinal Leo Jozef Suenens harshly for urging the practical implementation in church structures of the collegiality affirmed by Vatican II. "Invoking a logic presumed to be conciliar and in virtue of a collegiality that the Council had never understood in that sense," he wrote, "some—not content to criticize the pope's work—seem to wish to submit his activity as primate and supreme master of the church to the control or the approval of the bishops."

In the years that followed, Felici continued to redraft and try to persuade the bishops to accept what he now calls a *lex fundamentalis*, a fundamental law that would be the church's constitution, with maximum stability, superior to all other positive church laws, and valid for all Catholic churches, not just the Latin church. He told the 1974 Synod of Bishops that a poll taken among Catholic bishops had shown a slight margin in favor of this project, without revealing that fewer than half of all bishops had been polled. One analyst of the document has said that it implies that cardinals are part of the "divine constitution" of the church; that its concept of church-world relations reflects that contained in the fascist concordat between Italy and the Holy See; and that if it comes into effect, Vatican II will have died and the Sacred Scripture will have been exiled.

With the years, he tends to become more imperious. In the early 1970s, he was assigned to talk to a meeting of the Brazilian bishops instead of Cardinal Jean Villot, who had fallen sick. He spoke for ninety minutes, telling the bishops they should shape up and take a stronger line against dissidents. They were highly offended, and one got up and said they were in no mood for a *fervorino* (lecture). Felici just walked out and took the next plane back to Rome. Shortly after, at the 1974 Synod of Bishops, he was even more indiscreet. After Dr. Philip Potter, Secretary-General of the World Council of Churches, spoke to the Synod Fathers, Felici broke diplomatic protocol by attacking the guest for—in substance—

being a Protestant and trying to use the ecumenical movement to relativize the one authority named by Christ, the Catholic church.

In years, he is still papabile, and there is nothing he would love better than to be pope, if only to justify his view of what has happened and will happen to the church, namely that all these rebels against authority will melt away, leaving only men like himself rocklike in their fidelity to the tradition of Cardinal Ottaviani. But he has made too many enemies ever to hope to get two-thirds of the votes plus one. What he can do is to hold together the solid conservative bloc and probably rally to it some waverers who have come under his influence at the Vatican Council and subsequently. That could easily produce at least forty votes, the number required to prevent the election of a candidate unacceptable to a particular group. The conclave would then be forced to settle for a compromise alternative.

Cardinal Ermenegildo Florit

Identified as a liberal at Vatican II, but—like many of the Council Fathers—withdrawing to more conservative positions in dealing with the concrete problems of his own diocese, Cardinal Florit was born at Fagagna, archdiocese of Udine, in northeastern Italy near the Yugoslav border, 5 July 1901. He studied in the local seminary, then went to Rome and obtained a laureate in theology at the Lateran. After ordination to the priesthood in 1925, he did graduate work for two years at the Biblical Institute, then the only progressive center of higher ecclesiastical learning in Rome.

After two years in parish work in the Udine diocese, Florit returned to Rome to teach Scripture at the Lateran, where he also headed the theology faculty and later became prorector. In 1954 he was made coadjutor to the archbishop of Florence, whom he succeeded as archbishop in 1962. The cardinal's hat followed in 1965. Florit is a member of the curial Congregation for the Causes of Saints; and of the Commission for the Revision of the Code of Canon Law.

The author of many works on Scripture themes, especially related to Formengeschichte and other new concepts of interpretation, Florit at Vatican II was spokesman for the majority on the commission that rejected Cardinal Ottaviani's original proposal to distinguish two separate sources of revelation, Scripture and tradition. "Scripture is the norm of tradition," he said. "There is nothing in tradition that is not found at least implicitly in Scripture." On poverty he said, "Let us stress the close connection between the priesthood and poverty. Priests must be concrete proof of what the church of the poor is. . . . If there has to be only one poor person in a rich parish, it should be the priest." But a more conservative streak showed up on occasion. Thus, of atheism he said that it is by its nature wicked. "No conciliation with it is possible; any form of collaboration would be dangerous. The philosophical theories of our time have led to atheism and scientism. The problem of evil is the chief obstacle to accepting God."

At the 1967 Synod of Bishops, Florit supported the proposal that "there should be constantly in Rome what the Eastern church calls the Synodos endemousa, that is, some members of the College of

Bishops taking their place in turn beside the pope ... as the supreme executive and decision-making council of the universal church, to which all Roman curial offices would be subject."

During his first years in Florence, he came under the influence of Mayor La Pira, an ascetic and devout Catholic who promoted the same kind of radical reform of socioeconomic structures as demanded by the Italian communists. When there were labor disputes, Florit would come out into the streets to support the workers and seek a reconciliation. The impact of La Pira was, nevertheless, limited. What Florentines most remember is Florit's tenacity as auxiliary and later as archbishop to "restore order" in a diocese in which—on the style of Pope John—his predecessor had let all flowers bloom. This involved the silencing, the dismissal, or the removal of very many priests. Isolotto, the most famous grassroots Catholic community in the world, whose creation La Pira had made possible, was pushed by Florit to the breaking point in 1969, when he called on the civil authorities to oust the priests he had ordered transferred from the Isolotto church but whom the community wanted to stay.

People who know him well say that for him dialogue has only the place his "paternal bounty" accords it; that he will not be guided by the people, hews strictly to the letter of canon law, and insists that he has to answer for his actions only "before God and my superiors." In an analysis of the political stands of Italian bishops, the ecumenical weekly published in Rome, *Com-Nuovi Tempi*, said that "the most clamorous fact was the discovery of a warm letter of recommendation written by Florit for Mario Tuti," the fascist extremist who shortly before had machine-gunned two policemen to death. "One must remember," it added, "that the present leaders of the Italian Catholic church were educated under fascism and on the wave of the Concordat, that no bishop was ever dismissed for complicity with Mussolini, and that the Cold War and the anticommunist crusade of Pius XII still constitute the cultural foundations of the vast majority of the leaders of the Italian church."

Today Florit stands openly with the ultraconservative majority of the Italian bishops.

Cardinal Sergio Guerri

Born at Tarquinia, north of Rome, 25 December 1905, Cardinal Guerri studied at the minor seminaries of Montefiascone and Viterbo, then entered the Roman major seminary in 1923, obtained laureates in philosophy and theology at the Lateran and a licentiate in canon and civil law at the Apollinare.

Ordained a priest in 1929, he worked for a time in his native diocese of Tarquinia, then returned to Rome to teach at the Urbanianum, from where he moved in 1940 to become substitute secretary to the Institute for the Works of Religion, the Vatican financial institution that administers capital funds intended to promote religious purposes. In 1948 he was moved up to the post of assistant secretary of the Commission of Cardinals for the Administration of the Goods of the Holy See, and in 1951 he became its secretary. This office consists of two sections: the ordinary section which is responsible for the annual worldwide collection for the Holy See known as Peter's Pence, and of the patrimony of the Holy See in general; and an extraordinary section set up in 1929 after Pius XI signed the Lateran Treaty with Mussolini to handle the funds paid to the Vatican by Italy under that treaty. Guerri was put in charge of this extraordinary section in 1961.

In 1968 he was named assistant president of the Pontifical Commission for Vatican City State, a post he still holds. The following year he was ordained a titular bishop and made a cardinal. He is a member of the Congregations for the Eastern Churches, and for the Evangelization of Peoples (Propaganda Fide). With Bishop Paul Marcinkus of Chicago, he is regarded as the "brain" of the Vatican financial empire, and as such he wields immense power. Little is known of him except that he owns some ranches in Latium, close to the Via Aurelia and not far from Rome. A typical curial product, he can be counted on to vote with the curial bloc in a papal conclave.

Cardinal Albino Luciani

Son of a migrant laborer, Cardinal Luciani was born at Forno di Canale, diocese of Belluno, between Venice and the Austrian border in northeastern Italy, 17 October 1912. After study in the local minor and major seminaries, he received a laureate in theology at Rome's Gregorian University, and was ordained a priest at age twenty-three.

Following some years of parish work, he became professor of dogmatic theology and vice-rector of the Belluno seminary in 1937, gradually adding various offices in the diocesan chancery. He was named bishop of Vittorio Veneto in 1958 and moved as archbishop and patriarch to Venice in 1969. The red hat followed in 1973. He is a member of the Congregation for the Sacraments and Divine Worship.

Both at the Vatican Council and subsequently, he has maintained a low profile. He is culturally well prepared to deal with the problems of the contemporary world and has been strongly supportive of the decisions of Vatican II, but without wishing to move dynamically forward from that base. He approves of Pope Paul's policies, including his stand on birth control, is opposed to worker priests, women priests and the grassroots community movement, even in its more moderate manifestations. Like most of his Italian colleagues, he regards the rights and interests of the church as taking precedence over those of the individual, and he insists that Catholics must vote for a Catholic political party. In fact, he was the leader of the integralist bishops in the 1976 election campaign, when they came out strongly for a solid Catholic vote for the Christian Democrats. At the same time, he is an open and friendly person, a man of considerable cultural flexibility and free from Italian provincialism. At a time when most Italian bishops looked with disfavor on the programs of the German and Dutch bishops at Vatican II, he maintained dialogue, participating in many of their meetings.

Cardinal Mario Nasalli Rocca di Corneliano

The son of a count, Cardinal Nasalli Rocca was born at Piacenza, southeast of Milan in northern Italy, 12 August 1903. He studied in Rome's minor and major seminaries, and at the Apollinare where he obtained a laureate in canon law. He then went to the Pontifical Ecclesiastical Academy for the study of diplomacy and other courses preparatory to a career in the Roman Curia.

In 1927 he was ordained a priest by his uncle, Cardinal Giovanni Battista Nasalli Rocca di Corneliano, archbishop of Bologna. Within a short time he became a Canon of St. Peter's, Rome, and a Secret Chamberlain in residence to Pope Pius XI, a post he continued to occupy for more than thirty years under four popes. In 1969 he was ordained a titular archbishop and named a cardinal. He is a member of the Congregations for the Sacraments and Divine Worship, and for the Causes of Saints; and of the Secretariat for Non-Believers.

With Cardinals Opilio Rossi and Giuseppe Paupini, he is identified within the Curia as part of the group "loyal to the pope." He is a typical curial bureaucrat whose primary purpose is to support and maintain the system, and as such his vote would be for the curial candidate in a papal conclave. His hobby is collecting rings and pectoral crosses.

Cardinal Silvio Oddi

Born at Morfasso, diocese of Piacenza, southeast of Milan in northern Italy, 14 November 1910, Cardinal Oddi entered the minor seminary of Piacenza at age eleven, studied philosophy and theology at the major seminary, and was ordained a priest at age twenty-three. He then went to Rome for a laureate in canon law at the Angelicum and a diploma from the Pontifical Ecclesiastical Academy where he studied paleography and diplomacy.

Recruited into the Vatican diplomatic corps, he went to Iran as an aide to the apostolic delegate in 1936, then to Lebanon in 1939. During World War II he was assigned to the apostolic delegation for Egypt and Palestine, with the special task of tracing prisoners of war and informing their families. This was followed by periods in Istanbul and Belgrade, and in 1953 Oddi was ordained a titular bishop and assigned to Jerusalem as apostolic delegate. His activities there included an agreement with the Orthodox patriarchs to permit major repairs to the Church of the Holy Sepulcher. He was also deeply involved in work for the Arab refugees in Jordan and the Gaza Strip.

In 1956 he returned to Cairo to arrange with the Egyptian authorities, after the British withdrawal, for the future of the Catholic schools in which a hundred thousand pupils—composed in equal parts of Catholics, Orthodox, Protestants, and Moslems—were educated. In 1957, Egypt established diplomatic relations with the Vatican and Oddi became internuncio to Egypt. After special missions in 1961 to the Dominican Republic and Cuba, Oggi was named nuncio to Belgium and Luxembourg, his final post before being recalled to Rome and made a cardinal in 1969. He is a member of the Council for the Public Affairs of the Church; of the Congregations for the Bishops, for the Eastern Churches, and for the Causes of Saints; of the Segnatura Apostolica, the highest Vatican tribunal; and of the Commission for Vatican City State. A good diplomat with a practical approach to problems, he is strictly a servant of the system; and in a papal conclave would vote with the curial bloc.

Cardinal Pietro Palazzini

Born at Piobbico, diocese of Cagli, in the Apennine Mountains of central Italy, 19 May 1912, Cardinal Palazzini entered the local minor seminary at age eleven, four years later moved to the Roman major seminary and was ordained a priest at age twenty-two. He continued to study at the Lateran and other Roman institutions for a further eight years, gaining laureates in theology and in canon and civil law, and diplomas in librarianship, custody of archives, paleography, and diplomacy, and the qualifications needed to function as a procurator in the Causes of Saints, and as an advocate before the Vatican's matrimonial tribunal, the Roman Rota.

In 1958 he was named secretary of the Congregation of the Council (now, for the Clergy) and president of the Center for the Preservation of the Faith in the same Congregation. In the following years he was named consultor to the Commission for the Faithful Interpretation of the Code of Canon Law, to the Holy Office (now Congregation for the Doctrine of the Faith), and to the Congregation of the Sacraments. Additional offices included the presidency of the Disciplinary Committee for Vatican City State Employees, membership of the Commission for Latin America and of the Oversight Committee for the Archives of Italy, and also of the Commission for the Cinema, Radio, and Television.

Made a titular archbishop in 1962, the red hat followed in 1973. He is a member of the Congregation for the Eastern Churches; of the Segnatura Apostolica, the highest Vatican tribunal; and the Commissions for the Revision of the Code of Canon Law, and for the Interpretation of the Decrees of Vatican Council II.

At Vatican II, he was one of the prophets of doom to whom Pope John referred in his opening address. Henri Fesquet of *Le Monde* later in the Council described his uninformative answers to questions on the future of the Curia at a press conference as "characteristic of an exclusively juridic and static mentality." This juridic and static mentality is evident in his many books on theological subjects and his copious writings in the *Osservatore Romano*. All his work is derivative, matching Newman's description of a Roman theologian more than a century ago as one who can quote the opinions of thirty or forty other theologians. He was caught out in

1976 as having included in a book he had published the previous year verbatim passages of the Vatican document on sexuality which was not issued until after his book but to which he had access in its preparation.

A leading supporter of Opus Dei in Italy, he tried to protect the Italian manager of Lockheed when the Lockheed bribery scandals broke. He is a friend of the leaders of the right wing of the Curia, Cardinals Felici and Oddi, and as such would be a solid part of the most reactionary group in the Curia at a papal conclave.

Cardinal Salvatore Pappalardo

A little known but important member of the Italian hierarchy, Cardinal Pappalardo has a quality that, in a political situation that could easily develop in Italy, would make him the man of destiny for many cardinal electors. For more than a decade, no subject has occupied so much news space and violent differences of opinion as what the Italians call the "historic compromise." This is the proposition that, given the steady growth of the socialist and the communist vote in Italian elections, the day will arrive when the Christian Democrats—the leading party in a centrist coalition since 1946—will be faced with the choice either to enter a formal coalition with the Left or withdraw into opposition and hand over the reins of government to the Communist Party.

Most of the Italian cardinals are simply unable to face this dilemma, and if the Left were to come to power would in all likelihood exert all their influence in a negative and uncooperative opposition to the government. The resulting situation would be comparable to the stalemate that existed from the unification of Italy in 1870 to the Lateran Treaty of 1929, when the Vatican finally recognized the legitimacy of the Italian state in return for the concessions made by Mussolini in the Treaty and the accompanying Concordat. Pappalardo as pope would—in the opinion of some serious Vatican watchers—be capable of carrying out the "historic compromise," that is, of finding a modus agendi with whatever party or parties of the Left came to power, whether with or without a coalition with the Christian Democrats. This he would do, not because of theological or ideological considerations, but because he is a man of power and government who knows how to deal with realities pragmatically, and also a managerial type who makes his decisions stick.

Pappalardo is a Sicilian, born in Villafranca Sicula, in the diocese of Agrigento, 23 September 1918. His father was a policeman. From the local classical school, he went to the major Roman seminary for philosophy and theology, was ordained at twenty-three, received laureates in canon and civil law, and in theology, after studies at the Pontifical Ecclesiastical University and the Lateran. Courses in preparation for curial service followed at the Ecclesiastical Academy, and he joined the Secretariat of State, of which the present Pope Paul was then *sostituto*, in 1947, being assigned to the division of Extraordinary Ecclesiastical Affairs (relations with governments) headed by Monsignor Domenico Tardini. Pius XII insisted on acting as his own secretary of state, so that the *sostituto* or assistant was the day-to-day head of operations, making the decisions within the policy guidelines laid down by the pope. Pappalardo worked in the Secretariat until 1965, simultaneously teaching church diplomacy at the Pontifical Ecclesiastical Academy. When Pope John died in 1963, he was assigned to the secretariat of the College of Cardinals and became one of the very select group of noncardinals who participated in the work of the conclave at which Paul VI was chosen.

In 1965, Paul named him archbishop and sent him as pronuncio to Indonesia. That was the year in which an attempted left-wing coup was defeated by the army, bringing General Suharto to power and ushering in a bloodbath in which in a few years an estimated 300,000 people were slaughtered. It was a situation that called for tact and energy in the protection of the lives and rights of the Catholic community, and Pappalardo was the ideal man for it.

In 1970 he was recalled to Rome to become president of the Pontifical Ecclesiastical Academy and to take up again his former work as professor of diplomacy in that institution. Within some months, however, the see of Palermo in Sicily fell vacant, and Pappalardo accepted the offer to take charge of what was not only a difficult diocese but an assignment that many who had reached his level in the curial hierarchy would regard as a backwater.

Named a cardinal in 1973, he is a member of the Congregation for the Oriental Churches.

Theologically, he lines up with the center in support of Vatican Council II, avoiding equally a progressive interpretation or an interpretation based on preconciliar attitudes and concepts. He is rated a good spiritual pastor. He tries to avoid condemning any of his priests who protest against defects of the church, and he strongly favors reform of the methods and content of catechetical instruction. He believes that it is not necessary or usually effective to use a heavy hand against dissent. In consequence, while he approves *Humanae Vitae*, he would tend to be yielding with people who ignore or disapprove. He is definitely close to the poor of his

diocese, a large proportion of the inhabitants subject to high unemployment, malnutrition, and neglect.

He supports social equality and justice, but because of the em-
barrassment a strong stand on land reform might cause the ruling
Social Democrats, he soft-pedals this vital issue. He lines up with
most Italian cardinals in insisting that it is the duty of every
Catholic to vote for the Catholic party, and he would place the
rights and interests of the church before those of people. He
strongly supports the general policy lines of Pope Paul, favors the
maintenance of the Vatican structures in their present form, but is
less enthusiastic than Paul about developing understandings with
the Eastern European regimes. He has knowledge of and respect
for cultures other than European, but his level of cultural preparation for dealing with the contemporary world—if acceptable—is
not striking.

Cardinal Giuseppe Paupini

Born at Mondavio, diocese of Fano, on the Adriatic coast of central Italy, 25 February 1907, Cardinal Paupini studied at the local minor and major seminaries, and was ordained a priest at age twenty-three. He then went to Rome and obtained a laureate in canon law at the Lateran. After some years of work in Catholic Action and of teaching at the seminary in the diocese of Fano, he returned to Rome in 1939 to enter the Vatican diplomatic service. After World War II, he went to Honduras and Nicaragua as chargé d'affaires, and then to Cuba in the same capacity.

Recalled to the Secretariat of State in 1951, he was ordained a titular archbishop in 1956 and sent as internuncio to Iran. A year later he was transferred to Latin America as nuncio to El Salvador and Guatemala, and in 1959 to Colombia. Recalled to Rome and made a cardinal in 1973, he is head of the Apostolic Penitentiary, the curial office that deals with censures and dispensations reserved to the Holy See, and with all matters related to the concession and use of indulgences. He is a member of the Congregation for the Causes of Saints; and of the Commission for Vatican City State.

An undistinguished diplomat, whose allegiance is to the pope and the curial system, Paupini would be a solid member of the curial bloc in a papal conclave.

Cardinal Michele Pellegrino

Although no longer considered papabile because of ill health and his advanced age, Cardinal Pellegrino retains enormous moral prestige among non-Italian cardinals and could play a significant role in a conclave. But within the Italian hierarchy he has few supporters because of his courageous and consistent support of justice and human rights not only in society but in the church. "A white fly among Italian bishops" is one admirer's description of him.

Born in Centallo in the northwestern part of Italy not far from the French border 25 April 1903, Pellegrino decided "at an extremely early age" (in the words of his official biographer) to become a priest, a goal he achieved at age twenty-two. His higher studies were all in northern Italy, outside the stultifying atmosphere of the Roman universities. He has laureates in literature and philosophy from the Catholic University of the Sacred Heart, Milan, and a laureate in theology from the theological faculty of the University of Turin.

His first pastoral activity was as spiritual director of a seminary, and it was followed by a period in the diocesan chancery. He then went back to the University of Turin for further studies of early Christian literature, as a result of which the university made him professor of that subject. His academic reputation led to his induction to membership of the Roman Pontifical Academy of Theology and of the Academy of Sciences of Turin. Author of many works, both scientific and popular, he was for a time president of the Commission for Educational and Cultural Activities of the Italian Conference of Bishops.

He attended Vatican Council II as a peritus (expert adviser) but was named archbishop of Turin in 1965 in time to participate as a member in the Council's final session. He quickly emerged then and afterwards as a totally new kind of bishop for Italy, brilliant, dynamic in his leadership of a big industrial diocese, and identified as a prophetic defender of "intelligence," a quality downgraded by the church—especially in Italy—since the Enlightenment. He encouraged his priests to specialize in philosophy, history, biology and physics, because of the close relation of these disciplines to theology and the contribution they would give to the creation in the church of a Weltanschauung appropriate to contemporary needs and aspirations. This was in line with his very first address to the Council in which he stressed the duty of the church to permit full freedom of research. "The importance of historical research is evident from its subject matter, which is man himself. . . . Moreover, historical research is closely connected with the knowledge of the history of salvation." Having cited several instances in which ecclesiastical authority had moved against both priests and laymen, and even bishops and cardinals, without "due reverence for human dignity," he concluded, "If each one knows that he is permitted to express his opinion with wholesome freedom, he will act with the straightforwardness and sincerity that should shine in the church; otherwise the abominable plague of dishonesty and hypocrisy can hardly be avoided."

In 1966, the year after he had been named Archbishop of Turin, he wrote in his diocesan paper under his well-known pseudonym of *Homo Novus* that reform of the Curia and of the College of Cardinals should be part of a single plan. The College, he said should consist of the presidents of bishops' conferences. They would have all the privileges of cardinals, including the election of the pope, but their mandate would pass to their successors when each ceased to be president. This, he argued, would prevent a dangerous dualism between the Synod of Bishops and the Roman congregations (the Curia). It would permit the collegiality proclaimed at Vatican II to be effectively exercised. It would ensure universal representation. And it would provide for constant renewal by the elimination of older people and the influx of new members.

It looked for a time as if Pope Paul would adopt at least part of this program. But the resistance of the Curia proved too strong. The directive on papal elections that finally emerged was noteworthy only in that it excluded cardinals aged over eighty from the conclave. Curial reform was cosmetic, leaving it to the curial members to discipline themselves. A typical appeal is found in Paul's address to the Curia in February 1975: "Don't harbor sentiments of superiority and pride vis-à-vis the world's bishops and the people of God. You must be self-critical and know the analysis which the church and society makes of you."

Pellegrino returned again and again to what he regarded as

central: the implementation of collegiality and the obligation to respect everyone's right and dignity. In an interview in 1969, he chided the press for having failed to clarify the basic issue, namely, that the principle of collegiality proclaimed by the Council had not yet found concrete and specific ways to be applied, ways that would influence effectively the life of the church. On secrecy, he said that every person has a right to respect and privacy, but if what is at issue is a problem, it should normally not be kept secret. On choosing bishops, he said that "participation of the Christian community should in the nature of things be involved, once we recognize the principle of communion and coresponsibility."

Also in 1969, he intervened publicly on behalf of a conscientious objector named Fabrizio Fabbrini. Charged with disturbing a religious ceremony because he had stood up in the church to challenge a priest who was insisting that the Jews were deicides, Fabbrini had been acquitted by the judge of first instance, then retried on the demand of the Ministry of Justice and found guilty by a judge who based his ruling on the church's teachings. In a strong letter to the press, Pellegrino pointed out the absurdity of a civil judge engaging in a purely theological argument and basing his decision on his conclusions. "Absurd and grotesque," he wrote. "It is no longer the church that turns over the condemned person to the civil arm, but now the secular power formulates judgments and calls for punishment on theological grounds." Pellegrino is in fact strongly pacifist. In 1973 he presided at the opening of the international assembly of Pax Christi.

Almost alone among Italian churchmen, he rejects the claim that Catholics are bound in conscience to vote for a Catholic party. Speaking to the diocesan pastoral council in June 1976 on the eve of the national elections, he took a nuanced but firm stand in opposition to Pope Paul and Cardinal Poma, who by their condemnations of other political choices had made clear their stand that it was the duty of all Catholics to vote for the Christian Democrats. Political pluralism, he said, is "both legitimate and necessary when temporal choices are at stake." Everyone has "his own head and must think with his own head."

Not only did he keep his distance from the Christian Democrats, but he was equally careful to avoid dependence on big business, refusing to accept donations from Fiat and other industrialists known to be financial supporters of the Christian Democrats. In a sermon he preached in 1974, he stressed the increasing difficulty caused by rising prices for the old people and even for those who had a job, while at the same time "there is the rich man who sends his billions (of lire) abroad instead of using them to produce work in his own country and help the community."

He was highly supportive of lay councils in his diocese, and there is not a single instance of a clash with any of the worker priests or other progressive priests in Turin. He similarly encouraged and worked with the priests' council and used his influence to increase the prestige of the national conference of bishops. He would like to see more lay participation in the church's life, including the liturgy; and while he has not expressed himself on the subject of women priests, some who know him well believe he is open on the subject. He is less supportive of the Vatican as an institution than most of his colleagues. He also has reservations about its policy of promoting relations with the East European regimes, particularly because his progressive views do not include an openness to Soviet-type socialism. He supports *Humanae Vitae* but without stressing the issue.

What is most characteristic of the man is his commitment to social justice, equality, land reform, and an identification with the poor and marginalized people of Italy and the world. A good administrator as well as a good pastor, he had the sophistication and political astuteness to implement major programs of reform in the church in Turin. This combination of qualities, combined with an unusually broad culture and an appreciation of the need to incarnate the church in all the cultures of the world, marks him as a leader whose views will carry weight in the selection of a successor to Pope Paul.

Cardinal Sergio Pignedoli

As a chaplain in the Italian navy in World War II, the future Cardinal Pignedoli had an experience not paralleled by any other member of the college of cardinals, an experience that by a strange coincidence started him on his way to membership in that college. The cruiser on which he was serving in the Mediterranean received a direct hit that threw the young priest into the sea. He stayed afloat until picked up and brought back to Italy, to be welcomed by Monsignor Giovanni Montini, then Sub-Secretary of State at the Vatican and now Pope Paul VI. Then and there, his naval career ended and he became a member of Montini's staff.

Born at Reggio Emilia in northcentral Italy 4 June 1910, Pignedoli studied at the diocesan seminary, received a laureate in literature at the Sacred Heart University, Milan, a licentiate in church history at the Gregorian and a laureate in canon law at the Lateran. After ordination to the priesthood at age twenty-three, he spent three years as vice-rector of the major seminary of Reggio Emilia, then four years as chaplain to the students of the Sacred Heart University, Milan, before becoming a naval chaplain in 1940.

After the war, while engaged in a variety of activities in the Curia, he became chaplain to the Association of Italian Explorers and vice-chaplain general of Italian Catholic Action. He served as secretary-general of the Central Committee for the observance of the 1950 Holy Year, after which he was named archbishop and sent as nuncio to Bolivia. Four years later he was transferred as nuncio to Venezuela, only to be called back the following year to Italy to become auxiliary to Montini who had just been banished by Pius XII from the Secretariat of State and made archbishop of Milan without receiving the customary parting gift of a cardinal's hat.

Montini had been his original patron, and the two men recognized that they had much in common and could be helpful to each other. However, they never did become close personal friends. One of a group of foreign correspondents covering the Vatican recalls that he and seven of his colleagues several years later, when Montini had succeeded John, invited Pignedoli to join them for a social evening. As the evening progressed, tongues loosened.

"What did you think of Pope John," someone asked. Pignedoli answered: "Oh, I loved that man," then launched into a long paean of ecstatic praise. "And Paul?" came the next question. The answer was limited to three stiff words: "I admire him."

In Milan there was no falling-out between Montini and Pignedoli, but after five years they agreed to a parting of the ways, realizing that they had differing views on the job to be done by the church in Milan. Pope John had by this time succeeded Pius XII, and one of John's first acts was to rehabilitate Montini by making him a cardinal. Montini arranged to have Pignedoli sent to Lagos, Nigeria, as apostolic delegate for Central and West Africa. The working arrangement between the two men continued both before and after Montini became pope. Pignedoli planned the program for Montini when in 1962 Pope John asked Montini to make an extended trip in Africa, the first time in history that a European cardinal had visited that continent. Two years later, Montini as pope sent Pignedoli as apostolic delegate to Canada, a country in which he made many friends and in which he is still remembered especially for his parting gesture in 1968. When recalled to Rome, he traveled all the way across Canada and up into the Yukon in a Volkswagen, visiting every priest on his route and saying good-bye to hundreds of friends.

From Canada he went to Saigon, to preside as papal representative at an extraordinary assembly of the bishops of Vietnam called to deliberate on church policy in a country already ravaged by years of war against the Japanese and the French, and since 1954 divided in two and already entering into what would be the most bloody and devastating of all its unhappy experiences. After the meeting, he returned to Rome to become secretary of the Congregation of the Missions (Propaganda Fide). The titular head, Cardinal Gregorio Agagianian, had effectively ceased to function because of ill health, so it fell to Pignedoli to reorganize and revitalize the Congregation, a task he carried on with general approval until named a cardinal and head of the Secretariat for Non-Christians in 1973. Meanwhile, he had brought from India Archbishop Simon Lourdusamy of Bangalore and trained him as his assistant. Lourdusamay replaced him as secretary when he moved to the Secretariat for Non-Christians.

In addition to being president of the Secretariat for Non-

Christians, Pignedoli is a member of the Congregations for the Sacraments and Divine Worship, for the Evangelization of Peoples (Propaganda Fide), for the Causes of the Saints, and for Catholic Education. He is also a member of the Secretariat for the Union of Christians.

Everything went very well for Pignedoli in his new post until early 1976 when he was guilty of a gaffe that could destroy the career of a papal diplomat, especially one like Pignedoli who has not hidden his hopes of one day becoming pope. The incident occurred in Tripoli, Libya, where he was head of the papal delegation for a seminar of Islamic-Christian dialogue, the first encounter in thirteen centuries of official representatives of the two religions. Things went so smoothly for the first four days that Pignedoli was caught napping on the fifth and final day when politics raised its ugly head. Proposals were introduced for a joint Islamic-Christian struggle against exploitation of the Third World by the industrialized countries, against racism, for the freeing of Palestine, all this combined with a joint crusade against atheism and communism. This was followed by a final statement, apparently read too hastily and sketchily by the four Catholics who formed part of the drafting committee. After it had been issued, Pignedoli and his team realized that two paragraphs condemning Zionism, affirming the Arab character of Jerusalem, and demanding Israeli withdrawal from all occupied territories, went beyond the official Vatican position on these delicate points.

Pignedoli tried to save face by issuing a "clarification" that only the Vatican could give substantive approval to the final statement, an approval that—needless to say—was never given. No official reprimand followed, but memories in the Curia are long, and Vatican watchers believe that Pignedoli's prospects of becoming pope have declined seriously.

If he should in fact overcome the handicap, here is the kind of pope he would be in the view of insiders. He is regarded by many as Pope Paul's "adopted son," but a more open and positive person in many ways. He would strongly favor the measure of decentralization of decision making represented by national and regional conferences of bishops, and by diocesan councils of priests. He would be strongly supportive of Vatican Council II and would welcome more lay participation in the life of the church, including the administration of the sacraments.

As a liberal Catholic, he believes it is possible through mediation to find room within the church for all. In consequence, he doesn't think that excommunications have any positive value, and he is not interested in condemning people for their beliefs or views. On the question of women priests, he is probably less intransigent than Pope Paul but would be unlikely to change the traditional exclusion of women from the priesthood. He favors the teaching of *Humanae Vitae* in its condemnation of "artificial" methods of contraception, though perhaps not quite as strongly as Pope Paul does. He is somewhat cool toward worker priests, though not definitely opposed. He is strongly opposed to any form of racism, has considerable familiarity with other cultures, and does not share the bias of Cardinal Felici and various other Italian prelates in favor of European culture as intrinsically superior.

On such issues as land reform and social justice, which many Italian cardinals tend to soft-pedal so as not to embarrass the Christian Democrat government, he has a good record. As for the grassroots communities that have become a major feature of church life—and often a source of deep conflict—in Italy since Vatican Council II, he favors those in good standing with their bishops but is against the so-called spontaneous or nonapproved groups. At the same time, he seems to have a real concern for the poor and marginalized city-slum and rural dwellers, a growing proportion of Italy's population.

He shares the common opinion of his Italian colleagues that a Catholic is bound to vote for a Catholic party, where there is one, and he would tend to be more concerned for church rights and interests than for those of people, though less so than many around him. And like nearly all Italian—and many non-Italian—cardinals and prelates, on the issue of abortion he refuses to accept the distinction deeply rooted in the Catholic theological tradition between law and morality. Finally, his level of cultural preparation to face the problems of the contemporary world is, as cardinals go, above average.

Cardinal Ugo Poletti

Although the pope is bishop of Rome, the other functions he performs force him to leave the running of the affairs of his own diocese to a vicar-general who is also a cardinal. That has been the job of Cardinal Poletti since 1973, and his sense of duty to the pope and the institution has caused him to do a number of unpleasant things that do not seem to reflect his own better instincts. But in this he is true to his training. He is in full agreement with the policy lines of Pope Paul, and he believes the rights and interests of the church as conceived and formulated by the institution take precedence over those of individuals, including himself.

Born at Omegna, diocese of Novara, not far from Milan in north-central Italy 19 April 1914, he entered the diocesan minor seminary at a very early age, then passed to the major seminary and was ordained at age twenty-four. After eight years in administration in the diocesan seminaries, he became pastor of one of Novara's biggest parishes. He was also active with Catholic Action, both youth and adult sections. In 1951, he was named assistant vicar-general of the diocese of Novara, vicar-general in 1954 and auxiliary bishop in 1958.

Six years later, Paul VI started him on the first of several church activities on the national level as president for Italy of the papal missionary works. This work included visiting all the dioceses of Italy and participating in conferences in Italy and elsewhere.

In 1967 Poletti was named archbishop of Spoleto, and two years later he was called to Rome as assistant to Cardinal Angelo Dell'Acqua, then vicar-general of the diocese, whom he succeeded in that office on his death. Poletti is a member of the Congregations for the Clergy, and for the Sacraments and Divine Worship. He is also a member of the Pontifical Council for the Laity.

His concept of his job is to be the shadow of the pope and to carry out his directions as transmitted in part directly, but also in large part by the curial processes of decision making. Although his cultural preparation is modest, he is a hard worker with a reputation for dependability and obedience. As bishop of Spoleto, he has been very social-minded, and it was consequently no problem for him when he was instructed in his first years in Rome to stress socially progressive activities. However, when it was later decided to lean more toward the right because of the growing leftist influence in Rome, he still had little or no difficulty in executing his orders.

An example of Poletti at his best was his dealing with Father Gerard Lutte, pastor of Prato Rodondo in the zone of Magliana on Rome's outskirts. Here slum dwellers had been given low-cost and below-standard housing by the city government. In 1971, the occupants decided to take direct action, occupying vacant lots to prevent speculative building that would leave the area without land for schools and playgrounds. This created problems for Immobiliare, the enormous construction complex that built Watergate in Washington, D.C. It was then controlled by the Vatican and may still be indirectly under Vatican control. Poletti did everything possible to protect Lutte and find compromise solutions to the issues. But later he was forced to take a hard line with Abbot Franzoni, who was not only a social activist but a theologian who raised embarrassing questions for the Vatican.

As a result of his new hard line, he has come in for harsh criticism from progressives. In October 1975, he was condemned by 250 representatives of twenty-five grassroots communities on the charge that his overriding concern is to maintain the influence church authorities and their allies exert over the allocation of welfare assistance, health care, and aid to private schools, and their ability to manipulate the city finances and engage in real-estate speculation. Anyone who criticizes the church for holding on to power, they said, is struck down by him.

One measure of church influence on the city of Rome is that religious communities own property to the extent of fifty-one million square meters, while the debt-ridden municipality owns only four million. Church holdings affect the price of building sites, and the money of many religious institutions is invested in building societies, a decisive factor in the opinion of some observers in the "pillage of Rome" during the thirty years following World War II. The church owns thirty clinics with 2,959 beds reserved mostly for the wealthy, and church clinics are not available in the slums where they are most needed. Its kindergarten, grade and high schools serve 15 percent of school-age children, again heavily weighted toward the privileged.

Poletti thinks of himself as being in line with Vatican II, while interpreting it according to his preconciliar theological formation. While totally faithful to Paul, he has a somewhat lesser commitment to the Vatican as an institution. In spite of his background in Catholic Action, he has little sympathy with the grassroots communities, even those in good standing with their bishops, is opposed to worker priests, and even more strongly to the idea of women priests. He does not seem to be close to the poor in Rome, nor does he raise issues of structural reform. He could possibly come forward as a compromise candidate in a stalemated conclave, but the result of his election could hardly be other than to confirm the status quo.

Cardinal Antonio Poma

As president of the Italian Bishops' Conference, Cardinal Poma has taken an intransigent line in favor of church intervention in Italian politics. This has made him enemies, so that he is not a likely candidate for the papacy. It has also made him friends whose votes he will continue to influence even if—as is likely—Cardinal Benelli replaces him as president of the Conference in 1978.

Born at Villanterio, diocese of Pavia, just south of Milan in northcentral Italy, 12 June 1910, Poma studied at the local minor seminary, then transferred to the Lombardian major seminary in Rome and obtained a laureate in theology at the Gregorian. He returned to Pavia as secretary to the bishop, later taught dogmatic theology at the seminary and also was its rector from 1947 to 1951, when he was made auxiliary to the bishop of Mantua. Two years later he took full charge of the diocese when the bishop retired. In 1967 he was made coadjutor with right of succession to Cardinal Giacomo Lercaro, archbishop of Bologna, succeeding as archbishop when Lercaro resigned the following year. He was made a cardinal in 1969. He is a member of the curial Congregations for the Clergy and for Catholic Education.

Lercaro had bitter enemies in the Curia because he had been pushing liturgical reform in Bologna too fast for their liking, and they even persuaded Pope Paul that he should be made to resign. He came to Rome, was made to wait weeks before seeing the pope, but finally was vindicated. However, the pressure had been too much for him, so he decided to resign anyway. Poma was picked to follow him as a friendly but reserved person, good-mannered, kind and humble; and above all in complete accord with Pope Paul's policies. For these same reasons, Paul used his influence with the Italian cardinals and bishops to have them choose Poma as president of the conference of bishops, knowing he could trust him to do what Paul wanted without betraying the fact that he was acting as the pope's mouthpiece.

Poma's commitment to the view that the church's rights and interests take precedence over those of the individual caused him to urge the conference to take a firm stand on the two major Italian political issues: the call for a constitutional amendment on divorce, and the obligation to vote for the Christian Democrats in order to keep the communists out of power. The conference was in fact deeply divided on these two issues, not so much because of any theological conflict as because many of the bishops believed that a strong line would be counterproductive. The constitutional prohibition of divorce going back to Pius XI's agreement with Mussolini had done little to check the breakup of marriages but had caused untold suffering to abandoned wives and children. The worsening social conditions of industrial workers and rural peasants were driving voters steadily to the Left, and particularly since Pope Paul began to welcome the Russian leaders to the Vatican, the cynicism of the average Italian about the motivation behind the bishops' anticommunism has grown enormously. In fact, Poma could rally only 40 percent of the bishops to support his extreme stand, which included a threat to excommunicate lay Catholics who ran on the lists of the Communist Party, this in spite of the fact that Pope Paul in a public audience deplored the existence of such traitors. A small number of bishops openly opposed Poma, while the majority expressed reservations. The end result was to water down the resolutions.

Poma is against further change in the church and wants to keep controls firmly in episcopal and papal hands. He says little about social justice, does not seem too close to the poor of his diocese, opposes worker priests, women priests, grassroots communities, or similar expressions of new growths developing charismatically within the people of God.

Cardinal Opilio Rossi

Although born in New York, Cardinal Rossi is from the diocese of Piacenza, southeast of Milan in northern Italy, as are Cardinals Nasalli Rocca, Oddi, and Samorè. Shortly after his birth 14 May 1910, he was brought to Piacenza, where in due course he entered the minor seminary, then went to Rome and obtained a laureate in canon law at the Apollinare. After ordination to the priesthood at age twenty-three, he did specialized studies for entry to the Vatican diplomatic service at the Pontifical Ecclesiastical Academy, then joined the Secretariat of State as an aide to Monsignor Montini, now Pope Paul VI, in 1937. Sent to the nunciature in Brussels as secretary in 1938, he transferred to the same position at The Hague the following year. After the Nazi occupation of Belgium and Holland in June 1940, he went to Berlin as assistant to the papal representative, returning to Holland in 1945. From 1948 to 1951 he was part of the papal mission in Germany, and when the mission became a nunciature in 1951, he served there as Counselor.

Ordained a titular bishop in 1953, he went as nuncio to Ecuador, and to Chile in 1959. Two years later, the nuncio to Austria died, and Rossi was transferred to replace him. That was his final post. In 1976 he was recalled to Rome and made a cardinal. He is president of the Pontifical Council for the Laity and of the Commission for the Family. He is also a member of the Council for the Public Affairs of the Church; and of the Congregations for the Bishops, and for the Sacraments and Divine Worship. He is a curial bureaucrat; and while not an ultraconservative, he is unlikely to take any initiative in a papal conclave except as part of the curial bloc.

Cardinal Antonio Samorè

An old-fashioned and consistently reactionary theologian, Samorè was born at Bardi, diocese of Piacenza in northcentral Italy, 4 December 1905. He entered the diocesan minor seminary at age eleven, and five years later moved to the major seminary for eight years of study and a laureate in theology. Later he obtained a laureate in canon law at the Lateran. He was ordained in 1928. After three years in parish work in his native diocese, he entered the papal diplomatic service, being posted to Lithuania.

In 1938 he spent some months in Switzerland, then returned to work at the Vatican during World War II. In 1947, he went to the United States as counselor in the apostolic delegation, and in 1950 he was made archbishop and sent as nuncio to Colombia. In 1953 he was again posted to Rome, this time as secretary of the section of the Secretariat of State dealing with "extraordinary ecclesiastical affairs." In this post he was involved principally with Latin America, an area in which Pius XII took particular interest in the 1950s, seeing it as the logical place for expanded missionary activity with the exclusion of missionaries from China and the negative outlook for other parts of Asia and for much of Africa.

In 1955 Samorè was a member of the preparatory commission for the first meeting of the General Conference of Latin American Bishops (CELAM). When, however, CELAM was given its direction and tone by such progressive bishops as Manuel Larraín of Chile, Dom Helder Camara of Brazil, and Sergio Méndez Arceo of Mexico, Samorè set out immediately to get control of it by setting up at the Vatican the Commission for Latin America (CAL), of which he was at first vice-president and later president. CELAM's stated purpose of "adapting pastoral activity to contemporary needs" was effectively aborted by CAL until Vatican II, when the Latin American bishops in a series of discussions and maneuvers succeeded in reestablishing their autonomy, thus preparing the way for CELAM's prophetic commitment to renewal at Medellín in 1968. A small slip of the tongue played a big part in Samorè's defeat by the Latin Americans during Vatican II. At a meeting of the Latin American bishops with Pope John, Samorè gave an overview in Italian of the hemisphere in which he referred disparagingly to *Uruguay e Paraguay e tutti gli altri guaii* ("Uruguay and Paraguay and all the other disaster situations"). The play of words on the final syllable of the names of these two countries which sounds exactly like the Italian *guaii* was understandably resented by the Latin Americans and lost Samoré many friends.

Samorè is an intelligent theologian but totally within the framework of Roman theology which claims to be the only allowable theology and in consequence is unable to reconcile itself to the theological pluralism that is characteristic of the church since Vatican II, just as it was of the church before and even after the Council of Trent, when Thomists, Scotists and Suarezians fought each other merrily. Typical of Samorè's attitude is a warning against major liturgical changes at the 1967 Synod of Bishops: "Faithfulness to tradition is a basic element in the history of the church. . . . We should try to carry on the living worship of the past. The alternative would be to risk unleashing a veritable flood sweeping away everything in its path, without the possibility of saving anything or turning back."

Named a cardinal in 1967, he was prefect of the Congregation for the Discipline of the Sacraments (now named for the Sacraments and Divine Worship) until 1974, when he became instead librarian and archivist of the Holy Roman Church. He is a member of the Council for the Public Affairs of the Church; of the Congregations for the Bishops, for the Eastern Churches, and for the Evangelization of Peoples (Propaganda Fide); and of the Commission for the Revision of the Code of Canon Law. He is an integral part of the conservative curial bloc of cardinals.

Cardinal Giuseppe Maria Sensi

The sixth of ten children, Cardinal Sensi was born at Cosenza in the extreme south of Italy, 27 May 1907. His father, a politician, was a member of the Directorate of the Popular Party and a director of Calabrian Catholic Action; his mother, the Marchesa Andreotti-Loria. After study at the seminary in Cosenza, he went to Rome for a licentiate in philosophy and a doctorate in theology and canon law at the Lateran. Ordained a priest at age twenty-two, he did graduate work at the Pontifical Ecclesiastical Academy in preparation for a Vatican diplomatic career.

His first post was in Bucharest where he went in 1934 as secretary to the nunciature, moved to Berne, Switzerland, in 1938, and during the war years participated in the Vatican efforts to end the slaughter and to help the victims. In 1946 he went to Brussels for a year as Counselor in the nunciature; then, after a short stay in Rome, went as Counselor to Prague. He returned to Rome in 1949 to work with Monsignor Montini (now Pope Paul VI) in the creation of a new International Section of the Secretariat of State for relations with international organizations. In this capacity he worked with the international Catholic organizations, until sent to Paris in 1953 as the Vatican's Permanent Observer at UNESCO. In 1954, he led the Vatican delegation to UNESCO's general assembly in Montevideo.

Ordained a titular archbishop in 1955, he was sent as nuncio to Costa Rica, to be transferred the following year to Jerusalem as apostolic delegate. From there he went to Dublin as nuncio in 1962, and to Lisbon in 1967. Made a cardinal in 1976 and recalled to Rome, he is a member of the Congregations for the Eastern Churches, and for the Evangelization of Peoples (Propaganda Fide).

He is known in Rome as a lover of fast cars, identifiable in the recent past in his Porsche, and now in a red BMW 3000. In true curial style, he identifies his interests and those of the Curia with the interest of the church. In a papal conclave, he would be part of the curial bloc.

Cardinal Giuseppe Siri

"An archconservative's archconservative, one of the founders of the *Coetus Patrum* [a group seeking to block all reform or updating] at Vatican II, and unregenerate." Such is the description of Cardinal Siri, archbishop of Genoa, given by one who has followed his career close-up.

Born at Genoa 20 May 1906, Siri studied philosophy and theology in the diocesan seminary, then went to Rome for the final two years of theology at the Gregorian, and was ordained a priest at age twenty-two. He received a laureate in theology the following year, then became professor of dogmatic theology in the Genoa seminary at age twenty-four. In 1944 he became auxiliary to the archbishop of Genoa, and he succeeded as archbishop two years later. Made a cardinal in 1953, he is a member of the curial Congregations for the Clergy and for Catholic Education; and of the Commission for the Revision of the Code of Canon Law.

Even before Vatican II began, Siri made his position perfectly clear. In an interview with the Italian magazine *Orizzonti*, he said the Council would have to deal with very important doctrinal matters, the first task entrusted by Our Lord to his church being the teaching of truth. The church, he said, is confronted with pernicious doctrines and serious errors. As to the powers of the laity, they must continue substantially to be those traditionally accepted and defined by Our Savior when he established the sacred hierarchy, or as Pius XI had formulated Catholic Action, to be footsoldiers eager to carry out every order given by the clergy. He was unbending on the issue of the de-Westernization of the church, an attitude he shares with Cardinal Pericle Felici. "The West has not to be repudiated in any way; but the West must adapt itself better to the needs of all the others." This philosophy was at the foundation of the colonial era, as well as of Fascism and Nazism.

His many interventions during the Council were all directed to block progress and promote the passage of conservative or at best ambiguous statements. He resisted the introduction of the expression, the universal priesthood of the faithful, even though solidly based in the New Testament, because he claimed it would cause confusion. On the statement on the church in today's world, he complained that it did not contain a word about relativism, indifferentism, or laicism. "The church must not neglect her own problems in favor of the world." In private he criticized Pope John bitterly as the cause of all the unrest in the church. "It will take forty years to undo the harm John did the church in a few years," he reportedly said. He is also quoted as having described the Council as "an attack of insanity of Pope John." His final summing up of the Council was that its texts, even though accepted and approved by the pope, were not infallible. "They will never bind us."

At the 1967 Synod of Bishops he returned to his favorite topic, the need for a new Syllabus of Errors. He said it was the duty of the Synod to denounce the perils of our times: subjectivism, materialism, Pelagianism; and he warned against "an idolatry of apostolic works," which he called the secularization of the church. Forgetting his own repudiation of the Council's teaching, he said that people should accept not only the solemn magisterium of the church, but also the non-infallible magisterium, claiming that all doubts would be removed if everyone was sure about what Rome was saying.

Carlos Falconi, long a member of the Curia and one of the most informed of Vaticanologists, has said that Siri was Pius XII's choice to succeed him, and that in the conclave that elected Pope John, Siri was fully supported by the five top leaders (nicknamed the Pentagon) of the curial bloc as endowed with all the qualities calculated to ensure his becoming a second Pacelli. The likelihood of his being picked to follow Paul is minimal, but he will be a powerful leader of the most reactionary elements in a papal conclave.

Cardinal Corrado Ursi

While theologically conservative, Cardinal Ursi has an outstanding commitment to social reform, and this trait has served to endear him to the great masses of the poor in Naples, where he has been archbishop since 1966.

Ursi was born in Andria directly east of Naples near the Adriatic coast of southern Italy, an area of utter poverty and depression, 25 July 1931. His parents were storekeepers. He studied at the local minor and major seminaries, was ordained a priest at age twenty-three, and almost immediately began administrative work as vice-rector and later rector of the local major seminary. After twenty years in these posts, he was made bishop of Nardò in 1951, and ten years later archbishop of Acerenza.

Moved to Naples in 1966, he quickly gained the headlines by a number of unusual moves. First of all, he turned over all the gifts received at his installation to a fund destined to cancel debts and pay off obligations of poor people. Then he started to tour parishes in the poor quarters of the city, and when he learned that someone was sick, he would pay a visit, making a note of the person's name. A week or ten days later, he would call the pastor and enquire about the health of the individual. And if the pastor didn't know, he was told to get over there and find out. The message quickly got around that the new archbishop wanted the priests pounding the streets, not reading their breviaries in the sacristy.

The mayor and council of the city came to offer him a Cadillac and the customary police escort. He declined firmly. Then he learned of some dilapidated shacks down by the railroad. Two years earlier, money had been voted to replace them, but nothing had happened. He sent for the mayor and said he expected action within six months. He got it. Then he engaged an army colonel to prepare a big map of the diocese, showing every parish, every school, every convent, every diocesan institution, so that he could keep a running score of what was happening in each place.

A constant theme of his preaching is the disgrace of waste when so many are in want. In his 1969 Lenten pastoral, he called on the people to stop turning the "sacraments of the faith" into "sacraments of feasting," and not to spend at the coming Easter as much as it had been their practice to spend at Christmas, at first communions, at marriages, and on other religious occasions. "With so many homes in shocking disrepair, with such high child mortality, with so many unemployed, so many orphans, so many people condemned to underdevelopment, what a burden on the Christian conscience, on the Christian community! And still, last Christmas, for the birth of the poor Christ, what crazy expenses! It is an insult to the poor, an insult to Christ."

Ursi is highly supportive of Pope Paul's policy lines, agrees with *Humanae Vitae*, believes that Catholics should vote the party line, and believes—though less firmly than many of his colleagues—that the church's rights and benefits should be given precedence over those of the individual. While not enthusiastic about worker priests, he is less opposed than most Italian cardinals, and he identifies very definitely with the poor people of his diocese living on the edge of destitution.

He is a member of the curial Congregation for Catholic Education. His education and experience, limited entirely to the south of Italy, may account for the fact that he is not regarded as a serious candidate for the papacy.

Cardinal Egidio Vagnozzi

A Vatican diplomat who throughout his career has been consistently archconservative, Vagnozzi was born in Rome, 2 February 1906. After study in the Vatican minor seminary and the Roman major seminary, he was ordained a priest at age twenty-three. Two years later he graduated from the Lateran with laureates in philosophy, theology, and canon law.

Entering the papal diplomatic service, he was assigned to the apostolic delegation in Washington, D.C., rising to the grade of counselor. In 1942, he moved to Lisbon in the same grade, and shortly afterwards to Paris, where he stayed until 1948. After a visit to India in 1948 to arrange for the establishment of diplomatic relations with the recently created state, he was made an archbishop in 1949 and sent to the Philippines as apostolic delegate, becoming nuncio in 1951 when the Philippines established diplomatic relations with the Vatican. From there he returned to the United States in 1958, as apostolic delegate. This was his last diplomatic post. Recalled to Rome, he was made cardinal in 1967 and appointed president of the Prefecture of the Economic Affairs of the Holy See. This was a big disappointment to him. Earlier he had thought of himself as in line for the papacy, and he counted at least on getting a major post in the Curia. What he ended up with was a sinecure, the title and salary without effective control of the operations of this major Vatican financial institution. He is a member of the Congregations for the Eastern Churches and for the Evangelization of Peoples, and of the Segnatura Apostolica, a Vatican court.

At Vatican II, in the opening debate on the draft document on liturgical reform, he criticized the very progressive draft as badly constructed and full of loose definitions. He said it should be reworked on the basis of Pius XII's Mediator Dei, a traditionalist encyclical, and sent to the Theological Commission headed by his friend and fellow archconservative, Cardinal Ottaviani. When the Council discussed birth control, Vagnozzi defended the most traditional position, and it is believed he was responsible for bringing in the reactionary United States Jesuit John Ford as an expert. He similarly cooperated with Archbishop Philip Hannon of New Or-

leans in his unsuccessful efforts to have eliminated from the
statement on the church in today's world references to "have" and
"have-not" nations and a condemnation of nuclear weapons as
disparaging to the United States. Several United States bishops
complained bitterly in private that Vagnozzi was once again inter-
fering in the internal affairs of the United States church.

When Pope Paul, just before the end of the Council in 1965, took
part with the non-Catholic observers and Council Fathers in an
unprecedented interdenominational "Liturgy of the Word," in St.
Paul's Outside the Walls, Vagnozzi persuaded a number of United
States bishops to join with Archbishop Dino Staffa and others in a
message to the pope expressing amazement at the encouragement
he had given to what they had all been taught to believe was a
communicatio in sacris—a grave sin—with heretics.

Earlier, in 1962, as apostolic delegate in Washington, he had
sent an instruction to the United States bishops to refuse permission for any public lecturing on Teilhard de Chardin, and to take
other similar measures "to discourage the current wave of interest,
so that it will die a natural death." This, he said, was "the unofficial
but firm will of the curial head of the Holy Office, Cardinal Ottaviani."

Although disappointed that he did not reach the top in his
career, he remains a company man, a firm part of the reactionary
bloc in the Curia.

Archbishop Agostino Casaroli

Born at Castel San Giovanni, diocese of Piacenza, Italy, 24 November 1914, Caseroli had the typical seminary and Roman university preparation for a career in the Roman Curia. He has specialized in Vatican relations with the socialist regimes of East Europe, and he has pursued vigorously and with considerable success the policy of "opening to the East" initiated by John XXIII and continued by Paul VI.

Caseroli's substantive position is secretary of the Council for the Public Affairs of the Church in the Secretariat of State. He is also president of the Pontifical Commission for Russia, consultor to the Congregation for the Doctrine of the Faith and to the Commission for the Revision of the Code of Canon Law, and member of the Commissions for Latin America and for the Pastoral Care of Migrants and Tourists.

Asia

F or the first time in history, Asia will have a significant voice in the choice of a pope at the next papal conclave. When Pope Paul was elected in 1963, Asia had only three cardinals, one each from China, Japan and the Philippine Islands; and there were still only three in 1969. Now the number has grown to thirteen: three from India, two from the Philippines, one each from Japan, China, Korea, Vietnam, Pakistan, Sri Lanka, Indonesia, and Samoa.

Specific conditions vary greatly from country to country in this vast region, but there are several major factors that dominate the priorities of almost all these cardinals. Asia is a land of ancient cultures and highly developed religious systems. During the entire colonial period which coincided with the major modern missionary expansion of the Latin church, the centralized control of Rome prevented an adaptation of the European style of church life to the realities of a totally different world. Catholicism remained for most countries a foreign element, one identified by many with the colonial regimes which generally favored and gave financial support to the Christian missions for health and education purposes, and at times even for strictly religious and proselytizing activities. In addition, the common attitude of Rome and of the missions was to limit the number of indigenous priests by imposing unreasonably high standards and insisting on a complete transculturation that left them more at home with the European clergy than with their own people.

To change that negative image demands radical transformation not only of the liturgy but of life-style, and most of the Asian cardinals see this as a top priority. In the years immediately after Vatican II, Rome authorized on an experimental basis a wide discretion. In India, for example, many devotional practices, prayers and scripture passages of Hinduism were incorporated or adapted. Since Cardinal James Knox, former archbishop of Melbourne, Australia, became head of the curial Congregation for the Sacraments and Divine Worship in 1974, he has been issuing warnings to go more slowly with such adaptations. For this and other reasons, a major concern of the Asian cardinals—as of the

Africans—will be to ensure that the next pope will give them more discretion in their efforts to make the church as much a part of their respective cultures as it is of the culture of Europe.

In addition, in all this region—except the Philippines—Catholics constitute a small minority, everywhere subject to the pressures brought to bear on a minority with different characteristics by the dominant majority.

The church is also openly persecuted because of its strong stand for human rights in the two right-wing dictatorships of South Korea and the Philippines, while in Vietnam it experiences the more subtle but very real pressures of socialist regimes. Survival in these circumstances requires a high level of esprit de corps, an avoidance of divisive pluralisms, a readiness to submit to decisions of those in authority, and the ability to mobilize the power of the opinion of Christians worldwide. This last factor, combined with the poverty that is characteristic of most Asian churches and consequent dependence on help from the Holy See, would encourage the cardinals to stay in the good graces of the Roman Curia and even to welcome a strong central authority in Rome to support them in times of crisis. In consequence, the Asian cardinals, who—with the exception of the reactionary Yü Pin resident in Taiwan—range from moderately to highly progressive in their personal outlooks, will likely be cautious in a papal conclave, keeping their views to themselves until they can see clearly who is coming out on top.

Cardinal Thomas B. Cooray

Born into an extremely poor family at Periyamulla Negombo, archdiocese of Colombo, Ceylon (now Sri Lanka), 28 December 1901, Cardinal Cooray lost his father while very young, and his widowed mother had to raise the two children of the marriage. Cooray studied at Saint Joseph's College, Colombo, and at the University of Colombo, before entering the major seminary, from which he went to Rome for theology. He joined the Oblates of Mary Immaculate in 1924 and was ordained a priest in 1929. With a B.A. in fine arts from the University of London and laureates in philosophy and theology from Rome's Angelicum, he returned to Colombo to teach at Saint Joseph's College, and later to become also rector of the Oblate student residence. In 1945 he was made coadjutor to the archbishop of Colombo, whom he succeeded as archbishop in 1947. He was named cardinal in 1965, and he is a member of the curial Commission for the Revision of the Code of Canon Law.

At Vatican II he revealed what has been a continuing concern, that no action be taken that would seem to lessen the authority and dignity of the pope, even proposing that any criticisms of the Curia—because "it works in the name of the Holy Father"—should be submitted in writing to ensure that they did not become matters of public knowledge. At the 1969 Synod, he was one of a minority opposed to any implementation of collegiality that would weaken the primatial function of the Holy See and lessen unity in the church. Informed observers said he took this stand, not because he was personally conservative, but because he lives in a poor region where the strength of non-Christians is growing and where the threat of neocolonialism is real. He believes he needs a strong central power to protect the church.

That he is in fact theologically open had been demonstrated at the 1967 Synod. There he complained that seminary education continued to follow the principles of the Council of Trent excessively, isolating seminarians from the life of the surrounding civil and parochial community, and stifling their personality. He also urged a radical decentralization of the lawmaking processes in the proposed new Code of Canon Law. He has shown great concern for the divulgation and implementation of the decrees of Vatican II, had a pastoral convention at work for a year to develop a series of recommendations that were nearly all confirmed by a provincial synod. Praising the work, he said it would take "much courage, spirit of faith, and sacrifice" to implement the decisions.

Like the typical cardinal from a poor country in which Christians are a minority and regarded as a foreign element, he would see his interests best served by a pope who would be socially progressive, willing to allow local churches to make appropriate cultural and liturgical changes, and yet retain a strong central power in Rome to protect him in times of crisis.

Cardinal Joseph Cordeiro

Born at Bombay 19 January 1918, Cardinal Cordeiro attended Saint Patrick's school, Karachi, then graduated from the University of Bombay. As an adult, he entered the major seminary of Kandy, Ceylon (now Sri Lanka), and was ordained a priest in 1946. After two years in parish work and teaching at Hyderabad, India, he studied at Oxford, England, for a Diploma in Education. On returning to India, he was named rector of the diocesan seminary and head of Saint Francis' School, Quetta. In 1958 he was named Archbishop of Karachi. He was a member of the preparatory commission for Vatican II, and of various commissions and subcommissions of the Council, and he was also a member of the Synods of Bishops of 1967, 1969, and 1971. Made a cardinal in 1973, he is a member of the curial Congregation for the Evangelization of Peoples (Propaganda Fide); of the Secretariat for Non-Christians; and of the Council Cor Unum created in 1971 to promote human and Christian progress.

A specialist on Islam, Cordeiro approved at Vatican II the creation of a wider area of cooperation between Catholic and other Christian missionaries, deploring the negative impact of previous competition. Other interventions at the Council and the Synods of Bishops tended to be more cautious. Thus he warned against a danger of "a false sense of collectivism" if adaptation of the liturgy was not kept within defined limits.

His situation as head of one of the most impoverished dioceses in the world obliges him to be conscious of the need for the church to identify itself more with the poor. At the same time, his weakness in an overwhelmingly Moslem country forces him to look to a strong central power in Rome to support him. So for him, probably the ideal candidate at a papal conclave would be a socially progressive but theologically conservative cardinal.

Cardinal Justinus Darmojuwono

Simple appearing but a man of deep substance, courageous and bright. Such is the description by one who knows him well of Cardinal Darmojuwono, who was born at Godean, archdiocese of Semarang, Java (Indonesia), the son of Moslem parents, 2 November 1914. He studied to be a teacher at a Jesuit school, and just as he was about to obtain his teaching diploma at age eighteen, he asked to be received into the church. Two years later he entered the Djakarta minor seminary for a 5-year course, then passed to the major seminary for philosophy and theology. When the Japanese overran Indonesia in 1942, the foreign missionaries who were his teachers were interned, but Indonesian priests were available to help him complete his courses, and in 1947 he was ordained a priest. After some years of teaching and parish work, he went to Rome in 1954 for courses in missiology at the Gregorian. He returned to Indonesia for parish work until 1962 when he was named vicar-general of Semarang, becoming archbishop of Semarang a year later. In 1967 he became the first Indonesian and also the first convert from Islam to join the College of Cardinals. He is a member of the curial Congregation for the Sacraments and Divine Worship, and of the Secretariat for Non-Christians.

His interventions at Vatican II revealed maturity of thought combined with a progressive outlook. His primary concern was the document on the church in today's world, and as spokesman for the Indonesian bishops he urged that what was wanted was not a monologue in which the church expressed itself to the world but a dialogue that treated the world with respect and on a level of equality. "There is a deep unity in all created things that tends toward salvation. Let us respect the laws that are proper to all terrestrial activities." At the 1967 Synod of Bishops, speaking of a marriage of a Catholic and a Protestant, he said the *cautiones*, the unilateral promises by the Protestant to have all children raised as Catholics, should be abolished. The church, he said, should declare openly that the spouses have a true and common responsibility for their own religious life and that of their children. He also urged that bishops and conferences of bishops be given greater discretion.

Darmojuwono has made no effort to hide his disagreement with the position on birth control expressed by Pope Paul in *Humanae Vitae*, and Rome has shown its displeasure more than once. He was invited to the United Nations Population Conference in Bucharest in 1974, but the Vatican persuaded him to stay away in order to avoid a public break on the contraception issue. He is in a difficult situation, because as head of a minority church in a poor country in which strong prejudices against Christianity as a foreign influence exist, he needs the support of the Vatican, so he has to try to keep his views to himself. But he is both socially minded and progressive, and in a curial conclave would favor a candidate of like mind.

Cardinal Valerian Gracias

The first Indian ever to be made a cardinal is a tall graceful man who keeps in his chancery the saddest file in the world: the number who die of hunger each week in his archdiocese of Bombay. Cardinal Gracias was born in Karachi, now an archdiocese in Pakistan, then part of the diocese of Bombay, 23 October 1900. After early schooling at Saint Patrick's, Karachi, he went to the interdiocesan seminary at Mangalore, then to the Pontifical seminary of Kandy, Ceylon (now Sri Lanka), where he received a laureate in Theology.

Ordained a priest in 1926, he spent a year in parish work, then went to the Gregorian in Rome for further theological study and obtained the advanced degree of Magister Aggregatus. There followed seven years as secretary to the archbishop of Bombay, and gradually other tasks were added: ecclesiastical adviser to the Union of Catholic Students; assistant to the diocesan League of Catholic Action; synodal examiner; diocesan consultant; member of the editorial board of the *Messenger of the Sacred Heart*; editor-in-chief of *The Examiner*. His published books include *The Vatican and International Policy*; *Heaven and Home*; and *Features of Christian Life*.

Ordained a bishop and made auxiliary to the Jesuit Archbishop Thomas Roberts in 1946, he succeeded as archbishop when Roberts resigned in 1950. He was made cardinal in 1953, and he is a member of the curial Commission for the Revision of the Code of Canon Law.

In the extremely conservative era of Pius XII, Gracias was regarded as relatively progressive. The Vatican in the last years of Pius was dominated by five cardinals, four of them now dead: Canali, Pizzardo, Micara, Ottaviani, and Mimmi. They were known as the Pentagon. Montini (now Paul VI) was their strongest opponent in the Curia, and when Pius exiled him to Milan in 1954 without making him a cardinal, the Italian progressives were in the Milan-Bologna-Venice triangle: Montini, Lercaro, and Roncalli (later John XXIII). Outside Italy, these had the support of the French cardinals, and of a few others, of whom Gracias and Wyszyński were the most prominent.

Gracias adopted relatively open stands at Vatican II. For exam-

248

ple, he vigorously opposed the curial draft on the "two sources" of revelation, saying it needed so much amending that—like a tumbledown house—it would be better to start all over again. He strongly supported adaptation of the liturgy and urged a wide discretion for national conferences of bishops in the adaptations to be introduced in different countries and different linguistic and cultural settings. Another of his favorite themes was that the church should give preferential concern to the poor and work to eliminate misery from the earth. "The poor are the images of Christ, the living sacrament of Jesus."

The friendship of Gracias and Pope Paul was cemented when the latter visited India in late 1964 to preside at the Eucharistic Congress in Bombay. Paul had been deeply depressed by the serious conflict among the Fathers at the third session—just concluded—of the Council, and the extraordinary welcome given him not only by Christians but by Hindus and Moslems in Bombay restored his spirits. From that time on, he felt a sense of gratitude to Gracias, and Gracias responded by placing himself ever more firmly in the line of the pope as he grew more cautious and reserved in the years following the Council. When Paul picked him as one of the commission of seven cardinals to prepare the program for the 1969 Synod of Bishops, Henri Fesquet of *Le Monde* noted that Gracias had retained "to an outstanding degree the imprint of the Roman theology."

The result is that Gracias has become a firm supporter of the status quo in both church and state. He is traditionally Scholastic in theology, maintaining little interest in theological developments. He is lukewarm toward social justice, human rights and the status of women, and totally opposed to married priests or the ordination of women. He agrees that change is essential but that continuity is necessary, so that we should hasten slowly. He is loyal equally to the Holy See and to whatever government happens to be in power in India. He will not permit any changes until they have been sanctioned by Rome. His life-style is upper-class. Efficient, hardworking, decisive and receptive to reasoned argument, he can also be quite authoritarian. He has had conflicts with members of the clergy because of appointments he made and because of his choice of advisers. Some anonymous letters critical of his life-style and his resistance to collegial decision-making in his diocese circulated during his Silver Jubilee celebrations as a bishop in 1971, and these criticisms caused him severe emotional upset. He recovered after some time and has since led an active and effective life.

In India he strongly advocates a united church in the face of pressures under which Christian churches have labored since Independence (as explained above). This includes cooperation with the Syro-Calabar and Syro-Malankar rites, whose relations with the Latin rite had long been strained. (see Paracattil). But his influence is now mainly confined to the Roman Curia, and in a papal conclave he can be counted on to vote unquestioningly for the candidate promoted by the Curia.

Cardinal Stephen Sou Hwan Kim

A man who insists that the church must—like Jesus Christ—be biased in favor of the poor, Cardinal Kim was born at Tae Gu, Korea, 8 May 1922. After the normal ecclesiastical studies, he was ordained a priest in 1947, worked for a time in a parish, then as secretary to the bishop of Tae Gu, before going to Tokyo for advanced study of philosophy at the Jesuit Sophia University. On returning to Tae Gu, he edited the diocesan newspaper, then went to Europe for additional study and spent seven years at Münster, Germany, for specialization in the social sciences. Two years after his return to Korea, he was named bishop of Masan in 1966 and promoted archbishop of Seoul in 1968, then made a cardinal a year later. He is a member of the curial Congregation for the Evangelization of Peoples (Propaganda Fide), and of the Secretariat for Non-Christians.

For many years the South Koreans have lived under a despotic dictatorship which claims that its excesses are necessary to ensure a strong and united people in the face of the everpresent threat of invasion from the north. Although many Christians and a quarter of the bishops favor the repressive regime, Kim leads the progressive Christians as the only defender of human rights in a country in which all other opposition has been silenced. In 1973 he was one of 400,000 signatories of a request for revision of the Constitution. In a sermon that year he said, "Much is being done for development, but absolute priority is given to economic growth, and man has been reduced to the level of an instrument at the service of the economy. . . . Power has become absolute, and the fundamental rights of citizens are being violated by the authorities more and more each day. . . . The people and the government have been radically cut off from each other. That is our gravest problem. Why this gap? Because the regime has practiced an unbelievable policy of oppression. . . . The present system must be reformed, a system that seeks to eliminate the citizens systematically from a voice in the affairs of the nation, . . . to return to a truly democratic system, in which the people will be sovereign. . . . If the government continues in its obstinacy, the inevitable result will be a national catastrophe." What Kim here describes is the "development" model of the Chicago School of Economics imposed on Third World countries as a condition for United States aid either directly or through such institutions as the World Bank; and what Kim says of it is exactly the same as the Brazilian bishops have been saying for years about the socioeconomic results of its application by the military dictatorship in their country.

The dynamics of a repressive system bring a continual escalation of violence in order to maintain order without justice, and the result has been a strengthening of support for Kim in his opposition. In March 1976, the National Association of Priests for Justice held a Mass in the Seoul cathedral on the anniversary of independence, after which they issued a proclamation signed by many important citizens, Christian and non-Christian, which stated that victory over communism could be obtained only by the creation of a true democracy; and that therefore the emergency decrees should be rescinded, basic rights restored, political prisoners freed, and the courts made independent. It also denounced an economic policy that had handed the country over to foreign companies, while denying the right to strike or to unionize. President Park and his regime, they concluded, must go. Many of the signatories were quickly jailed. According to foreign press reports, Kim said in a sermon that those who had signed the proclamation had only done their duty.

Nine months later, in his Christmas address, Kim reaffirmed his stand. "The contemporary church," he said, "has not ceased to insist on the fact that true development, prosperity and peace are possible only where justice and the rights of man are respected. . . . This is a point on which it is necessary for us to convert ourselves profoundly. If we do not, . . . our society and our people in their entirety will end up losing all freedom and falling into slavery. Indeed, this is practically our fate already."

Kim made an extremely important statement on Asian problems at a meeting at UNESCO, Paris, 11 November 1977. All the Asian countries (other than Japan) think of themselves as being in "the process of development," he said, when in fact they are "on the way to greater underdevelopment and perhaps even on the road to antidevelopment." His analysis is that the capitalist model has as its result—"and perhaps even as its principle"—an increase in the gap between a minute group of economically rich, politically in control, and socially the masters, while the enormous majority is economically poor, politically objects, and socially instruments. This model simultaneously increases the foreign debts of the countries of Asia. As elsewhere in the Third World, so in Asia authoritarian regimes have emerged to defend this unjust distribution by force, and to render the citizens powerless even to protest. The result is an omnipresent, omniscient and omnipotent state.

In all of this, Kim has no political ambitions. His concern is pastoral and humanitarian. He is a heroic man risking his life daily in the cause of justice. His concept of the church is that it should, like Jesus Christ, be biased in favor of the poor, and that its leaders should express this concern in their life-style and priorities. This would place him in a papal conclave on the side of the progressives, and specifically in favor of a candidate committed to the social Gospel.

Cardinal Joseph Parecattil

Head of the Syro-Malabar rite with five bishops and a little more than a million members, a church that goes back in India to apostolic times and claims to have been founded by the Apostle Thomas, Cardinal Parecattil was born at Kidangoor, diocese of Ernakulam, state of Kerala, in the extreme southwest of India, 1 April 1912. He entered the minor seminary of Ernakulam at age sixteen, and three years later the major seminary of Kandy in Ceylon (now Sri Lanka), a seminary subsequently transferred to Poona, India. Having obtained a licentiate in philosophy and a laureate in theology, he moved to the University of Madras for a laureate in literature.

Returning to Ernakulam, he engaged in various parish ministries and was editor of the socioreligious diocesan weekly *Sathya Deepam* ("Light of Truth"). In 1953 he was made auxiliary to the archbishop of Ernakulam, whom he succeeded as archbishop in 1956.

At Vatican II, his interventions reflected his concerns as a member of a small rite within the church, and as a leader of Christians in a country in which they are a minority. When a draft document referred to the Eastern Christians as "the ornaments of the church," he expressed thanks for the honor but added he would prefer to be seen as an integral part of the church. When relations with non-Christians were under discussion, he commented, "Let us present Christianity as the fulfilment of everything members of other faiths find in their religion. Let us specify that missionaries must be disinterested and not succumb to proselytism. Furthermore, the church needs the values of other religions to become truly Catholic. Let us learn how to recognize the action of the Spirit in the whole world."

At the 1967 Synod of Bishops he opted for a single Code of Canon Law for Western and Eastern churches, with special applications left to the initiative of local churches. The general code should regulate such things as the hierarchy and the sacraments, leaving room for adaptation where desirable, for example, on the issue of clerical celibacy in the Eastern rites. On liturgical reform, he urged more variation and also more freedom in translating texts.

The sense is what is important, he said, and that means that the words must be adapted to the mental capacity and cultural assumptions of those to whom they are directed.

The Syro-Calabar rite had been extremely Latinized during the colonial regime in India, and it has been striving hard since 1960 to revive its older traditions. Parecattil has supported this renewal, while simultaneously seeking improved relations with the Syro-Malankar and Latin rites. At Pentecost 1969, he joined with Archbishop Mar Gregorios of the Syro-Malankar rite, Cardinal Gracias of the Latin rite, and many other bishops, in a concelebrated eucharist, a proclamation of solidarity that was well received. In that year also, he presided at the opening of a program of intensive theological formation for lay leaders at Kerala. It was the first initiative of the kind in India, and the reaction of other bishops was most favorable.

Parecattil is very much in favor of more independence for national hierarchies. All the Indian cardinals and most of the bishops believe it is essential to Indianize the liturgy so that Christianity will cease to appear as a foreign element in Indian society. Some years ago the Indian bishops were authorized to experiment with the introduction of various Hindu practices and sections of the Hindu sacred writings, but when Cardinal James Knox was transferred in 1974 from Melbourne, Australia, to Rome to head the Congregation for the Sacraments and Divine Worship, he sent a letter to the bishops advising them to slow down. All the cardinals resented this interference and the text of the letter was never made public, but all did in fact withdraw to a more cautious stand except Parecattil. He continues to press forward as best he can. In a papal conclave, his choice of candidate would be greatly influenced by the individual's attitude to decentralization. He certainly would not favor a candidate who sought to retain rigid curial control of all church activities.

As cardinal, Parecattil is a member of the Congregation for the Eastern Churches; of the Secretariats for Christian Union and for Non-Christians; and of the Commission for the Revision of the Code of Canon Law. He is president of the Commission for the Revision of the Code of Eastern Canon Law; and as such he reported at the 1977 Synod of Bishops on the Commission's progress. Within a conceptual framework very different from that of Cardinal Felici who is working on the Latin church's code, Parecattil stressed that the first principle of Eastern church law is subsidiarity, and in consequence they were concentrating on describing patriarchal authority, synodal rule, and the position of clergy and laity in each of the Eastern traditions.

Cardinal Lawrence Trevor Picachy

The son of an Indian army doctor and of a mother of Irish descent, Cardinal Picachy was born in western Bengal—where his father was stationed—at Darjeeling, 7 August 1916. He studied at the Jesuit College of Saint Joseph, Darjeeling, until 1934, when a major earthquake destroyed a large part of the building, then decided to follow his elder brother, who had joined the Jesuits and is now a pastor in Calcutta. Having completed his novitiate at Saint Stanislaus College, Hazaribagh, Bihar, he studied philosophy at the Sacred Heart College, Shembaganur, southern India, taught four years at Saint Xavier's, Calcutta, then did theology at Saint Mary's, Kurseong, in the Himalayas, and was ordained a priest in 1947.

His first ministry was in Calcutta, and it involved learning Bengali, the regional language. He held various posts, including that of rector, in Saint Xavier's, Calcutta. He then volunteered as a mission pastor at Basanti, close to Bangladesh, where in an immense territory among the thousand channels of the Ganges 3,500 Christians were scattered in a population of 3 million Hindus and Moslems. From 1960 to 1962 by jeep in the jungle and by canoe on the river he ministered to this neglected flock. He was then recalled to become the first bishop of Jamshedpur, state of Bihar, a diocese in which India's biggest steel making complex is located. He soon assumed many posts in the Indian hierarchy, vice-president of the bishops' conference, president of the bishops' commission for social communications, and president of the bishops' committee for priests and religious. He was in charge of church aid to the thirteen million who fled from Bangladesh to India during the Bangladesh war of secession from Pakistan. Made archbishop of Calcutta in 1969, he subsequently was elected president of the Indian bishops' conference, and it was at a meeting of its executive committee that he learned in 1976 that he had been named a cardinal. He is a member of the curial Congregation for the Evangelization of Peoples (Propaganda Fide).

At Vatican II, he kept a low profile but ranged himself clearly with the progressives. On the status of the laity he was particularly emphatic. Even though their vocation is in the world, he insisted, it is a call to be holy. "The duty of the apostolate for lay persons results from baptism and confirmation. Let us not speak only of the obedience of the laity to the hierarchy, but of their right and duty to act as adults." He criticized the text for overstressing the duty of the laity to obey and for overlooking the reality that the clergy needed their help. He also recalled the statement of Saint Augustine that, while bishops and pastors are shepherds in charge of sheep, they remain—in the sight of the Divine Good Shepherd—sheep along with their people.

According to sources close to him, he appears very simple but is a man of deep substance. After the Jesuit general chapter in the mid-1970s he assured a friend that he stood solidly with Father Pedro Arrupe, the Jesuit General. At that chapter, in which there was deep difference of opinion over the role of the Jesuits in the conciliar church, Arrupe had insisted successfully that the Society had to adopt a radical line. To be a Christian today, he said, one has to be for justice. That for many meant, as it had always meant, that they would be repudiated by their families and by the rich supporters of the Jesuit colleges, universities and other enterprises; but that was the choice Christ offered them. At a press conference in Rome during the October 1977 Synod of Bishops, Picachy repeated this message. He had made several efforts, he said, to make the Synod realize "the meaning of poverty in the context of actuality and not in the realm of morality." Poverty cannot be understood until it is seen. All this would place Picachy in a papal conclave on the side of the evangelical prophets, the small progressive group whose faith is not in power but in the Spirit.

Cardinal Julio Rosales

At the opposite end of the spectrum from the younger Filipino cardinal, Jaime Sin, the progressive archbishop of Manila, Cardinal Rosales was born at Calbayog, island of Samar (Philippines), 18 September 1906, the third of five children. His father died while he was young, and his mother sent Julio and two brothers to the seminary of Saint Vincent de Paul at Calbayog. Ordained a priest in 1929, he worked in various parishes until 1946, when he was named first bishop of Tagbilaran, island of Bohol, and from there he was promoted in 1949 to Cebu, the second most important see in the Philippines after Manila, as archbishop. He was named a cardinal in 1969, and he is a member of the curial Congregations for the Clergy, and for Catholic Education; and the Commission for the Revision of the Code of Canon Law.

At Vatican II he identified with the most reactionary and traditionalist elements. He was particularly eloquent in defense of a draft statement on priests which he had helped to prepare, and which was quickly rejected by the consensus of the assembly. Since the Council he has continued to adopt reactionary positions, unconcerned about the growing numbers of destitute people in the Philippines, kowtowing to the dictatorship, denouncing those who seek social change as dupes of the communists. At a round table of seven newly named cardinals, of whom he was one, held in Italy in 1969, he supported Cardinal Paul Yü Pin, the archbishop of Nanking, who fled to Taiwan with Chiang Kai-shek and has since lived there. "From the political viewpoint, our greatest fear is communist infiltration. We are neighbors of Vietnam. If Vietnam falls completely to the communists, the Philippines will be next. Unfortunately, this is a real threat, a threat capable of realization, and it will be realized if we do not start an authentic social reform." In spite of his assertion that authentic social reform is essential, his concrete actions and open support of the Marcos regime work against reform in society and in the church.

Cardinal Jaime L. Sin

Progressive, socially conscious, and a determined fighter for human rights which are being systematically violated by the Marcos regime, Cardinal Sin was born at New Washington, diocese of Kalibo, on Panay, one of the larger of the more than 7,000 islands that constitute the Philippine archipelago, 31 August 1928, the seventh of sixteen children. His father became a Catholic shortly after his marriage to a member of a Catholic family of long standing.

After public primary school, he entered the minor seminary of Saint Vincent Ferrer at Jaro, Iloilo, in 1941, but almost immediately he had to flee to the mountains to escape the Japanese invasion, and he spent the next three years in hiding at El Kalibo, where he continued the study of Latin under the tutorage of the local pastor. After the liberation of the Philippines in 1945, he returned to the Jaro seminary for philosophy and theology, and in 1954 was ordained a priest for the diocese of Capiz in northern Panay. In company with another priest, he spent the next three years visiting nearly a hundred parishes scattered through the mountains in which he had hidden during the war, preaching and promoting vocations for the seminary which the newly created diocese was building. In 1957 he became rector of the new seminary. Ordained a bishop and made auxiliary to the archbishop of Jaro in 1967, he was promoted to coadjutor and apostolic administrator of the same diocese in January 1972, and succeeded as archbishop the same year. Transferred to Manila as archbishop in 1974, he was made a cardinal in 1976. He is a member of the curial Commission for Social Communications.

His appointment to Manila represented a radical break with the policies of his predecessor, Cardinal Santos, a man of traditional piety and totally subservient to the regime and to big business. Within months of his arrival in Manila, Sin publicly protested the official use of torture by the regime against political suspects. Although the church in the Philippines is deeply divided, with many bishops following the reactionary stands of Cardinal Julio Rosales, archbishop of Cebu, Sin has substantial and growing support. Following a strike in October 1975, Marcos issued a decree banning all strikes, slowdowns, etc., controlling the activities of foreigners, requiring the approval of the Labor Secretary for any individual or group to help in any way an organization or group of workers, a cooperative, or a research institute specializing in labor problems. This order effectively excluded all church personnel, and in particular foreign missionaries, from engaging in any kind of social work. A few days later, thirty-seven priests at a regional meeting of the major superiors of religious orders issued a strong protest. Sin followed this up with a letter to Marcos on his own behalf and on behalf of the signatories of the protest, who within a week had grown to 2,000, including several bishops. "We protest," he said, "because this decree prevents us from performing our Christian and human duty to help the poor and suffering. If a group of workers lose their jobs, and their families are dying of starvation, . . . should we have to apply to the Labor Secretary before giving them a few centavos to buy food. . . . And if a priest wants to preach on the dignity of work and the rights of workers, . . . must he first also ask for a like permission?" When United States President Ford was in Manila the following month, 6,000 workers and clergy came into the streets to support the protest. Ten days later, Marcos withdrew the decree.

In a papal conclave, Sin's primary concern would be the stand of a candidate on human rights, basic reform of unjust socioeconomic structures, and commitment to dynamic leadership on behalf of the poor, powerless, and voiceless.

Cardinal Pio Taofinu'u

The first Polynesian bishop and cardinal was born at Falealupo, diocese of Apia, Western Samoa, 9 December 1923. His preparation for the priesthood began at Moamoa, continued at the seminary on Wallis Island and later at the major seminary of Green Meadows, New Zealand. A year after ordination as a priest in 1954, he joined the Marianist Fathers. He attended the second session of Vatican II in 1963 with the bishop of Samoa and visited the Holy Land before returning home. In 1966 he was named vicar-general of the diocese of Apia, and bishop of Apia in 1968. The diocese embraces three territories, American Samoa, a United States possession; Western Samoa, which is independent; and the Tokelau Islands, a New Zealand protectorate.

As bishop, Taofinu'u built many schools, as well as a theology institute to train lay catechists and permanent deacons, the first such initiative in all of Polynesia. He has also been active in efforts to raise the living standards of the people. Made a cardinal in 1973, he is a member of the curial Congregation for the Causes of Saints. His interests are those of most of the cardinals of Asia and Africa, the need to indigenize the church in order to make it more meaningful to peoples of Polynesian culture. For that reason, in a papal conclave he would support an open candidate. At the same time, in a position of weakness because of the great poverty of his people and shortage of clergy, he must keep his options open so as not to fall into disfavor with the Roman Curia.

Cardinal Joseph Marie Trin-nhu-Khuê

Born at Trang-Duê, archdiocese of Hanoi, 11 December 1899, Cardinal Trin-nhu-Khuê was ordained a priest in 1933. During the French regime, Hanoi was merely a vicariate apostolic, and in 1950 Trin-nhu-Khuê was made a bishop and appointed vicar apostolic. After the communist regime (which came to power following the 1954 Geneva Agreements) had consolidated its control of North Vietnam, the Vatican in 1960 decided to raise Hanoi to the dignity of an archdiocese and promoted Trin-nhu-Khuê to be its archbishop.

While many Catholics fled to the south, Trin-nhu-Khuê remained at his post and during the years of the conflict that ended with the reunification of Vietnam in 1976, his main concern was to keep the remaining Catholics united and lead them in a policy of adjusting to life under a communist government. The Hanoi regime did not break relations with the church, but the actual contacts were tenuous and difficult until the war had reached a point where the communists were confident that the country would soon be reunited. For the first time, Trin-nhu-Khuê was received by the prime minister, Pham Van Dong, for the New Year of 1976. Before he was made a cardinal, the Holy See consulted with the Hanoi regime and was given its approval. He was then allowed to go to Rome to receive the red hat in May 1976, and on his return, he was again received by Pham Van Dong. Speaking on Vatican Radio on that occasion, he said that his incorporation into the College of Cardinals signified the recognition by the Vatican of one Vietnam. He then praised the Vatican's "perfect understanding of the situation of his country and its church." As cardinal, he is a member of the curial Congregation for the Sacraments and Divine Worship.

A year later, in an interview with a representative of the National Catholic Reporter, he said that women in Vietnam do not want to be ordained priests. As for married priests, while not now authorized, he remains open to the possibility of changing that rule. The church in Vietnam, he added, does not oppose the government's birth-control program, but he urges the family to use the method of abstention and to be sure it does not upset the harmony of the family.

Trin-nhu-Khuê is an able politician who has managed to steer an astute course throughout the years. In a papal conclave, his overriding concern would be for a candidate who would support him in his flexible policy, ensuring that the substantial Catholic community can hold together while cooperating fully with the social policies of the communist regime.

Cardinal Paul Yü Pin

A man whose sense of his vocation in life has narrowed down to the dream of overthrowing the communist regime in China and restoring the rule of the Chiang Kai-shek dynasty with which he fled to Taiwan in 1949, Cardinal Yü Pin was born at Lan-si Sien, diocese of Kirin, in what was then Manchuria and is now part of China, 13 April 1901. Having become a Catholic at age thirteen, he studied for a year at a Jesuit university in Shanghai, followed by philosophy at the Kirin seminary. From 1924 to 1929 he lived in the Rome College of Propaganda Fide and obtained a laureate in theology at the Atheneum. He next studied canon law at the Apollinare, while simultaneously teaching Chinese language and literature at the Propaganda Fide College.

Returning to China after ordination to the priesthood in 1928, he began an administrative career in the Pekin diocesan chancery, while simultaneously becoming General Assistant of Catholic Action. He organized in 1935 the first Chinese national congress of Catholic Action. He also became inspector general of Catholic schools in China. In 1936 he was ordained a bishop and made vicar apostolic of Nanking, and when the Chinese hierarchy was established in 1946, he became Archbishop of Nanking. After moving to Taiwan in 1949 as the communists completed their conquest of the mainland, Yü Pin became one of Chiang Kai-shek's closest advisers, to the point that it was not easy to decide which of the two made decisions for the other, and Yü Pin was the arbiter of power after Chiang's death until his son consolidated his position.

In Taiwan, he used and continues to use all his influence at the Vatican to ensure that the Vatican does not break diplomatic relations, the condition that the Peoples Republic of China imposes on those who seek to establish diplomatic relations with it. At a round table of the seven new cardinals from the Third World (of whom he was one) in Rome in 1969, he said "The general problem seems to me to be about the same everywhere, not just in the Third World. But we Catholic Chinese have our own specific problem—to recover continental China now in communist hands, and prepare to rebuild it." And in October 1977, he toured the United States with a delegation from Taiwan asking for prayers and moral support for continued freedom from a communist takeover of Taiwan. Recognition of one China by the United States government, he said, would end the religious freedom now enjoyed by sixteen million Chinese on Taiwan. He also said that Pope Paul in two private audiences the previous month had again assured him that the Holy See will not withdraw diplomatic relations with the Republic of China on Taiwan.

Yü Pin has many friends among conservative circles in the United States. He exercises influence in such circles through his membership on the board of the lay-owned and professedly conservative Catholic weekly, *The Wanderer*. As a cardinal, he is a member of the curial Congregation for the Evangelization of Peoples (Propaganda Fide). In a papal conclave he would be a solid supporter of the most reactionary elements in the Roman Curia.

Africa

A frica is not only a vast continent, divided by many cultures, poor communications, and the linguistic, ideological and political obstacles created by the colonial period and persisting even where it has ended. The problems of the Coptic patriarch of Alexandria are totally distinct from those of his fellow cardinal, Owen McCann, in South Africa; and both face quite different issues from those presented by the growing trend to socialism, often with considerable hostility to Christianity as a foreign element, in many new countries of black Africa.

Notwithstanding all this, at the Vatican Council and subsequently, the church leaders all over Africa have discovered that many of their problems are similar. In particular, there is almost universal agreement on the need for a profound Africanization of the church in liturgy and structures, a trend already considerably advanced in many parts. A major influence on the votes of the African cardinals, who have grown in number from one in 1962 to five in 1969 and twelve today, will be the attitude of the candidates in a papal conclave toward decentralization of decision making in these areas.

Their concerns in this respect are identical with those of the great majority of the Asian cardinals, and they also share with them the complication that they want Rome to decentralize in their favor, yet at the same time remain strong to help and protect them in countries in which they form a minority dealing at times with hostile regimes and also at times with the strong and growing power of Islam.

Within the body of African cardinals there are significant theological and other differences, as a review of the individual profiles that follow will reveal. Yet the history of their cooperation at Vatican II and the Synods of Bishops suggests strongly that these differences will count for less at a papal conclave than their understanding of their common needs. They even have within their number a potential candidate for the papacy, Cardinal Gantin. His election would enthuse Africa and black people everywhere.

Cardinal Léon-Etienne Duval

A Frenchman who is an Algerian citizen and who identifies himself totally with the interests of Algeria, Cardinal Duval was born at Chênex, diocese of Annecy, close to the Swiss and Italian Alps in southeast France, 9 November 1903. He studied at the local minor and major seminaries and at the Gregorian in Rome, and was ordained a priest at age twenty-three. Two years later he was pastor at Saint Gervais, Annecy, taught at the Annecy major seminary from 1930 to 1942, then was named bishop of Constantine and Hippo (the diocese of St. Augustine) in Algeria. In 1954 he was moved to the metropolitan see of Algiers.

The first eight years of his rule in Algiers were dominated by the bitter struggle of the Algerians to free themselves from French control. Duval never hid his sympathy for the aspirations of the Algerians, and in a series of masterly pastoral letters, published in two volumes under the title *Words of Peace*, pleaded earnestly and ultimately successfully for an end to the savagery and bloodshed that characterized the war. One of the most world-minded of the church's leaders, he saw that the duty of Christians in an overwhelmingly Moslem country was to give witness, not seek to exercise power. He accordingly took the initiative in handing over all the Catholic churches, including the massive cathedral of Constantine, to the Moslems.

His sensitivity to the contemporary world dominated his interventions at Vatican II. "If we want the world to understand us, let us begin by understanding the world. Let us lay the foundations of an ethics of scientific research." On relations between rich and poor countries, he was already sponsoring positions that were then violently opposed by the United States and its major allies, but which have since become coin of the realm. Urging the strengthening of the draft statement on the church in today's world, he said, "It should indicate more clearly why a reform of international commerce is necessary; in its present form, it (international commerce) increases the differentiation between rich and poor nations. . . . Racism is only mildly reproved. . . . The horror of war is not enough emphasized, and the condemnation of total war is not clear. . . . The chapter should be more synthesized in form, in order to show how the problems of hunger, ignorance and peace are interrelated. . . . The Council should address itself to political and economic leaders, emphasizing the necessity of a world authority, as well as the backwardness of states that do not want to give any consideration to international institutions."

He spoke in similar terms at the 1967 Synod of Bishops, saying that today's Christians expect the church to be visible to all as a sign of justice and charity in the world, and they want it to repudiate the self-centeredness of so many believers. "The Gospel seems today to be imprisoned by protocol. It is the whole church and not just the pope that is called on to work for justice in the world. We must end the dispersion of forces that wastes our energies." At that Synod also, he supported the demand made by many of its members for a radical decentralization of the lawmaking process, as part of the reform of the Code of Canon Law.

At a Mass for the Christian delegates to the Conference of Non-Aligned Nations held in Algiers, September 1973, he said, "All believers and all men of good will rejoice in particular at the unanimity of the delegations to the Conference regarding the need to struggle with courage against every kind of racism and every kind of foreign domination. . . . The fact that the Third World has reached the full measure of its responsibilities will make necessary a renewal of the way of functioning of the United Nations. We salute in advance this happy innovation. It will be the expression of the universal vocation of that institution and will assure it the authority it requires for giving reality to the demands of peace."

Theologically open, highly ecumenical and a fighter for human rights and social justice, he is cool to curial control and has serious reservations about the *Humanae Vitae* teaching on birth control. In a papal conclave, he will be an important bridge between progressives of Europe and of the Third World.

Cardinal Dominic Ignatius Ekandem

The first priest of his diocese born within its borders, the first African bishop in West Africa in modern times, and Nigeria's first cardinal, Ekandem was born in 1917 in the most easterly part of Nigeria, at Obio Ibiono, Cross River State, diocese of Calabar. His father, a pagan, was head of a clan of the Ibibio tribe, and he wanted his son to learn to read and write, so he sent him to the only school in the village, the Qua Iboe Mission school. From there he went to a primary school run by the Presbyterian church at Itu and later to the Catholic school at Anua of the Irish Kiltegan Fathers of Saint Patrick. Here he was instructed in the Catholic religion and was baptized at age eight. He had a keen desire to learn but for a time remained undecided if he should become a doctor, a lawyer, or an engineer. Instead, he entered the minor seminary at Onitsha. Later, in his first sermon after ordination to the priesthood, he said he had achieved all his ambitions by having become a doctor to cure his people, a lawyer to defend them, and an engineer to build homes for them.

Although his father had not become a Christian, he approved his son's decision. With the strong support of Bishop James Moynagh of Calabar, who foresaw the urgent need to develop indigenous priests, Ekandem entered the major seminary of Enugu-Okpala in 1941, the first Nigerian to do so. Ordained a priest in 1947, he worked as assistant and later as pastor in the parish of Afaha Obong, then became rector of the diocesan minor seminary. In 1953 he was ordained a bishop and named auxiliary to Bishop Moynagh. He set out immediately to organize the Federation of Catholic Teacher Associations, for Nigerians studying in universities at home and abroad. He also was an active promoter of education for women, previously much neglected, and was responsible for starting a secondary school for girls. After Nigeria became independent in 1960, the federal government recognized his work by conferring on him the title of Commander of the Order of the River Niger.

In 1963, with the creation of the new diocese of Ikot Ekpene, Ekandem was chosen as its bishop. The final honor of the cardinalate came in 1976, and with it an appointment to the curial

Secretariat for Non-Christians. In this case, as in many of the new countries, the cardinalate represents a recognition of the importance of the church in a new country, and an honor which governments appreciate as increasing their international status. Ekandem has none of the specialized training which is the characteristic of members of the College of Cardinals. But some of the cardinals from the new countries have already shown that they possess valuable qualities. In particular, they are conscious of the need to de-Westernize the church if it is to grow and put down roots. In this Ekandem is no exception, so that in a papal conclave he would favor a candidate sensitive to his particular pastoral requirements.

Cardinal Bernardin Gantin

The son of a black railroad worker, Cardinal Gantin was born at Toffo, archdiocese of Cotonou, Dahomey (now People's Republic of Benin), 8 May 1922. For those who know him well, he is a man of profound spirituality. After primary studies in a school founded by Bishop Mario de Bresillac, a strong supporter of the development of an indigenous clergy, Gantin went to the preseminary, the minor seminary and the major seminary, to be ordained a priest at age twenty-nine. After two years teaching languages and other subjects at the minor seminary, he went to Rome for graduate study at the Urbanian and the Lateran, obtaining licentiates in theology and canon law. While working on his laureate dissertation, he was ordained bishop in 1957 and made auxiliary to the archbishop of Cotonou, whom he succeeded on his retirement in 1960.

That was the year in which Benin became independent of France, and the country was soon beset by a number of clashes which resulted in the overthrow of the constitutional government in 1963 and the establishment in 1965 of an extremely Leftist government which amended the constitution the following year to provide for a one-party state. Gantin had already had difficulties with the regime. It had sought to restrict the activities of the church and to harass priests close to Gantin and even the bishop himself, for reasons never fully clear but believed to be related to an ideology that stressed return to "authentic African civilization" by eliminating such foreign elements as Christianity.

After the 1965 coup, the pressures increased. Gantin sought to be conciliatory but firm. In a pastoral letter in 1966 he said he respected the will of the people as expressed in the referendum, but warned of risks ahead. While not opposed in principle to one-party government, "especially in our countries that are trying to reconcile the democratic way with the need for harmonious and rapid development," he warned that history shows the danger of drifting into a systematically totalitarian regime. He called on all in the upcoming elections to reject regionalism and tribalism, and even more the monied interests, and to vote for the best candidates.

Actually, Gantin had long been actively espousing the Africanization of Christianity. At Vatican II, in 1964, speaking in the name of all the bishops of Africa and Madagascar, he asserted that the missions must overcome the prejudice that sees evangelization as a disguise for foreign domination. "The church is at home in all cultures. All civilizations belong to God, who created them and loves them." And even earlier, in 1962, when Dutch-born Bishop Willem van Bekkum of Ruteng, Indonesia, called for the Christianizing of the feasts in which original socioreligious structures are preserved, stressed the value of spontaneity in the liturgy, and hoped that the languages of Asia and Africa might become "sacramental languages," Gantin congratulated him, saying, "You are our spokesman."

In spite of all his conciliatory efforts, pressures on him increased as the regime moved toward an openly Marxist-Leninist position (formalized in 1972) and as tribal discord grew. Accordingly, he was called to Rome to work in the Congregation for the Evangelization of Peoples (Propaganda Fide) in 1971, later moved to the Justice and Peace Commission, of which he became Prefect in 1977 immediately after being made a cardinal. His only visit to Benin since 1971 was in August 1977. The government press and radio had passed over in silence his being made a cardinal three months earlier, but when his visit was announced, it felt it had to make a gesture. Accordingly, the people were asked to welcome him. Twenty thousand thronged the airport, and enthusiastic crowds attended all ceremonies at which he presided for three weeks. But he ran into trouble when he said at a Mass, celebrated for those killed in an attack by mercenaries the previous January, that belief in eternal life was anchored in the conscience of the Christians of Benin. Arguing that such a statement undercut one of the bases of the regime, the government forbade him to participate in further public acts, keeping him effectively under house arrest until he went back to Rome at the end of August.

Even though lacking the specialized training that normally paves the way to the cardinalate, Gantin is a man of great sensitivity and an understanding of the contemporary world. His consistent optimism and confidence in people emerged again in a comment he made at the 1977 Synod of Bishops. "Hunger for God and thirst for God," he said, "are real among today's young people, in spite of appearances." Intelligent, social-minded and progressive, he will be a positive element with a big influence on most of his fellow Africans in a papal conclave. Nor can he be automatically excluded as himself a suitable candidate for the papacy. A black pope would be an inspiring gesture in a world in which whites are a shrinking minority. Gantin is one who could measure up to the responsibility.

Cardinal Joseph Malula

One of the benefits of being a cardinal is that it is a career in which violent death is rare. Until March 1977, when Cardinal Emile Biayenda was taken from his home in Brazzaville, People's Republic of the Congo, and killed, no cardinal had been assassinated since 1923. Biayenda's neighbor across the Congo river in Zaire, Cardinal Malula, carries his life in his hands every day. His relations with Zaire's volatile military dictator, Mobutu Sese Seko, have long been strained. But Malula, who was born at Léopoldville (now Kinshasa) in what was then the Belgian Congo, 12 December 1917, is a strong man and fearless.

After study in the regional seminaries, he was ordained a priest in 1946. He immediately moved into parish work in his native city, giving particular attention to the development of vocations and the training of lay leaders in anticipation of the transfer of power that occurred in 1960. Ordained a bishop and made auxiliary to the archbishop of Kinshasa in 1959, he succeeded as archbishop in 1964.

At Vatican II, he showed his open and progressive views, while always directing his comments to the situation in Africa. In a discussion on the need to recognize the rights of women in the church and in society, for example, he drew applause by denouncing tribalism and urging that the document insist on the dignity of women, who should be "neither the instruments of lust nor slaves." He was even more explicit on the needs of Africa at the 1967 Synod of Bishops. The basic problem in the Congo, he said, in opposing the curial draft listing doctrinal errors, is not so much the defense of the faith, as the search for ways to spread it and make it meaningful. What often stands in the way is a presentation of the evangelical message that has not been adapted to Africa's specific social and cultural needs. Pastoral changes should make it possible to integrate, to a far greater extent, the psychological, cultural and religious elements already existing in Africa.

Malula's problems with President Mobutu are a reflection of the power struggles in Zaire since it became independent. The country has more than 200 tribes, and tribal rivalries have played a large part in the civil wars, aggravated by the intrigues of Belgian mining interests. There is an estimated Christian population, mostly Catholic, of nine million in a total population of twenty-five million. This makes the cardinal a very important man, and Mobuto has at times threatened him, at times courted him. He sent him into exile for some months in 1972, then let him return, finally in 1976 made peace publicly again by conferring on Malula the National Order of the Leopard, from which he had ousted him when he exiled him.

Malula, meanwhile, continues to press forward for the modernization and Africanization of the church. In August 1977, he presided at a symposium on African theology, organized under the patronage of the Zaire bishops, at the theology faculty of the University of Kinshasa. The meeting centered on the theology of liberation in an African setting, stressing that its thrust was not solely socioeconomic, but basically theocentric, recognizing that God has not merely a cosmic function (creation) but a historic function, namely, to free his people from the existing sinful world structures. This emphasis fits in with Malula's constant insistence that the church must—like Christ—be biased toward and incarnated in the poor and powerless.

At a papal conclave, he would probably play a waiting game. While personally inclined to a highly progressive and evangelical position, he cannot afford to come out openly on the losing side in a clash with the Curia. But if a situation arose in which there was a nearly even balance between curial and anticurial forces, he would most likely go against the Curia and urge other Africans to do the same, on the ground that they would all be better off if freed from their present condition of subservience to Roman bureaucrats.

Cardinal Owen McCann

The first South African cardinal, McCann was born at Woodstock, archdiocese of Cape Town, 29 June 1907, the son of an Irish-born father and an Australian mother. After primary schooling with the Irish Dominican nuns at Woodstock, and secondary with the Marist Fathers, he went to the University of Cape Town and obtained a doctorate in the commerce department, in 1929. The following year he decided to become a priest and went to study at the Propaganda Fide College, Rome.

Ordained a priest in 1935, he worked in various parishes in the Cape Town archdiocese until 1940, when he became secretary to the vicar apostolic. From 1942 to 1948 he edited the national Catholic weekly, the *Southern Cross*, then returned to parish work for two years until he was made a bishop and named vicar apostolic of Cape Town. With the establishment of the South African hierarchy in 1951, he became first archbishop of Cape Town. The choice of McCann to head the principal archdiocese and thus be put in line for cardinalitial rank caused some surprise in South African church circles, where Archbishop Denis Hurley of Durban and Archbishop William Whelan of Bloemfontein were considered the outstanding churchmen. But it so happened that the Apostolic Delegate in South Africa at the time was opposed to promoting members of religious orders, and both Hurley and Whelan were Oblates. His recommendation was accepted by his friends in the Curia. Thus are cardinals made. McCann received the red hat in 1965. He is a member of the curial Congregation for the Evangelization of Peoples (Propaganda Fide).

Hurley was the most prominent South African at Vatican II, consistently supporting the aggiornamento of the church. McCann followed in the same line. Up to 1964, however, he left much to be desired at home, accepting without protest the progressive imposition of apartheid at a time when Hurley was leading not only Catholics but other South Africans in open protest. But when he was made a cardinal, the government neither sent an appropriate representative to the ceremony in Rome, nor did it give a reception on his return. From that time onward, he supported the protests of his fellow bishops, to the point of joining with them in February

1976 when they voluntarily placed themselves "outside the law" by opening their schools to blacks and whites on a basis of equality. And in 1977, he sent an open letter to the prime minister of South Africa, in which was set out a program of radical reforms in race relations. The letter, cosigned by eighty priests, said the country could avoid bloody confrontations only by implementing this program. He followed this letter up by opening Catholic buildings to shelter squatters driven from camps at Modderdam and Werkgenot, in the depth of winter in the southern hemisphere, their shacks destroyed by police bulldozers. This action of the cardinal exposed him to criminal charges which the regime has avoided pressing because of the now solid stand of the Catholic leaders.

At the 1967 Synod of Bishops, McCann made several good interventions. He called for a profound decentralization of the lawmaking processes as a concrete expression of collegiality. He also urged openness in discussion of theological and other church issues. But, generally speaking, he has little interest in or knowledge of theology. He follows a traditional ascetical life style and sees the pastoral work of the clergy as consisting primarily in encouraging people to say their prayers, go to the sacraments, and bring the children up in the same molds in which they themselves were formed. In a papal conclave, he would be very much in the middle, waiting for others to reach a consensus before committing himself.

Cardinal Emmanuel Nsubuga

Uganda's first cardinal, Nsubuga was born at Kisule, in what is now the archdiocese of Kampala, 11 November 1914. After study at the major seminary of Katigondo, he was ordained a priest in 1946. He was engaged exclusively in parish work until made vicar-general of Kampala in 1961 and archbishop in 1966. He was named a cardinal in 1976, and he is a member of the curial Congregation for the Evangelization of Peoples.

He is best known for three events: arranging the visit of Pope Paul to Kampala; the construction of a vast basilica in honor of the Ugandan martyrs; and the organization of several pilgrimages, in which Protestants and Moslems joined Catholics, to Rome for the Holy Year.

He has had his problems with General Idi Amin, who established himself as dictator in 1971 and has since then repeatedly shocked world opinion by his largescale massacres of suspected enemies and his other excesses. Amin jailed Nsubuga for two nights in 1972, then assigned him for a considerable time to forced residence (house arrest). Amin, however, allowed him to attend the 1974 Synod of Bishops in Rome, and to go to Rome in 1976 to receive the red hat. But he did not allow any Ugandan to accompany him.

Nsubuga has the reputation of being very conservative and closed-minded. With Cardinals Rugambwa of Tanzania and Zoungrana of Upper Volta, he constitutes the right wing of the church in Africa. In a papal conclave he would support the curialists.

Cardinal Maurice Otunga

The first Kenyan cardinal, Otunga was born at Chebukwa, diocese of Kisumu, in January 1923. From the Mangu high school, he went to the Kakamega seminary, then to the regional seminary in Kampala, Uganda, for philosophy, and to Rome for theology. Ordained a priest 1950, he taught theology for three years in the major seminary of Kisumu, and he also worked for a time as assistant to the apostolic delegate in Kenya. In 1956 he was ordained a bishop and assigned as auxiliary to the bishop of Kisumu, and in 1960 he moved to Kisii as bishop. In 1969 he was named coadjutor to the archbishop of Nairobi, succeeding as archbishop two years later. The red hat followed in 1973. Otunga is a member of the Curial Congregation for the Sacraments and Divine Worship.

With Cardinals Kim of South Korea, Cordeiro of Pakistan, and Malula of Zaire, Otunga belongs to the new theological movement identified as "the church of the poor," a development of the theology of liberation, and he is probably the most evangelical and radical of all of them. He is highly critical of the Romanization and centralism of present church structures, and inspired by Africa's own sense of the meaning of life. In a papal conclave he would definitely favor a progressive candidate to the extent that his church in a poor country would allow him to identify himself as anticurial. That is a problem he shares with many others of the Third World.

Cardinal Victor Razafimahatratra

A Jesuit and one of sixteen children, Cardinal Razafimahatratra was born at Ambanitsilena-Ranomasina, archdiocese of Fianarantsoa, on the island of Madagascar (Malagasy Republic) off the east coast of Africa, 8 September 1921. His father had been a catechist for forty years, becoming superintendent of catechists for the region. Razafimahatratra went to the Christian Brothers primary school, then to the minor seminary of Fianarantsoa. In 1945 he joined the Jesuits, studied philosophy and theology at the major seminary of Tananarive, then taught in high schools for two years and was ordained a priest in 1958. After a course in catechesis at the Lumen Vitae center in Brussels, he returned to Madagascar as rector of the minor seminary of Fianarantsoa. In 1963 he became director of the Jesuit mission band in Ambositra. For six years he led thirty priests and numerous catechists in a program centered on development of the lay apostolate and improved methods of religious education. In 1969 he was named rector of the major seminary and the Institute of Higher Studies of Tananarive, and two years later went to Farafangana as bishop. There he formed a pastoral council of forty elected members, priests, nuns and lay people, to help in the five areas of his primary concern: local vocations, education, training of catechists, strengthening of the Christian family as the foundation of the church, and social action. In 1974 he was promoted to Tananarive as archbishop, and in 1976 he was made a cardinal. He is a member of the curial Congregation for the Evangelization of Peoples.

The specific needs of the church in Madagascar and his training at Lumen Vitae would combine to sensitize him to the need to adjust liturgical and other church practices to the cultural and nationalistic attitudes of this recently decolonized republic. This would tend to make him favor a progressive and decentralizing candidate in a papal conclave.

Cardinal Laurean Rugambwa

The world's first black cardinal, Rugambwa was born at Bukongo, diocese of Bukoba, Tanganyika (now Tanzania), 12 July 1912. When he was eight years old, he was received into the church with his parents and the entire family at the Kagonodo Mission. After a prolonged course of studies, he was ordained a priest at age thirty-one. After some years as a missionary in East Africa, he went to Rome to study canon law at the Propaganda Fide College and emerged with a laureate. In 1951 he was ordained a bishop and made vicar apostolic of Lower Kagera. When the Tanzanian hierarchy was established in 1953, he moved to Rutabo as bishop. There he established the National Union of Saint Augustine to form a Catholic lay elite in his diocese, and many of its members have subsequently risen to important positions in politics and government. Named a cardinal by Pope John in March 1960, he was transferred to the diocese of Bukoba some months later, and in 1968 to Dar-es-Salaam as archbishop. He is a member of the curial Congregation for the Causes of Saints, and of the Commission for the Revision of the Code of Canon Law.

At the start of Vatican II in 1962, the African bishops formed a single secretariat and chose Rugambwa to head it. In spite of the great diversity within the African continent, its bishops made every effort to speak with one voice, and even though Rugambwa tended to be personally conservative, he spoke with the progressive voice of the group. He was particularly emphatic about the urgent need to Africanize the liturgy in Africa and otherwise to eliminate the colonial holdovers. Foreign missionaries, he insisted, had to know the cultures, philosophies and ideologies of the country in which they worked. They should live like the people and respect their laws and customs. As an example of the underlying assumptions of much church thinking, he pointed out that even so progressive a document as that on the church in today's world was addressed to the mind-set and problems of the developed countries and consequently failed to speak to Africans or other Third World peoples.

Rugambwa joined with the other Tanzanian bishops in approving the Arusha Declaration, the 1967 government statement of policy proclaiming socialism as the goal toward which Tanzania was advancing. They praised in particular its stress on respect for the person. But like most of the bishops, Rugambwa's subsequent attitude has been mainly one of waiting to see how things turn out. He is basically a conservative person, not able to adjust easily to change. Indeed, with Cardinals Nsubuga of Uganda and Zoungrana of Upper Volta, he forms the right wing of the church in Africa. In a papal conclave, accordingly, he would be sympathetic to the curialists, although the specific needs of his church would make him want a pope willing to decentralize authority.

Cardinal Stephanos I. Sidarouss

The Coptic Patriarch of Alexandria, Cardinal Sidarouss, was born in Cairo 22 February 1904. Ordained a priest in 1939, he was made a titular bishop in 1947 and Patriarch of Alexandria in 1958. The patriarchates date back to the very early days of the church, each patriarch having authority over all the bishops of the territory included in the patriarchate. In the case of Alexandria, this extends to the whole of Egypt. Most of the several million Christians in Egypt are Copts not in union with Rome. The number of Copts who acknowledge Sidarouss as their head is small, probably fewer than 50,000. The reason he was made a cardinal is that at Vatican II the Eastern patriarchs claimed that under ancient church protocol they took precedence over cardinals, and to provide a compromise it was decided to make the major patriarchs cardinals as well. As cardinal, Sidarouss is a member of the curial Congregation for the Eastern Churches; and of the Commissions for the Revision of the Code of Canon Law, and for the Revision of the Code of Eastern Canon Law. His impact and influence are minimal. His biggest concern is to stay in the good graces of the Roman Curia, on whose support he is totally dependent for survival.

Cardinal Hyacinthe Thiandoum

An active and progressive spokesman for the church in Africa at the four sessions of Vatican II and at the subsequent Synods of Bishops, Cardinal Thiandoum was born at Poponguine, archdiocese of Dakar, the most westerly point of Africa in what is now Senegal, 2 February 1921. His father was a catechist. After secondary school, he entered the Dakar regional seminary and was ordained a priest in 1949. After four years in pastoral work in Dakar, he went to Rome for two years and earned licentiates in philosophy and sociology at the Gregorian. On his return, he was put in charge of Catholic Action, then made pastor of the cathedral and later vicar-general of the diocese. He became archbishop of Dakar in 1962, and a cardinal in 1976. He is a member of the curial Commission for Social Communications.

At Vatican II he stressed the urgency of liturgical reforms that would take account of cultural differences, with special stress on African religious practices. He was active in ecumenism and in social communications, becoming a member of the press committee with responsibility for Africa. At the 1971 Synod of Bishops he made an important personal statement that emphasized the continuity of the Synods with the Council. He intervened repeatedly on the ministerial priesthood, stressing the benefits of celibacy as a sign; also on the need for free expression and action of citizens in favor of justice and peace, on the right of people to self-determination, on the immorality of violence, on church cooperation in development programs, and on violations of justice and human rights in Southern Africa. Subsequently, he condemned with equal forthrightness the efforts of Portugal to retain its hold by brute force on Angola and Mozambique.

Thiandoum is highly social-minded and had no difficulty in accepting the official policy of moving the country toward socialism, particularly because of the influence of President Leopold Senghor, an extremely cultured and intelligent man, a theologian and poet of distinction. Thiandoum has been active in building bridges to Islam, the religion of 80 percent of Senegalese. As far back as 1963, he was urging at the Council that ecumenism be extended to non-Christian religions (as it later was). He pleaded

especially for ties with Islam which claims Abraham as a forerunner and has many traditions from both the Old and New Testa-
ments.

Thiandoum stands out as one of the most important of the African cardinals. His support of progressive candidates at a papal
conclave would influence greatly the decision of many of his fellow
Africans.

Cardinal Paul Zoungrana

Born at Ouagadougou, Upper Volta, 3 September 1917, Cardinal
Zoungrana was first taught by the White Sisters, then went at age
eight to the minor seminary at Pabré, where he studied classics
followed by philosophy for ten years, then transferred to the major
seminary at Koumi, near Bobo-Dioulasso. He was ordained a
priest in 1942. In 1948 he became a member of the Congregation of
White Fathers, then went to Rome and obtained a laureate in
canon law at the Gregorian in 1952. After that, he studied sociology at the Catholic Institute of Paris.

Returning to Upper Volta, he taught canon law at the Koumi
major seminary, and simultaneously engaged in parish work as
supervisor of the pastoral experience given to the seminarists
along with their theoretical studies. In 1959 he was assigned to
establish a relief and social information service in Bobo-Dioulasso.
Named archbiship of Ouagadougou in 1960, he received the red hat
in 1965. He is a member of the curial Congregations for Religious
and Secular Institutes and for the Evangelization of Peoples
(Propaganda Fide).

One of his first actions as bishop was to make a study of the
manhood initiation rites of the local tribes, with the intention of
ultimately Christianizing them, and at Vatican II he shared the
concern of other African bishops for Africanization of the church.
He also played a positive part in working out arrangements to
modify a system that had grown up in Africa giving mission
societies almost total autonomy from the bishops, insisting that
the time had come to place control in the local church. One of his
strongest interventions was in favor of a new deal for the poor
countries in their trading relations with the rich countries, which
he denounced as one-sided in favor of the rich. "Let us say clearly
that superfluous riches belong in justice to the poor."

He returned to these issues in a talk at a symposium of African
bishops at Kampala in August 1969, just before Pope Paul's visit to
Uganda. "It must be clearly understood that our own being is not to
be conferred on us from outside. We can regret that the weight of
certain international organizations is used to affect the pastoral
line in our dioceses and regions, not in the function of the real

needs of the apostolate, but rather in accordance with a precon-
ceived program that has been legitimated exclusively by outside
interests. All these forms of teleguidance could more easily be
avoided if there was a pan-African episcopal organism." He was
here referring in particular to efforts by Europeans and North
Americans to get the Africans to take the lead in a campaign for
married priests on the ground that Africans are not celibates, and
also to call for a change in birth control rules. His view, shared by
many Africans, is that these are not African concerns but strictly
those of the developed West.

His personal theological outlook is conservative, and he is linked
with Cardinals Nsubuga of Uganda and Rugambwa of Tanzania as
the right wing of the church in Africa. The role he has played,
nevertheless, indicates that his awareness of pastoral needs in his
country takes him to what are generally regarded as progressive
stands. In a papal conclave, he would most probably stay in line
with his fellow Africans.

Australasia

A lthough they occupy a substantial part of the land area of the world, Australia being almost as big as the 48 adjacent states of the United States, and New Zealand considerably bigger than Great Britain, these remote and recently established nations do not have an impact on the world scene comparable with their size or even their population (13.5 million and 3.2 million respectively). Although the Catholic church is a major and respected denomination in both countries, it suffers from the same limitations as the countries themselves, and in its isolation tends to be derivative in theology, looking to Europe for guidelines and following emotionally a generation or two behind the worldwide church in attitudes and practices.

Each country has one resident cardinal elector, and Australia has a second in charge of a curial office in Rome. The resident cardinals are middle-of-the-roaders, followers rather than leaders. The curial cardinal is very much at home as part of the traditionalist curial machine. New Zealand's Cardinal Delargey will vote against any curialist candidate, but other than that, the three Australasians are not expected to make a major impact in a papal conclave.

Cardinal Reginald John Delargey

The firstborn and only son in a family of six of Irish origin, Cardinal Delargey was born at Timaru, diocese of Christchurch, New Zealand, 10 December 1914. His father was a bank official. After primary schooling with the Sisters of Notre Dame des Missions at Napier, he went to the secondary school of the Marist Brothers at Auckland, then to the major seminary at Mosgiel for philosophy, and to the Urbanian in Rome for theology.

Ordained a priest in 1938, he started to work in a parish in Auckland, specializing in work with young people. He introduced the Young Christian Worker movement to Auckland and was its director for many years. Ordained a bishop in 1958 and assigned as auxiliary to the bishop of Auckland, he succeeded to that see as bishop in 1970. Transferred to Wellington as archbishop in 1974, he was named a cardinal in 1976. He is a member of the curial Congregation for the Evangelization of Peoples (Propaganda Fide).

Delargey attended the four sessions of Vatican II, having already participated in the preparatory commission charged with a statement on the laity. Throughout he maintained a low profile. He is fully in tune with the church in his country, a country enjoying a high standard of living, a beneficiary of the capitalist system, and only recently beginning to experience the social problems that have developed in older capitalist countries. Brought up in the most triumphalist and legalistic period in the church's history in the second quarter of the twentieth century, he has no sense of the urgency of change that dominates the thinking of many in the nuclear age. On one important issue, nevertheless, his mind is made up. He is militantly opposed to the domination of the Roman Curia and of the Italians in general. It has been said of him that even if the other electors unanimously supported an Italian candidate, he would still cast a protest vote for a non-Italian.

Cardinal James Robert Knox

An Australian-born member of the Roman Curia, Cardinal Knox was born at Bayswater, archdiocese of Perth, Western Australia, the second of three children of John Knox and Emily Walsh, both born in Kilkenny, Ireland. His father had first settled in Melbourne, Eastern Australia, on arrival from Ireland early in the century, then crossed the vast empty continent several thousand miles as part of a camel caravan, burying two of his ten companions on the way. The lure of gold had brought them to Western Australia, and it was as a gold miner that the cardinal's father worked for many years. The cardinal's mother died when he was nine, and he was raised by an uncle and two aunts.

After primary education, Knox was apprenticed to a tailor in Perth, but after a year he was encouraged by a Benedictine priest to go to New Norcia for secondary schooling at the college of Saint Ildephonsus directed by the Marist Brothers. From there he went to the seminary of the Abbey of New Norcia, and in 1936 the Abbot sent him to Rome to study in the Propaganda Fide College. After ordination to the priesthood in 1941, he remained a further nine years in Rome. After several years as an assistant to Giovanni Battista Montini (now Pope Paul) in the Secretariat of State, he went to Tokyo as assistant to the apostolic delegate in Japan. Ordained a titular bishop in 1953, he was an apostolic delegate in various African countries for three years, then went to New Delhi in 1957 as Internuncio to India, Burma, and Ceylon, remaining there until 1967 when he was named archbishop of Melbourne. Lacking pastoral experience and emotionally and theologically ill-attuned to the postconciliar church, he resigned in 1974, the year after he had been named a cardinal, and returned to Rome as Prefect of the Congregation of the Sacraments and Divine Worship. He is also a member of the Council for the Public Affairs of the Church; of the Congregations for the Bishops, for the Eastern Churches, for the Evangelization of Peoples (Propaganda Fide), and for Catholic Education; of the Commissions for the Reform of the Code of Canon Law, and for the Reform of the Code of Eastern Canon Law; and of the Office for the Administration of the Patrimony of the Holy See.

In conformity with the instructions of Vatican II, and under pressure from the world's bishops expressed at the Synods of Bishops and in other ways, the Congregation for the Sacraments and Divine Worship had in the late 1960s and early 1970s given wide discretion to national conferences of bishops to adapt many liturgical forms to make them more meaningful to the people in the different linguistic and cultural areas of the world. The arrival of Knox in 1974 coincided with a major withdrawal by the Roman Curia, a concerted effort to regain the strict controls it had exercised on all church activities around the world. Knox had no difficulty in fitting into this restrictive pattern.

In India, for example, he has caused much resentment by warning the Indian bishops to pull back on their experimentation in introducing spiritual and cultural elements of Hinduism into Christian worship. But the most widely commented action was his rebuke of Bishop Carroll Dozier of Memphis, Tennessee, for the communal rite of reconciliation he organized in his diocese in December 1976. Leading Catholic journalist Monsignor Salvatore J. Adamo, commented as follows: "Cruelly and bluntly, the head of the Congregation for the Sacraments, the Australian Cardinal James Knox, accused Dozier of violating norms 3, 5, and 10 of the decree governing the practice of general absolution. The rough rebuke was not sent directly to Dozier, but to the head of the National Council of Catholic Bishops with instructions that it be distributed to all his fellow bishops. The idea was to humiliate Dozier before his peers and ruin his reputation. The idea was to stop anyone else from duplicating the Memphis rites. Finally, the idea was to emphasize that even a national hierarchy that shepherds some fifty million sheep can be ordered around like sheep themselves by these mini-popes." And the late Don Thorman, publisher of the *National Catholic Reporter*, added: "I was personally appalled by the Byzantine maneuverings of Cardinal James Knox. . . . It is a prime example of what retired Archbishop Fulton J. Sheen, I believe, once called 'sacred politics.' "

A polished diplomat, but a machine man who can be ruthless when instructed to bring bishops back into curial step, Knox can be counted on to follow the hard curial line in a papal conclave.

Cardinal James Darcy Freeman

Born at Sydney, Australia, 19 November 1907, Cardinal Freeman received his primary education from the Brothers of the Christian Schools, then studied in the minor and major seminaries of Sydney and was ordained a priest in 1930. He worked in various pastoral and administrative activities in the archdiocese of Sydney, for many years as private secretary to Cardinal Norman Gilroy, then archbishop. In 1956 he was ordained a bishop and assigned as private secretary to Cardinal Gilroy. In 1968 he was sent as bishop to Armidale, which—like Sydney—is in the State of New South Wales. Three years later, he was back in Sydney as archbishop, following the resignation of Cardinal Gilroy at age seventy-five. He was made a cardinal in 1973.

Although he participated in Vatican II, he did not assume any position of leadership, usually voting with the progressives. Without graduate education in theology, and trained in the conventional wisdom of the old-style seminary, he had more to learn than to contribute. However, he has the reputation of being personally open, sympathetic to social progress in the restricted sense in which the concept is understood in highly traditionalist Australia. In a papal conclave, he can be expected to follow a moderately progressive line.

SOURCE NOTES

The accumulation of data for this book involved combing the files of scores of magazines and newspapers in many languages, for some of them going back as far as the 1950s. The most important were *Informations Catholiques Internationales* (Paris); *Osservatore Romano* (Vatican City), especially issues of 12 January 1953, 15 December 1958, 28 March 1960, 26 January 1961, 22 February 1965, 16 June 1967, 5 March 1973, 24–25 May 1976, and 27–28 June 1977; *COM-Nuovi Tempi* (Rome); The *Tablet* (London); *Herder Correspondence* (Germany); *National Catholic Reporter* (Kansas City); *Latinamerica Press* (Lima); *Latin American Political Report* (London).

Books that provided major information and guidance included:

Andrews, James F. ed, *Paul VI: Critical Appraisals*. Encino, Calif.,: Bruce Publications, 1970.

Antoine, Charles. *L'Eglise et le Pouvoir au Brésil*. Paris: Desclée de Brouwer, 1971.

Bruneau, Thomas C. *The Political Transformation of the Brazilian Catholic Church*. New York: Cambridge University Press, 1974.

Clancy, John G. *Apostle for Our Time: Pope Paul VI*. New York: Kennedy, 1963.

Congar, Yves; Küng, Hans; O'Hanlon, Daniel, eds. *Council Speeches of Vatican II*. New York: Sheed and Ward, 1964.

Falconi, Carlos. *Pope John and the Ecumenical Council*. Mountain View, Calif.: World, 1964.

——— *The Popes in the Twentieth Century*. Boston: Little Brown, 1967.

Fesquet, Henri. *The Drama of Vatican II*. New York: Random House, 1967.

Hatch, Alden. *Pope Paul VI*. New York: Doubleday-Echo, 1966.

Laurentin, René. *L'Enjeu du Synode: Suite du Concile*. Paris: Seuil, 1967.

Martin, Malachi. *Three Popes and the Cardinal*. New York: Farrar, Straus and Giroux, 1972.

McKenzie, John L. *The Roman Catholic Church*. New York: Holt, Rinehart & Winston, 1969.

Murphy, Francis X., and MacEoin, Gary. *Synod '67: a New Sound in Rome*. Milwaukee: Bruce, 1968.

Rynne, Xavier. *Vatican Council II*. New York: Farrar, Straus & Giroux, 1968.

Wiltgen, Ralph. *The Rhine Flows Into the Tiber*. New York: Hawthorn Books, 1967.

Zizola, Giancarlo. *Quale papa?* Rome: Borla, 1977.

Annuario Pontificio. Vatican City: Libreria Editrice Vaticana. (Vatican official yearbook, updated annually).

Between Honesty and Hope. Maryknoll, New York: Maryknoll Books, 1967. (Major documents on church in Latin America).

SELECTED NAME INDEX

ARCHBISHOPS

Gary MacEoin, who has written for such magazines as *Life* and *McCalls,* received his Ph.D. from the National University of Ireland and worked as a reporter and editor of two Irish dailies before becoming an American citizen twenty-five years ago. He is an authority on Ireland, conflict, and world development and has also authored many books on Latin America, including *No Peaceful Way: The Chilean Struggle for Dignity.*

The Committee for the Responsible Election of the Pope is a group of laypersons in business, government, and education dedicated to conveying the needs and opinions of today's church to tomorrow's leaders.